A Celebration of Poets

EAST
GRADES 4-6
SUMMER 2009

creativeCOMMUNICATION
A CELEBRATION OF TODAY'S WRITERS

A CELEBRATION OF POETS
EAST
GRADES 4-6
SUMMER 2009

AN ANTHOLOGY COMPILED BY CREATIVE COMMUNICATION, INC.

Published by:

1488 NORTH 200 WEST • LOGAN, UTAH 84341
TEL. 435-713-4411 • WWW.POETICPOWER.COM

Authors are responsible for the originality of the writing submitted.

ISBN: 978-1-60050-297-2

FOREWORD

"The times they are a changin'."

When Bob Dylan coined this phrase, his times were changing. It was 1964 and a much different world than we have today. However, to every generation the times change. The students today cope with issues that earlier generations could not even conceive. Each generation has its own unique problems. Today we have terrorism, the economy, the environment, swine flu and the list goes on.

However, the hopes of each generation is one thing that is constant. Everyone wants to make it through the stresses of school, have positive relationships, and generally succeed in life. The writings in this book give the reader an insight into each of these students. We are allowed to view, if only for a moment, what is important to each author.

It has been a joy to have published student essays and poems for over 15 years. For each contest, students send in their hopes and dreams of becoming a published writer. As most of the entries in our contests are not invited to be published, we congratulate the students that were selected to be included in this book.

We hope you enjoy reading what our authors have decided to share. As our "times change" we have hope, as our youth care about their world and want to make it a better place.

Thomas Worthen, Ph.D.
Editor
Creative Communication

WRITING CONTESTS!

Enter our next POETRY contest!
Enter our next ESSAY contest!

Why should I enter?
Win prizes and get published! Each year thousands of dollars in prizes are awarded throughout North America. The top writers in each division receive a monetary award and a free book that includes their published poem or essay. Entries of merit are also selected to be published in our anthology.

Who may enter?
There are four divisions in the poetry contest. The poetry divisions are grades K-3, 4-6, 7-9, and 10-12. There are three divisions in the essay contest. The essay divisions are grades 3-6, 7-9, and 10-12.

What is needed to enter the contest?
To enter the poetry contest send in one original poem, 21 lines or less. To enter the essay contest send in one original non-fiction essay, 250 words or less, on any topic. Please submit each poem and essay with a title, and the following information clearly printed: the writer's name, current grade, home address (optional), school name, school address, teacher's name and teacher's email address (optional). Contact information will only be used to provide information about the contest. For complete contest information go to www.poeticpower.com.

How do I enter?
Enter a poem online at:
www.poeticpower.com
or
Mail your poem to:
    Poetry Contest
    1488 North 200 West
    Logan, UT 84341

Enter an essay online at:
www.studentessaycontest.com
or
Mail your essay to:
    Essay Contest
    1488 North 200 West
    Logan, UT 84341

When is the deadline?
Poetry contest deadlines are April 13th, August 18th, and December 2nd. Essay contest deadlines are February 17th, July 15th, and October 19th. Students can enter one poem and one essay for each spring, summer, and fall contest deadline.

Are there benefits for my school?
Yes. We award $15,000 each year in grants to help with Language Arts programs. Schools qualify to apply for a grant by having 15 or more accepted entries.

Are there benefits for my teacher?
Yes. Teachers with five or more students published receive a free anthology that includes their students' writing.

For more information please go to our website at **www.poeticpower.com**, email us at editor@poeticpower.com or call 435-713-4411.

TABLE OF CONTENTS

States included in this edition:

Alabama
Arkansas
Connecticut
Delaware
Florida
Georgia
Kentucky
Louisiana
Maine
Maryland
Massachusetts
Mississippi
New Hampshire
New York
North Carolina
Pennsylvania
Rhode Island
South Carolina
Tennessee
Vermont
Virginia
Washington D.C.
West Virginia

Summer 2009 Poetic Achievement Honor Schools

* Teachers who had fifteen or more poets accepted to be published

The following schools are recognized as receiving a "Poetic Achievement Award." This award is given to schools who have a large number of entries of which over fifty percent are accepted for publication. With hundreds of schools entering our contest, only a small percent of these schools are honored with this award. The purpose of this award is to recognize schools with excellent Language Arts programs. This award qualifies these schools to receive a complimentary copy of this anthology. In addition, these schools are eligible to apply for a Creative Communication Language Arts Grant. Grants of two hundred and fifty dollars each are awarded to further develop writing in our schools.

Arthur I Meyer Jewish Academy
West Palm Beach, FL
Arlene S. Colavito
Dr. Potente*
Lisa Rochefort*

Avon Grove Intermediate School
West Grove, PA
Kelley Crist*
Kathy Di Domenico*
Brian Yohannan*

B'nai Shalom Day School
Greensboro, NC
Dawn Ross*

Bedford Middle School
Bedford, PA
Lisa A. Cessna*

Berry Middle School
Hoover, AL
Cheryl Thomas*

Blue Ridge Middle School
Purcellville, VA
Lee Martin*
Virginia Walker

Bnos Malka Academy
Forest Hills, NY
Beverly Fruchter*

Caldwell Elementary School
Benton, AR
Jo Anne Zachary*

Canterbury School
Fort Myers, FL
Lee Maes*

Captain Nathan Hale Middle School
Coventry, CT
Adrienne Manzone
Laura Myslinski*

Chickahominy Middle School
Mechanicsville, VA
Kathleen Martin
Cynthia Sinanian*

Christ the Divine Teacher Catholic Academy
Pittsburgh, PA
Lucille Bishop*

Covenant Life School
Gaithersburg, MD
Denise Griney*

Discovery School @ Reeves Rogers
Murfreesboro, TN
Kristy Mall*
Melissa Pepelea

E T Richardson Middle School
Springfield, PA
Kate Walton*

East Shore Middle School
Milford, CT
Richard Hribko*

Fishing Creek Elementary School
Lewisberry, PA
Claire E. Richcrick*

Foxborough Regional Charter School
Foxborough, MA
Charlotte Sheer*

Freedom Area Middle School
Freedom, PA
Patricia A. Donaldson*

Gulfview Middle School
Naples, FL
Susan M. Keehner*

Hamilton Avenue School
Greenwich, CT
Darlene Angotto*
Catherine Byrne

Harmony Community School
Harmony, FL
Esther Ruth Gilbert
Christina Kading

Haynes Academy for Advanced Studies
Metairie, LA
Sandra DeMers
Janet C. Gubler
Faye Haley*
Wendi Majeau
Leslie Straight*

Hillcrest Elementary School
Holland, PA
Kelly Weiss*

Jamestown Elementary School
Jamestown, PA
Tammy Bugher
Christy Smith

Kelly Lane Intermediate School
Granby, CT
Olive Gianakos*
Stephanie Stupienski*

L Ray Appleman Elementary School
Benton, PA
Miss Lutkiewicz*

Lake Noxen Elementary School
Harveys Lake, PA
Wendy Garrety*
Mrs. Krogulski*

Linkhorne Middle School
Lynchburg, VA
Sheri Bosta
Nora Kluender*

Meadow Park Elementary School
West Palm Beach, FL
Jill Ostaffe*

Mclville School
Portsmouth, RI
Mrs. Andrews
Erin Costa*
Sue Frost
Danielle Laurie

Morton Middle School
Lexington, KY
Judy Lowry*

New Garden Friends School
Greensboro, NC
Brad Harrell*
Neil Swenson

Normandin Middle School
New Bedford, MA
Jodie Braun*

North Albany Academy
Albany, NY
Loretta Fantroy
Mike Pulsar

Our Lady of Grace Elementary School
Pittsburgh, PA
Brenda Serbicki*

Pike Creek Christian School
Newark, DE
Alice Agostinelli
Amanda Parks

Public School 207 Rockwood Park
Howard Beach, NY
Denise Close*

Riverside School
Riverside, CT
Tressa Torre*

Southern Pines Elementary School
Southern Pines, NC
Jennifer Reynolds*

St Agatha School
Brooklyn, NY
Rosemarie Paredes*

St James School
Montgomery, AL
Norma Jo Roberts*

St Stephen's School
Grand Island, NY
Daniela Schmidt*

Stackpole Elementary School
Southampton, PA
Stephanie Badulak*

Suffern Middle School
Suffern, NY
Ellen Weller*

Tucker School
Lowell, AR
Melissa Bender
Steve Berens
Donna Sparks*

Warrenton Middle School
Warrenton, VA
Amy Kuhler*

Watsontown Elementary School
Watsontown, PA
Jodie Danowsky
Becky Geiger
Jenn Harer
Alison Newman
Dana Pick
Eric Rockey
Marcia Saam

West Frankfort Elementary School
Frankfort, NY
Melissa Rocco*

Weston Middle School
Weston, CT
Dana Goetz*

Youngsville Elementary School
Youngsville, NC
Susan Stallings*

Language Arts Grant Recipients 2009-2010

After receiving a "Poetic Achievement Award" schools are encouraged to apply for a Creative Communication Language Arts Grant. The following is a list of schools who received a two hundred and fifty dollar grant for the 2009-2010 school year.

Arrowhead Union High School, Hartland, WI
Blessed Sacrament School, Seminole, FL
Booneville Jr High School, Booneville, AR
Buckhannon-Upshur Middle School, Buckhannon, WV
Campbell High School, Ewa Beach, HI
Chickahominy Middle School, Mechanicsville, VA
Clarkston Jr High School, Clarkston, MI
Covenant Life School, Gaithersburg, MD
CW Rice Middle School, Northumberland, PA
Eason Elementary School, Waukee, IA
East Elementary School, Kodiak, AK
Florence M Gaudineer Middle School, Springfield, NJ
Foxborough Regional Charter School, Foxborough, MA
Gideon High School, Gideon, MO
Holy Child Academy, Drexel Hill, PA
Home Choice Academy, Vancouver, WA
Jeff Davis Elementary School, Biloxi, MS
Lower Alloways Creek Elementary School, Salem, NJ
Maple Wood Elementary School, Somersworth, NH
Mary Walter Elementary School, Bealeton, VA
Mater Dei High School, Evansville, IN
Mercy High School, Farmington Hills, MI
Monroeville Elementary School, Monroeville, OH
Nautilus Middle School, Miami Beach, FL
Our Lady Star of the Sea School, Grosse Pointe Woods, MI
Overton High School, Memphis, TN
Pond Road Middle School, Robbinsville, NJ
Providence Hall Charter School, Herriman, UT
Reuben Johnson Elementary School, McKinney, TX
Rivelon Elementary School, Orangeburg, SC
Rose Hill Elementary School, Omaha, NE

Language Arts Grant Winners cont.

Runnels School, Baton Rouge, LA
Santa Fe Springs Christian School, Santa Fe Springs, CA
Serra Catholic High School, Mckeesport, PA
Shadowlawn Elementary School, Green Cove Springs, FL
Spectrum Elementary School, Gilbert, AZ
St Edmund Parish School, Oak Park, IL
St Joseph Institute for the Deaf, Chesterfield, MO
St Joseph Regional Jr High School, Manchester, NH
St Mary of Czestochowa School, Middletown, CT
St Monica Elementary School, Garfield Heights, OH
St Vincent De Paul Elementary School, Cape Girardeau, MO
Stevensville Middle School, Stevensville, MD
Tashua School, Trumbull, CT
The New York Institute for Special Education, Bronx, NY
The Selwyn School, Denton, TX
Tonganoxie Middle School, Tonganoxie, KS
Westside Academy, Prince George, BC
Willa Cather Elementary School, Omaha, NE
Willow Hill Elementary School, Traverse City, MI

Grades 4-5-6

Top Poem Grades 4-5-6

The Miniature World

Gentle hum of the singing breeze
Quiet song sways the grass of the miniature world
Tiny workers gather for their queen
Leaves and crumbs: a colony's feast

Humble guards rush from their hive
Swarming to protect their sweet treasure
Down below a red lady buzzes by
And green acrobats jump through the forest

Artists spin away on their new masterpiece
A complicated design of delicate thread
Water walkers glide over the water
Appearing as ice skaters

As the breeze blows the jungle
It gusts through tiny kingdoms
Creates waves on the water
And gently sways the miniature world

Rachel Bouldin, Grade 6
Blue Ridge Middle School, VA

Top Poem Grades 4-5-6

My Farmer

My granddad works now and then
His old wrinkled face smiles
With his aged yellow teeth
I hold his sticky sweaty hand
As if it was for the first time.
He says "Listen to the crickets"…I do.
The skin glows on his bald silky head,
The rest of his skin is brown and peach like a ripe onion.

His worn, red, broken down barn is still there.
Morning to dawn he crops his grains and corn.
The morning air smells like
Dew and blossoming flowers.
The wide open field is full of memories
That we cherish.
The house is still surrounded by laughs.
His barn is veteran, but not as old as him.
I can picture the old ideas of his inventions
Crumpled on his desk.

He says "I love you"
I say "I love you too"
I love…My Farmer.

Maddie Driscoll, Grade 4
Goshen Elementary School at Hillcrest, KY

Top Poem Grades 4-5-6

Jazz

I love to hear the sound.
The smooth improvisation.
It talks to me,
causing my body to dance.

I dance all night
'til the sound of passion
fades away.

The horns are gone
The happiness is gone
and we hear silence
as the smooth, swift
waves of music
drift into the open field.

Eli Fribush, Grade 5
New Garden Friends School, NC

Top Poem Grades 4-5-6

Mountains and Valleys

High mountains in the distance.
Snowy caps on the tips of the mountains.
The sky is blue over the hills.
Bright flowers like
   Ruby
         Bronze
               Sherbet pink
The birds are chirping in the distance.
Low in the valley I hear the wind
   Whistling in my ear.
The grass swishing side to side.
The ground rumbling beneath me.

Dana Gisonno, Grade 6
Suffern Middle School, NY

Top Poem Grades 4-5-6

Write from My Soul

Gliding that pencil across the page,
Gives me a certain feeling
A feeling of which will not go away.
When I hear that story, whispering to my mind,
My heart beats and I cannot stay away from the paper.
Even if I try to resist, the story pours out
And beckons for me to follow, into a world that I control.
I sit at my desk and put my pencil to the paper —
The story seems to unravel itself and all my troubles melt away,
And I feel as calm as the sea at daybreak.
I fall into a dream, where the pages of a story fill my mind,
And the sun and moon dance to the rhythm in my head,
As my feelings burst out into the heart of the story.
The words pop off the page, the feelings become real,
And the characters come alive!
I feel when I'm sitting at my desk with a pencil in my hand,
I can truly write —
Write from my soul.

Rachel Grant, Grade 4
Crestwood Elementary School, KY

Top Poem Grades 4-5-6

Gentle Hands

Gentle hands hold you tight
They give out love with all their might
Giving their own sentimental feeling
Hands are great for healing

Grandparents' hands give their life stories
Mostly filled with pride and glory
They leak with the surprise of wisdom
Now looking at their graceful freedom

Mother's hands as soft as butter
As gentle as they are they might as well flutter
Hands for tucking you into bed
Holding them you know you have nothing to dread

Father's hands are warm and strong
They make you feel safe and secure for so long
They can help you build your toys and dreams
And fill your life with unforgettable themes

There are many gentle hands everywhere
Finding them takes time and care
They're God's greatest gift for you to find and give
To fill every day with joy that will help you live

Samantha LeBlond, Grade 6
Captain Nathan Hale Middle School, CT

Top Poem Grades 4-5-6

Twilight

Some call them dusk and dawn
Others call them the time of the fawn,
The time when young deer
Frolic and play
In the cool mist of night
Or spring like colors of a new day,
The time when birds sing to bring forth the day
And keep the dark syrup of night at bay

For twilight comes twice,
To bare the cloak of darkness
And to introduce the play of day,
It's the fog that hides the sparkling confetti of night
And the colorful curtain that reveals
The shining, golden sun.

Emily Leibiger, Grade 4
John Lyman School, CT

Top Poem Grades 4-5-6

Nature

I look into the aqua water and see a reflection of the leaves
colored bronze, emerald and amber, crackling on the copper trees.
The teal water speaks to me, telling me to jump in,
as the remarkable, stunning leaves fall from the trees and float away.
The grass nearby is a mossy, damp forest,
with golden leaves turning mahogany as they break, die and fracture.
As I follow the leaves downstream birds are chirping
and the water is flowing calmly down the stream.
The turquoise water smells so fresh, it's overwhelming.
I jump in with the leaves and swim down the stream.

Tonianne Magnelli, Grade 6
Suffern Middle School, NY

Top Poem Grades 4-5-6

A Dog's Extreme Joy

The dog pulls me to the coast,
That is one of the things she adores the most.
The dog feels she is late,
And doesn't want to wait.
The dog arrives wagging her tail,
And woofs "hello" at an innocent snail.
The dog's leash falls to the ground;
She rockets away without a sound.
The dog only hears the ocean's beat,
Chases the birds, feeling complete.
The dog's face is glowing with joy,
This is better than playing with some toy.
The dog's happiness explodes as she runs free,
Her liveliness is a sight to see.
The dog eventually gets tired and wants to nap,
But maybe take another lap.
The dog changes her mind and sits in the sand,
With her beaming face, she looks just grand.
The dog and I leave, an extended grin on her face,
We keep a happy but weary pace.

Arabella Reece, Grade 6
Oyster River Middle School, NH

Top Poem Grades 4-5-6

Spring Kingdom

Swooping butterflies
Catching bugs as they head toward me,
My little warriors,
I peer over hills
Covered with yellow daffodils,
My detailed carpet,
White, puffy clouds
Flowing gently in the sky,
My sun blanket,
Tweeting birds
Making up their own song as they go
My talented orchestra,
Butterflies and birds,
Flowers and clouds,
My kingdom!

Rachael Russell, Grade 6
Blue Ridge Middle School, VA

New York City
A hundred windows
Buildings crashing together
Traffic lights shining
Batsheva Maksimov, Grade 4
Bnos Malka Academy, NY

I Don't Know!
I don't know
what to do,
I'm really bored
How 'bout you?

I'm waiting for
a call from you,
but while I'm waiting
what shall I do?

I'm so bored,
I want to play,
Hurry up
I haven't got all day!

I'm sitting here
so very bored,
I think I'm now
getting ignored.

It's now 9 pm
like I said,
never mind
gotta go to bed.
Matthew Keating, Grade 4
Nelson Place Elementary School, MA

Ghosts
Ghosts
White, scary
Floating, levitating, spooking
Hollow ghoul of fright
Monster
Hala Van Nostrand, Grade 6
Kelly Lane Intermediate School, CT

Darkness
Darkness surrounds me
Going everywhere I go
Darkness is watching
Danielle Isgett, Grade 6
Westview Middle School, SC

Ground Hog
Pointy as needles
Prickly as a porcupine
Hands soft as pillows
Leah Tova Solaimanzadeh, Grade 4
Bnos Malka Academy, NY

Blue
I sit,
at the edge,
of a creek.
I see blue.
Shining in the sun.
Glimmering,
on the rocks
and over.
I look up,
at the sky
and see blue.

Clouds in the shape
of tuna.
Swimming in the ocean.
Eating the smaller fish.

As the clouds
turn over the sun,
everything turns
Black.
Austin Hicks, Grade 5
New Garden Friends School, NC

Life
Although I lived a meaningful life
Today I died a painful death
So here I am all alone and dead
But I am still alive in my head
But I still mourn for one last breath
Wes Orred, Grade 6
Kelly Lane Intermediate School, CT

Unseen Beauty
The midnight flower blooms.
One by one they open
A picture perfect scene.
The dawn breaks and midnight is over.
An unseen beauty.
Tosin Onaolapo, Grade 6
Sandy Spring Friends School, MD

Dolphins
Dolphins
Flipping, jumping, squealing,
Swimming through the sea,
Jumping every wave,
Looking up at me,
Racing every boat,
Attacking every shark,
Beating up a whale,
Avoiding every net,
No one is taking the lives
Of these animals anymore.
Celia Frattarelli, Grade 6
Indian Valley Middle School, PA

Ice Cream
Cherries and chocolate swirls
Chocolate chips and creamy curls
Chocolate fudge as sweet as can be
Any kind is good for me.

Rocky Road and Mint Chocolate Chip
All these flavors make me skip
Vanilla, Sherbet, and Cookies and Cream
Too many flavors I have to scream
Any flavor it doesn't matter
But today I'll have Cake Batter.
Will Laverty, Grade 6
Linkhorne Middle School, VA

Places
Down the stairs,
Out the door,
See the bears,
See them roar.

Through the hallway,
Out the back door,
See the bay,
See the shore.

Across the land,
Through Main Street Way,
See the band,
See them play.

As you and me,
Can more than well see,
The places you've gone,
The places you'll see,
Everywhere will have something special!
Lexi Lewis, Grade 5
Hinesburg Community School, VT

Soccer
S uper fun
O ut of this world
C alling out helps your team
C ool looking game
E ager to play
R un fast to get the ball
Morgan Mayers, Grade 4
Lincoln Elementary School, PA

Beach
B each
E xcellent
A wesome
C ool
H ot
Teresita Lantes, Grade 4
Bayshore Christian School, FL

Math Class

I was assigned a math problem today.
It feels like a probability essay.

Maybe I'm bored, maybe I'm spacing.
I just can't believe a hard problem I'm facing.

I cannot believe that this problem's so lame.
If I don't get it right I'll be taking the blame.

There never was a good thing about math.
If I tell the teacher that she'll unveil her wrath.

My mechanical pencil ran out of lead.
Maybe because it tap-taps on my head.

I think I'll pretend that I have have the flu,
The funny thing is, it's just 2 + 2.

Amanda Vousden, Grade 6
Captain Nathan Hale Middle School, CT

Sammy

There once was a man from Miami
We're pretty sure his name was Sammy
He left for a little
For the reason was a riddle
And came back with a girl named Tammy

Kyle Mays, Grade 6
Canterbury School, FL

The Dog

Doggy, dog, the fearless knight
In the darkness lays the night,
You watch and guard your master
Are you sweet or a disaster?

Does the master know that you
Are full of sadness and blue?
Beware the knight's striking bite
For you're no coward, you're a knight

Little creature? Sweet and loved?
Is this creature ever shoved?
Don't be scared of its sharp teeth
Is their beauty like a sharp sheath?

Licks your face as a greeting,
Protects you, heart is beating,
They know how to get back home
Why do they rarely like to roam?

Doggy, dog, the fearless knight
In the darkness lays the night,
You watch and guard your master
Are you sweet or a disaster?

Melissa Lu, Grade 4
Maureen M Welch Elementary School, PA

Hiding from the World

Is this how it's supposed to be?
Am I left alone for eternity?
Will all I do is hide myself,
because I'm not meant for my own world?
They won't ever like me.
They just want to hide me
Because they're afraid of my strength.
They won't ever see me,
    the real me.
They won't ever understand what I'm hiding.
And why I'm hiding…
    from the world.

Kayla McKellar, Grade 6
Gulfview Middle School, FL

I Wonder

I wonder how the sun rises and sets
how the wind blows east to west

I wonder how many galaxies there are
all I know is that they're really far

I wonder how many people there are in the world,
how many teenagers, adults, boys and girls

I wonder how airplanes fly
and how wings keep birds up in the sky

I wonder how the world is formed
and the world being warmed

Anum Sheikh, Grade 5
Public School 2 Alfred Zimberg, NY

The Stars

Being five you know your place,
One of the younger kids.
But when you're ten,
You feel confused of where you fall.

Are you younger or older?
It'll always be a mystery.
Until the next year when you become,
A little older, just like me.

When you reach the age of twelve,
You'll realize what you were supposed to be.
But until then I'll keep hidden,
The secrets you'll soon learn of.

So live your life,
And have some fun!
Forget about this until the time comes.
To when you learn what you are,
Chill out and watch the stars.

Megan Bennett, Grade 6
Kelly Lane Intermediate School, CT

School Is Out

school is out for the summer
some people think it is a bummer
but some people are very glad
as for me I am not mad!

Katelyn Kerr, Grade 4
Glenwood Elementary School, MA

Hockey

Ice hockey
Snow to shovel off ice
Putting on ice skates
Lace up skates to the top
Put on hat
Put on gloves
Now it is time to play hockey
You skate around with your friends
The hockey game is 5 on 5
The goalie is very good
At the end of the game it is tied at 2
You go into a shoot out
On the third try you score
Your friends are piling on you
You're on the snow
It is the end of the day
Your friends have to go

Zachary Cooney, Grade 6
St Stephen's School, NY

Fluffy Snow

Snow comes at a very special time.
It's winter when it comes to mind.
You always think of a lamb.
For me I think of Bethlehem,
And what the Lord has done for me.
It reminds me of the shining star
That shines above us all.
Rain at first but then it freezes in midair.
Sometimes it gets stuck in your hair.

Samantha Bramigk, Grade 4
Bethesda Christian Academy, NC

Secret Garden

Behind these walls is
A very special place.
No eyes have seen it,
Except for the ones on my face…
Though I am very fortunate
To have what I have,
I am still always unhappy,
And oh so very sad.
So though I am in my closet,
Closing my eyes,
I feel like I am in a garden
And not just trying to hide.

Rachel Wohl, Grade 6
Canterbury School, FL

I Am From…

I am from fields of grain, bacon and eggs in the morning before church
I am from Clorox and Windex
I am from love and passion
I am from "don't back talk me" and "I love you"
I am from singing in the choir on Sunday morning
I am from grassy plains
I am from "Jed's BBQ" after church on Sunday mornings
I am from the calm waves of the ocean
I am from my daddy's grave and sadness
I am from books of glory and peace to the Earth
I am from death and sorrow
I am from wisdom
I am from telephones ringing day and night
I am from hog jowls and watermelon
I am from horses to donkeys to ponies
I am from the country
I am from curiosity and questions
I am from "do you want to have a tea party?"
I am from screaming babies and time out

Heather Hinson, Grade 4
Brier Creek Elementary School, NC

Basketball Game

Ten seconds left in the championship basketball game
The other team shoots and scores
My team is down by two
We take it out of bounds and pass it in
Oh no! The ball was almost stolen, but our point guard still has it
He dribbles up the floor
He passes to me at the three point line
BEEP! There goes the buzzer
One moment to aim and I let it fly
It's getting closer to the net
It comes down and
SWISH!
I made the winning shot
My team is going crazy
We are the winners of the championship
Here comes the huge trophy
My team and I are so happy as we wait for next season

Quinn Carey, Grade 6
St Stephen's School, NY

Teal

Teal is the air and fragrance of the breezy wind in the spring.
Teal is the sparkling grass on the edge of the shore.
Teal is the smell of cheese sticks.
Teal is the aroma of the cleanest, freshest springs in rainforests.
Teal is the color of the trees on the darkest day of the year.
Teal is the smell of food went bad.
Teal is lights beeping and flashing on a computer.
Teal is the wind spirit's leafy hair.
Teal is the luminescent lights at the bottom of the ocean.
Teal is a fresh peaceful color that can envelop someone in serenity.

Quinlan Davis, Grade 5
Princeton Elementary School, ME

Peace

peaceful waters flow down the river,
gently lining the grassy valley,
although the clouds are a light baby blue,
today they turn a gray, murky black.
tree branches swaying all,
peace to the earth is pleasured.

Bridie Daley, Grade 6
Mary Ellen Henderson Middle School, VA

Baseball…

Baseball is a taste of fun,
When you step on the field, you get hit by the sun.
Baseball is the perfect sport,
I would rather play on the field instead of a court.
Baseball is really fun when you get someone out,
But it is even better when your fans give a shout.
Baseball is a game for everyone,
Your dad can play and so can your son.
When you play baseball you fall in love,
And don't forget to bring your glove.
Baseball is a game you can play in your yard,
And if it's raining you can go through your baseball cards.

Davis Brown, Grade 4
St Joseph School, KY

My Life

My life is best no wonder I succeed.
The bad I tend to disagree.
The good I always believe.
That's the wonders of being me.
It's ok if you disagree,
'cause I will still believe.

Do what you do and I'll do what I do.
I will try to help you if you shall need.
I can't force you but wish you knew
that living my life is really cool.

Believing is the key in order to succeed.
That's why I have hope.
That living my life therefore is no joke.

Setting myself up for higher goals for each year that I grow.
It's no wonder my life is sweet,
there are so many goals that one must reach.

Cody Marsden, Grade 6
St Camillus School, NY

The Pencils

In my backpack there are some broken pencils
It is so dark and something feels like a shark
Sometimes I hear a little bark
Sometimes a little human digs in here
I just hope he will grab me!

John Sklarz, Grade 4
West Frankfort Elementary School, NY

Summer

The joy of summer
Summer means swimming around
What a great season

The sun is so hot
I am sweating like crazy
Why is it so hot?

Noah C. Trainor, Grade 5
Our Lady of Grace Elementary School, PA

Daddy's Day

I wish I wish that I had,
The man of the house I call Dad.
One day I heard him say,
I'm sorry, I have to go away.

I went to my room with a tear in my eye.
Where is he going I don't know why.
The next day I walked home from school,
I decided to take a dip in the pool.

When I walked inside I said,
Where is Daddy he's not in bed?
My mom said "I'm sorry, Dear, he went away."
Wait, why can't he stay?

We got a call from his boss.
He said we had a great loss.
I asked if Daddy was ok,
But the answer I didn't want them to say.

The next day was Daddy's day,
And my turn was bad I had to say,
My daddy is not here today
Let's just say, heaven is too far away.

Kayla Smith, Grade 6
Captain Nathan Hale Middle School, CT

The Game

There's a game,
that brought me fame,
as my coach walked to the mound,
no one made a sound,
he made me pitch,
there were two quick outs,
in everybody's mind there were no doubts,
the score, fifteen to fifteen,
with bases loaded, what a scene!
My friend stepped to the plate,
I threw my pitch, he swung late,
the count was two strikes, three balls,
all ears were on the umpire's calls,
I started my wind up, I let the ball free,
then heard the umpire say "Strike three!"

Sam Milewski, Grade 4
Nelson Place Elementary School, MA

Brooklyn Bridge
Shimmering ripples
Light showing a reflection
Show off to the world
Tehilla Bracha Mammon, Grade 4
Bnos Malka Academy, NY

Vacation
V ery great
A wesome
C amp
A vacation
T o have fun
I nvestigate Alaska
O n visiting
N ote: Alaska was great!
Thomas Lake, Grade 4
Bayshore Christian School, FL

Ladybug
Chocolate chip cookies
Tiny as a fingernail
Flying on a leaf
Rivki Elias, Grade 4
Bnos Malka Academy, NY

Relay for Life
R esearch
E motions spread
L ove heals
A hand held up
Y our comfort

F ighting for your life
O perations you go through
R adiation that weakens you

L ooking to the future
I n hope for life
F ighting to find a cure
E mbraced with faith from God
Amanda DeCarolis, Grade 4
Sacred Heart School, PA

Water Park
W ater felt good
A ctivities were cool
T otally awesome water slides
E xactly fun with my cousins
R ocking music at park

P erfect
A wesome water
R ocking fountain
K icking diving board
Katie Tawzer, Grade 4
Bayshore Christian School, FL

Rain and Snow
Rain
Wet, cold
Falling, cleaning, dropping
Water, liquid, snowflakes, icicles
Blowing, melting, sticking
Soft, white
Snow
Justin Heron, Grade 6
St Agatha School, NY

The Way the Flower Blooms
Your hair is red
Your eyes are blue
The flowers are blooming
And so are you!
Your smell is sweet
And it makes me boil
Your taste is like strawberries
In the new spring soil!
Kalie Ertwine, Grade 5
L Ray Appleman Elementary School, PA

The Dog
There was a brown dog name Nibble
Who started each day with a kibble.
He chased after the cat
Who squashed him flat
And now he is lunch on the griddle.
Jacob Powell, Grade 6
Bedford Middle School, PA

Gift of Nature
Trees breezing in the air,
Birds make nests,
In the tree's hair.

Water flows all around,
Making its lovely sound.

Animals come from all over,
Greeting each other,
With the mysterious sound.

Bring them all together,
And they create the gift of nature.
Alyssa DiCandilo, Grade 6
E T Richardson Middle School, PA

Who? What? When? Where? Why?
Ms. Dorff
was teaching fractions
today
in the classroom
because it was our aim for the day.
Dominick Tristani, Grade 4
St Agatha School, NY

Free Fall
So,
Here I am
About to let go
Leave it all behind
Here I am
Just falling
My mind blank
Not noticing anything
Around me
It was time
To let go
So
I did I did
Let go

I fell
Olivia deLeon, Grade 6
Kelly Lane Intermediate School, CT

Frightened
I was never scared
Not even of bears
Till you came along
You frightened me

I always saw the light
At the end of the road
Till you came along
You frightened me

I never thought about death
Till you came along
You frightened me
I thought that was wrong

Now I'm scared of death
Death by you
Because you frightened me
That is sad but true
Jill Durso, Grade 6
Norton School, CT

My Dog Lady
M akes a lot of noises,
Y elps when people knock on the door,

D oes not like to do tricks,
O n the couch when we are not looking,
G reat at begging,

L azy when she is alone,
A lways in a good mood,
D igs like a machine,
Y ou're going to love my dog!
Brian Espinosa, Grade 4
Meadow Park Elementary School, FL

What Is White?

White is a mountain, all covered in snow.
White is cold, feeling the wind blow.
White is a peaceful swan, swimming around.
White is a lightning bolt booming with sound!
White is a ski racer zooming downhill,
Racing and racing with a lot of skill.
White is a beach, covered in warm sand.
White is white chocolate, not a bit bland.
White is crackling ice breaking under my feet.
White is a marshmallow, squishy and sweet.
White is peaceful, like a cooing dove.
White is vanilla ice cream, that I love!

Brad Bonser, Grade 4
Fishkill Elementary School, NY

Best Buds

He was with me forever
We were instantly friends
Until that terrible day
Which was a dead end.

He was with me forever
With his big brown eyes,
And fur as yellow as a lemon,
I couldn't say good-bye.

He was with me forever
And his cheerful heart
Told me that, us two
Couldn't be apart.

He was with me forever
Until he floated to the sky,
To become a peaceful angel
While I sat to cry.

Erika Button, Grade 5
Foxborough Regional Charter School, MA

Nightfall

The breeze is gently rocking,
The tall grass to sleep.
As the trees rustle around,
Trying to get in a comfy position.
The barn creaks with the sound of life.
As the cows moo their last moos for the day.
All the children lie in their beds as,
The sky turns as black as coal.
The moon appears along with,
Hundreds of twinkling stars.
This is the beautiful place of Canada.
The sound you hear is silence.
All except the crickets playing,
Their beautiful songs,
But this only happens in Canada.

Erica Hopkins, Grade 6
Captain Nathan Hale Middle School, CT

Am...

I wish for love and peace t...
I am courageous and ...
I feel brave and strong.
I am proud and daring.
I am valiant and helping.
I have a lot of freedom.
I am never discouraged.

Briana Ng, Grade 4
Coral Park Elementary School, FL

Runaway

The rainforest is my home in my eyes
My friends and family were all surprised
No one saw it coming
Even though I knew it was my becoming

I'm a stowaway, with no partners in crime
I hope to arrive in a matter of time
I know it won't be any time soon
But I stay optimistic and always assume.

Two years have gone, and the day finally came around
I was exhausted, and skinny, and was going downward bound
I set up my camp, and looked at my new home
And a feeling washed over me that I was alone

I'm only twelve, I shouldn't be alone
I'm not immature, but I just want to go home
I hope I find a ride, with natives I find
Kids mess up, right, time after time?

Kevin Bates, Grade 6
Kelly Lane Intermediate School, CT

Those Crazy Dogs

My neighbor has seven dogs
she buys them food which they eat like hogs
and every night before I sleep
I sit in my bed and weep and weep
because those dogs are barking pests
I can't get my nightly rest

Virginia McCarthy, Grade 6
Linkhorne Middle School, VA

Master of Terrors

His genre of film is inspiring
It's almost like he founded the term "Living Dead."
From night,
To dawn,
From day to diary.
George A. Romero
    has
        redefined
            the word
                ZOMBIE.

Tyler Donahue, Grade 6
Gulfview Middle School, FL

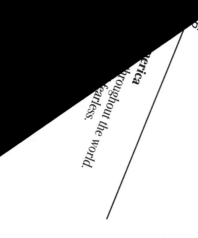

So he c... ...ead.
...ur. *Grade 5*
Westmont Hilltop ... chool, PA

Sadness the Snake

Sadness is a snake
Which binds around your soul.
When it strikes the venom goes deep.
How venomous will it be
When it bites you?
Mitchell Gray, Grade 6
Newport Middle School, NC

Racing

As I shut the door
I turn on the engine
I buckle my belt
I shift the transmission
I put it in reverse
I'm on the track
I'm ready
I'm set
Let's just hope
I don't crash.
Alex Moscone, Grade 6
Gulfview Middle School, FL

Snow

S omething that is fluffy.
N ever warm always cold.
O utside where it's cold
   we sled and play around.
W hite and fun to play in.
Kirsten Oakley, Grade 4
Bethesda Christian Academy, NC

Scooby-Doo

Scooby-Doo
Went to chew
A Scooby snack
And ate the whole pack.
Jade Sipes, Grade 6
Bedford Middle School, PA

Inside Each of Us

...e is a soul inside each of us deep within our hearts
...n't know where this poem ends but I sure know where it starts

...here it is sitting there right behind this door
But the door is locked, I can't go back I'm trapped within the core

I'm getting nervous not relieved
I'm scared to death afraid to breathe

Should I shout should I scream
I'm so alone I have no team

I feel the darkness I'm losing hope
Should I give up or should I cope

Then something shines it's a light
The door is open all is right

Caitlin Mongon, Grade 4
Mill Creek Elementary School, FL

Des Ott

Des
Fiery, friendly, caring, energetic
Daughter of Diane Carlton
Lover of horses, writing, and nature
Who feels happy when school is over, confident when we have tests,
and hyper when I'm with my friends
Who fears heights, roller coasters, and some bugs
Who would like to go to Mexico, Paris, and London
Resident of Arcadia Park
Ott

Des Ott, Grade 6
Morton Middle School, KY

5th Grade School Year

This school year was tough, I got through it
With all the home work, child labor on the playground

Three pluses, I made a lot of friends
I got good grades; my favorite subject is Social Studies
It was fun to learn about the wars and the important people and dates.

Recess is a lot of fun because of the new playground
Dances were a lot of fun and they have good music.
The parties where ok, but it was still fun to play all the day

Science was very fun such a blast, we made cars and rockets
All the experiment scum was such a mess.

The computer was fun the things an all programs
Gym was the best out of all it — all we did was have a great big ball!

Summer is here every one cheers
End of school is very near!

Jonah Maro, Grade 5
Waccamaw Intermediate School, SC

The Nature of Black

Black is the long razor sharp arrow
plunging deep through the heart,
of the massive buck
as he falls to his sudden demise.

Black is the strong ferocious bear
bolting swiftly towards it's prey,
shattering limbs beneath his huge paws
while ripping trembling flesh.

Black is the hungry lonely wildebeests
wandering the dry African plains,
cautiously searching
for tender green shoots of grass.

Black is the speedy slick rat snake
slithering round the smooth rocks,
quietly sneaking toward the old barn
to feast upon plump rodents.

Black is the enormous wild turkey
roosting on a branch of an ancient oak,
waiting for the sun to peek over the mountain
foraging for acorns and juniper berries.

Black is truly wild!

Will Gooch, Grade 4
Waynesburg Elementary School, KY

Family

The best thing you could ask for.
But sometimes it ends a snore.
Scream, scream, yell!

Brothers you can adore.
But sometimes they can war.
Bang, bang, boom!

Alex Novelli, Grade 5
Our Lady of Grace Elementary School, PA

Raindrops

Raindrops on the ground
Raindrops in the sky and clouds
Raindrops now on me

Kylee Conaway, Grade 6
Grandview Heights Christian Academy, PA

Alone

Sometimes I like to be alone, and sometimes I don't.
Most of the time I can't.
When I'm alone my world is different.
A bright light shines at the end of my dark tunnel.
A new friend enters my world.
"A soft light blue bird."

Jade Coffey, Grade 5
Southern Pines Elementary School, NC

Matt's Unlucky Day

One day Matt walked to school,
Thinking he was really cool.
He went to school looking his best,
Forgetting about the geography test.

After his test he did all his work,
Until they collected math homework.
Oh, he forgot his homework, what a shame,
But wait, just then, his mom came.

His mom had his homework what a surprise,
Then it was lunch time, it was pizza and french fries!
Poor little Matt he failed his test,
Even though he tried his very best.

Now after Matt got his grade,
He went to the nurse for first aid
After that the teacher gave him a perk,
But then he had more homework.

When he came home and took off his hat
He gave his dog a pat, pat, pat, pat.
Then he tried to play, play, play, play,
Trying not to remember his unlucky day.

Miguel A. Ortiz III, Grade 4
Nelson Place Elementary School, MA

Green

Green is grass
Green is somebody when they're ill
Green is sometimes the ocean
Green is a hopping grasshopper
Green smells like a honeysuckle vine
Green tastes like peppermint
Green sounds like a chomping alligator
Green looks like a bumpy frog
Green feels like poison ivy
Green makes me put on a tank top and go outside
Green is a Christmas tree

Ivy McGlaughlin, Grade 4
Lincoln Elementary School, PA

Best Friend

Next to you every moment
Beneath your feet sound asleep
At your window when you get home
In your room chewing up all your stuff
By the backdoor waiting to chase a squirrel
Inside your bathroom about to drink your toilet water
Beside you during a thunderstorm
For you when you're down and upset
On your bed taking up all the room
According to us,
MAN'S BEST FRIEND.

Jordan Nakayama, Grade 6
Berry Middle School, AL

Fish

I wish to be a fish,
But I am only human.

I wish to live in water,
But I am only a mammal.

I wish to be in the reef,
But I will implode.

My mind begs to be a fish,
But I would never last.

My heart longs to be with fish,
But I can't swim.

I know a job that I can do,
A marine biologist surely will do.

I now can be in the water.
I now can be with the fish.

But still cannot be in the reef.
I've reached my dream and career.
And now my life's complete.

Alyssa Smith, Grade 6
Discovery School @ Reeves Rogers, TN

Death

Death is an
indistinct hole.
It's raw,
horrifying.
It feels as if you
have fallen into a
profound, vital
slumber.
Death is like the
irreversible loss of
personhood.
Your heart
ceases to a stop.
You're no longer
a person.
You're lifeless.
So what's it going
to be?
Life or death?

Patra Banks, Grade 6
Holmes Middle School, NC

Cougar

The ready cougar
Waiting for prey to chase
With speed of hunger

Jakob Wassler-Beck, Grade 5
Avon Grove Intermediate School, PA

Army of the Brave

An army of soldiers
Mounted on their horses
Ready for battle
Facing death, of course.

But they will do it for their country
That they love so dear.
The enemy will flee
And run away in fear.

The army will face hardships;
Few will make it through.
The ones not so lucky
Have finished their journey too.

Alex Abernathy, Grade 6
Discovery School @ Reeves Rogers, TN

Nutmeg

N ever have I seen such
U nique craftsmanship
T o give to the world.
M arkings so beautiful
E very spot on her head. She's my
G reat goat Nutmeg, Ginger's kid.

Casey Bounds, Grade 5
St John Catholic School, MD

The Legendary Garden

I remember
    the garden smell.
Going
D
    O
        W
            N
the side of the house.
My mom in the grass,
Scooping out the dirt
Putting in the
flowers,
carrots, and
lettuce
    in the flower bed.

Nicole Angelo, Grade 6
Challenger Middle School, FL

Ponies

Ponies
fat, cute,
playing, galloping, running,
soft, fat tummy, tall, heavy,
kicking, squealing, biting,
fat, furry,
horses

Emilee King, Grade 4
Harmony Community School, FL

How I Hate the Morning Sun

O how I hate the morning sun,
how it's bright and not so fun.
I still would like to be asleep,
like some lucky little sheep.

Mornings are just not my thing,
I'd rather eat a LIVING THING.
Tonight is just so far away,
school takes up too much of the day.
Yes I do hate to dread,
but can't I just stay in bed?
Going to school is just so cruel.
O how I hate the morning sun.

Nicholas Clay, Grade 6
Chickahominy Middle School, VA

Features of Fall

Red, orange, yellow, and brown
swirling from the trees.
Dark gray smoke
rolling from the chimney
from the old house in the woods.
Carving huge orange pumpkins
into scary jack-o'-lanterns
sitting them on the front porch.
Colorful wild turkeys
roosting in the trees
sleeping for the night.
Chainsaws buzzing
cutting red oak and hickory
for cold winter mornings.
A plump juicy turkey
roasting in the oven
just for Thanksgiving dinner.
Feisty little fox squirrels
gathering walnuts and acorns
hiding them in their dens.
Fall is a wonderful time of year.

Chase Peel, Grade 4
Waynesburg Elementary School, KY

Polar Bears

Nature sings in me.
Polar Bears smile lightly
Earth is almost gone
Polar Bears waiting
For somebody to save them
Earth is almost gone
Sad enough to see
She sits by her mother sad
Earth is almost gone
She waits unhappy
Wanting, needing earth to cure
We have to save them

Mackenzie Leedy, Grade 6
Canterbury School, FL

I Am…

I am a child,
perhaps I seem young,
My temper is quite mild,
This fact I have sung.

I am a trilling bird
On a bright clear day.
I do not want to be treated like milk curds,
But one does not have to go with my way.

I am a swaying tree
Standing solidly in the ground.
I feel wind whistling through me,
For this I do not feel safe and sound.

As a child, I may seem young,
This fact I have already sung.

Jessica Ding, Grade 6
Haynes Academy for Advanced Studies, LA

Hilarious

Matthew
Lively, hilarious, positive
Sibling of Marissa
Lover of video games, vacations, dogs, and the outdoors
Who feels joy, love, and caring
Who needs enthusiasm, an accent, advice
Who gives love, gifts, and care
Who fears falling, getting stung, and failing a test
Who would like to see the moon, space, China
Beck

Matthew Beck, Grade 4
St Alexis School, PA

A Tribute to the American Soldiers

When there is war
Our hearts are sore
Just wanting peace
And wanting wars to decrease

Trying not to cry
It is hard when people die
I know just how you feel
Just pray to God and kneel

Everyone needs to be brave
No hiding in a cave
All of the American soldiers are in our hearts
Especially when war starts

Stop all the fights
Days and nights
We want peace
For we want all wars to cease

Alyson Mooney, Grade 4
Charles Campagne Elementary School, NY

Nothing But a Simple Concept

A unit of the sixth dimension,
Over infinite amounts.
Clouds of frustration over such a simple,
Simple concept.

From light years to time and space,
Examples of the tension between scientists
And the sixth dimension.
Not much to get but,

distance…

Ben Swanson, Grade 6
New Garden Friends School, NC

Him

As I pass him on the road so near,
I have a feeling of no fear,
I have missed him for all the years,
He is one of the few that I hold so dear.
I want him back and I want him back for good,
Why can't it be the way I think it should?
I have held on to his memories for so long,
Everyone says that I am wrong,
I miss him, I love him, and I want him back,
I am so sorry but that is that,
He is my dad,
Everyone says he's bad,
But I love him and miss him, and now I've lost my view,
So hear me that you need to,
Always love and cherish your dad,
Or he will be gone and that is bad.

Emily Jolly, Grade 4
Cave City Elementary School, AR

Football

Football is a popular sport,
Even most say it's "America's sport."
The team from Dallas, The Cowboys,
Is known as "America's Team."

53 players in the locker room,
53 players all with one goal,
53 players all wanting a ring,
All wanting to win the Super bowl.
It's not "how hard you hit" no,
It's "how hard you get hit, and get back up."

Football is a team sport,
There is no I in TEAM.
On Fridays its high school,
On Saturday its college,
On Sunday it's the pros.
What is Football?
Football is "America's sport."

Troy Pecoraro, Grade 6
Haynes Academy for Advanced Studies, LA

Dominic

D aring
O utstanding
M agnificent
I ntelligent
N ice
I nteractive
C aring

Dominic Bray, Grade 4
West Frankfort Elementary School, NY

It

It
licked Lucy
barked at Betty
jumped on Joey
It
drooled on Drew
wiped its paw on Wally
slobbered on Stacy
It
even laughed at Larry
made Megan mad
yelped at Yalanda
don't forget
It
had Hailey on her heels
chased after Chase
nibbled on Nelly
so
beware!
Because it could come
to your house some day.

Sagan Leggett, Grade 6
Ichabod Crane Middle School, NY

Flip

I can flip up
I can flip down
Flipping is fun
But not on the ground
You bump your head
You make big frowns
I'd rather do it in the pool
So, you won't look like a fool
I must admit
Flipping is fun

Chanelle Dupuis, Grade 5
Trinity Lutheran School, FL

My Cat

Loving and smart
sitting to care for me
like the best cat ever
if only she could live forever

Danielle Long, Grade 4
Black Fox Elementary School, TN

Lost Beauty

The wind blows, rustling through the trees.
The wind so warm but cool, the grass so wet,
The brush so green. Refreshing.

The cooling mist is over. All it is, is ashes.
From the burning trees no more do the bugs crawl. The silence is unnatural.
The birds are gone, no more of a forest,
Now a large barren wasteland. Where there seldom is movement.
The river is dry, there are no frogs. No more plants because of us humans.

How I miss the beauty of those woods.
And how the trees would chat, and how I watched it flourish with plants and animals.
Maybe someday it shall grow back greener and fuller than it was before.
The beauty was stunning,
I was always happy sitting with my true friends.

Jordyn Fairbanks, Grade 6
Blue Ridge Middle School, VA

Do You Know…?

Bombs, guns, fire, destruction
Do you know what it was like?
Do you know what it was like to get treated like dirt?
Do you know what it was like to be free?

Do you know what it was like to have your name like a curse?
To get marked with a star and get sent away,
To a camp where pain and suffering are its' priorities?

Do you know what it felt like to get cramped into a room deadly gases seeping in?
Where tears of agony and fear come from innocent eyes?
And one man laughing cruelly at his near perfect world.

Maryanna Antoldi, Grade 6
Sacred Heart School, MD

The Fairies

I sit alone in the grass so green,
Wishing I had someone to play with, besides me.
When I see a fairy flying hither and a twitter,
I watch with wide eyes as it comes down to me and whispers,
"Come with me into the trees, and we can fly against the breeze!"
I say, "I can't! I have no wings!"
She looks at me in her odd little way,
Then sprinkles fairy dust on me, and
I soar up, and away!
I fly high and low then do a twirl,
Then I swing on a branch with the fairy girl.
For the rest of the day we fly in the warm spring air,
As I pretend I am an acrobat,
In a circus or county fair.
Then suddenly I wake up from my happy dream,
And though I feel sad,
In my eyes there is a gleam,
Because now I know what it is like
To experience a fairy dream!

Sarah Ferris, Grade 6
Covenant Christian School, FL

Bye Bye Winter Hello Beautiful

I peer out the slightly frosted window.
Oh how I look forward to hearing that first ambitious crow.
In the streets soon I will shout to all those out there,
"Winter's over! Winter's over!"
Now I lay here and merely ponder.
The snow sprinkles all about the ground.
Yet it does not make the slightest sound.
Wintery,
Snowy,
Wait what is that I see infinitely glowing?
It's the sun! The sun is showing!!!
The sun's coming up for the first time in days!
No more Santas, no more snow, no more sleighs!
The spring is coming!
Tag and kickball, everyone soon should be playing!!!

Nichole Dahlen, Grade 6
Mellon Middle School, PA

Sadness

Sadness is like the color blue,
It sounds like rain dropping to the ground,
It smells like dew drops on a spider's web,
It tastes like the ocean salt water,
It looks like blueberries that just got picked,
Sadness feels like a thunderstorm.

Nicolette Jones, Grade 4
Sacred Heart School, PA

Frightening Night

The darkness of the night
filled the room with no light
My spine shivered with fright
at this indescribable sight
I hear the creak of the door
and sudden footsteps on the floor
And this feeling deep inside of me gnaws at my core
this ominous premonition I've never felt before
What came to be
a nightmare in reality
Is a dark haunting figure I suddenly see
and slowly, and quietly, it starts walking towards me

Aubrey Bouchard, Grade 5
Edgeworth Elementary School, PA

The Sunset

As the sun sets
There's only a pinch of light
It shines upon the slide and monkey bars
Slowly, slowly
The darkness settles upon the sky
I lay upon the grass
And look up at the sky
As the stars twinkle
It's like they're talking

Shayla Leeney, Grade 4
Riverside School, CT

Love

Love.
A word we take for granted.
Every night, we say I love you.
But do you mean it?

I say I love you every night.
I mean it.
But would you say I love you if you didn't mean it?

You could, I guess.
You could lie through gritted teeth.
You could.

I love. I love life.
I love the sand, the sky, the grass, and the clouds.
I love animals. I love my family. I love the trees.
I love everything that I can love.

I love the stars that dance at night.
I love the wind that whispers good night.
I love the world, and everything on it.

I'll do anything to keep it all going.
Those lives before mine.
No one will or can change it.

Elizabeth Profaci, Grade 6
Garrison Forest School, MD

How the World Should Be…

I wish the world was all 100% peace
I wish there was no fighting
I wish we could all get along
I wish there were no bullies
I wish there were not power-hungry demons
I wish there were all helping angels
I wish that we all believed in and trusted God
I wish we all believed in and trusted the Holy Spirit
I wish we all believed in and trusted Jesus

Steffen Janser, Grade 6
Kelly Lane Intermediate School, CT

Money Can't Buy Everything, Joy

Money can't buy everything
Joy is a thing that can't be bought,
No matter whom you are or what you thought,
Joy is a feeling and a great one too,
But, I wouldn't expect to hear that from you,
You are just one of those people,
Who simply can't understand,
Why even though you spend a fortune,
Your life is so bland.
Yes joy is a feeling and a great one too,
I hope you can find it,
Now that I have shared with you.

Gene O. Desideraggio, Grade 6
Kelly Lane Intermediate School, CT

My Fifth Grade Year

Math — Adding, subtracting, and fractions — these are the things that make contraptions, I have some questions on algebra, and it isn't fun. Thank goodness — I'm on the last question — that means I'm almost done.
Social Studies — I really like social studies; it is my favorite subject, this I know is correct, Alaska was connected with Russia at the beginning of time, then they broke away without any sign.
Reading — I don't like reading; I'm not very good, but I need to read, I really should, my favorite book of all is Robin Hood, but this year it was hard to choose, they were all really good.
Science — I made a rocket and a car — they both didn't go very far.
Art — Painting, coloring and clay, these are the best parts of the day.
We went to the state and art museum, some day I want to go back again.
P.E. — Poison ball, running, and capture the flag, these are the things that make me glad.
Music — Guitars, pianos, and brass instruments are fun to play,
The plays and the bands made my day.
CAI Lab — Math and reading is what we do,
Sometimes my scores make me look like a fool.
Guidance — We talk about drugs or safety, sometimes Mr. Cook goes crazy.
Spelling — Entrepreneur, geology, and factor,
These are the words that bring no laughter.
Friends — Ethan, Jack, Zach, Grayson, and Nate,
These are my fifth grade friends from 2008.

Aubrey Gauthier, Grade 5
Waccamaw Intermediate School, SC

The Beach

It speaks the language of the ocean.
Splash, splash
It borders the ocean with two skies.
Water is connected to the sky.
It hits the horizon when exchanging places.
Fire will touch the mountains behind the water.
The white horizon will come again.
Foolish blue waves crash against the shore, piling over each other.
Illusion covers the ocean in a blanket.
A cut line whirls across the sea.
BAM!
It hits its target.
Grains of sand with crystals that capture the colors of the sunset dance like the Northern Lights.
Black water is fierce like an unblinking eye.
Air, which was silently growing, goes wild.
In a room inside an oyster the sheen of a pearl waits to be discovered.
Crystallized starfish are frosty stars.
A twinkling legendary music is locked in time inside a shell.
A heavy, unfolding ribbon of seaweed embraces its surroundings.
Sand dollars, medallions of sunlight are flowers shaped like the moon.
Someday, sometime in a million years my memory will bring the beach back.

Faith Gray, Grade 4
Quest Elementary School, NY

Respect

Everyone needs to show respect to everyone
You could show respect by listening to what people have to say
Respect is important because if you show respect to someone they will show respect to you as well
You could also show respect by doing what you're told
Or even just listening to people when they're talking
And by respecting their wishes

Alysha London, Grade 5
Jamestown Elementary School, PA

The Sign

The sign says you can't play golf
Or dance and shout, "Ole!"
It says you can't play soccer
Or teach your dog ballet.

You can't jump or run or even play,
You can't dance or jog or scream "Hooray!"
'Cause that's what the sign says.

The sign says you can't wear dresses
With purple polka dots.
It says you can't eat candy,
'Cause then your teeth will rot.

You can't build or plant or eat some pie,
But I just stare and laugh and sigh.
'Cause I know I've broken every rule
They say here on this sign!

Brooke Aubin, Grade 5
Briggs Elementary School, MA

Chants

Walking along the heated sand
The hot dry wind pursued us
Nothing to eat or drink
And only the clothes we have on our back
The hot dry wind pursued us
Not a living creature or plant to be found
The hot dry wind pursued us

Kristal Huber, Grade 6
Kelly Lane Intermediate School, CT

5th Grade

Last summer nothing to do every day,
Yet so many opportunities.
August the first day of school is the worst day of school.
Mornings speeding down the hall,
I try to beat the BRINGALINGALING!!
September waiting for my birthday, like a desert waits for rain.
October I see all the scary monsters, I become one myself.
November having lots of fun, eating lots of turkey,
Don't want to go to school, and do any worky.
December Christmas time is almost here,
Time of laughter and time of cheer.
New Year staying up late and eating lots of BBQ,
I was so tired, I saw my dad and said "who are you?"
February everyone is happy, and cares for each other,
Loving all of their sisters and their brothers.
March Leprechauns attack,
Everyone but Jack.
April I told my sister she's getting old,
She hit me and then got told.
May summer time is here
School's over and I am glad my time is free time.

Jack Sanders, Grade 5
Waccamaw Intermediate School, SC

Alex

A thletic
L arge imagination
E nthusiastic
X -tra special

Alex Reid, Grade 4
West Frankfort Elementary School, NY

Kangaroo

Bounces and pounces like most animals do.
Has a pouch on the front of it too.
Eats plants green and leafy.
Lots of different kinds of species.
Groups of them live in Australia.
This animal is the kanga…ROO!

Emma Thomas, Grade 4
Pike Creek Christian School, DE

Things I Like

Things that I like
are riding my bike.
My mom and my dad
always make me glad.
I don't want to be a fool,
so I go to school.
Homework isn't fun
I get a ton.
I like hockey
and the movie *Rocky*.
Skateboarding on a ramp
and going to camp.
Playing with my brother
cooking with my mother
and most of all helping others.

Nico Stelitano, Grade 6
Christ the Divine Teacher Catholic Academy, PA

Spec of Time

As time passes slowly and slowly
time gives changes around the world
the shadows change
the Earth orbits
nature blossoms
slowly and slowly the time passes
it never goes back and
it always goes forward

Sitting by a tree
I can see the shadows
skinny lines of branches
there are no more leaves
to fall on the ground
except for one little leaf
on the tip of the branch
barely falling but never does

Yuto Iwakuma, Grade 6
Haynes Academy for Advanced Studies, LA

Bride

My dad is going to marry,
He is very occupied.
And on the contrary,
I really like the bride.
Beside the fact she's nice,
It's not that big a sacrifice.
To spend one-thousand dollars,
To get married more than twice.
Sabrina Kopf, Grade 6
Kelly Lane Intermediate School, CT

Honesty

Honesty is the
Sparkle
In your heart
And what makes you
Shine.
Honesty is
Pride.
It means to be
Brave,
And to do the right thing
When no one is
Watching.
Honesty is standing
Up
For what you
Believe in.
Honesty is joy
And peace
And happiness.
Honesty is temptation,
And being able to resist it.
Princess Lane, Grade 6
J E Holmes Middle School, NC

White

White is snow
It tastes like water
It sounds like crunching
It smells like winter
It looks like ice
It makes me feel joyful
Savannah Hughes, Grade 4
Black Fox Elementary School, TN

Day and Night

Day
Bright, loud
Shining, living, moving
Cloudy, happy, still, starry
Sleeping, snoring, dreaming
Dark, silent
Night
Nicole McCartin, Grade 5
Avon Grove Intermediate School, PA

I Really Want a Pet

I really want a pet,
But I don't know what to get,
I want something small,
That could fit into a ball.

I really want a pet,
But I don't know what to get,
Now I've found a mouse,
My mom goes EEEK!
Get it out of the house!

I open the door,
And I fall onto the floor,
To see my mother's blouse,
Squishing my little mouse!

Now I'm really mad,
And also a little sad,
My mom said no more pets,
So I think I'll be a vet.
Zane Denmon, Grade 6
Lake Noxen Elementary School, PA

Black Sand Beach

Black sand and emerald sand,
The waves carrying the sand away.
The bright sun is like a lamp's light
Shining on the dark sand.
Does the wave have feelings?
I wonder
As I see the black waves crashing.
Emma Schaale, Grade 4
Riverside School, CT

Fat Old Lady

Once there was a fat old lady
Her middle name was Cady
Her shoes were small
When she hit the wall,
She said, "My this tree is so shady!"
Emory McVeigh, Grade 6
Linkhorne Middle School, VA

My Star

The sky so large above our heads
Not only stars and planets live
Where God lives, I'm sure
That one star is my Father's
Twinkling and waiting for
Someone to join in
I wish to see this star
When I'm in God's hands
For my star awaits me
Twinkling and waiting
Nikita Singh, Grade 6
Canterbury School, FL

Art!

Art is wonderful and peaceful.
You escape from the world
and go into your own fantasy.
You feel like you have the whole world
in the palm of your hand.
You can paint,
sculpt,
or draw.
Art has a variety of ways
to escape the everyday world.
You paint from your heart.
Sculpt your dreams
and draw your plans for life.
Art is a magical
and wonderful thing.
Amanda Brianne Brown, Grade 6
Gulfview Middle School, FL

My Kitten Sparta

Today I went in my room.
I saw my kitten, Sparta, on my bed.
He was curled up in a ball.

Sparta, why do you curl up
Into a ball and just lay there?
Your pretty eyes are closed.
Don't you want people
To admire your eyes?

And your fur! Why do you crawl
Into the blankets and hide
Your soft fur?
Don't you want people to pet you?

Your purr sounds good.
Don't you want people
To hear your lovely voice?
It makes a pleasant humming sound.

Sparta, all of your pretty features
Are being cooped up.
You shouldn't do that.
You are being selfish.
Laura Carrara, Grade 6
Hinesburg Community School, VT

Summer and Winter

Summer
Hot, warm
Swimming, biking, vacationing
Pool, beach, Canada, Alaska
Snowboarding, skiing, snowing
Icy, cold
Winter
Johnelly Fabian, Grade 6
St Agatha School, NY

Let Me Tell You About the Seasons

Winter, Spring, Summer, Fall
Those are the seasons — I love them all.

Winter is cold and Spring is misty,
Summer is warm and Fall is windy.

Take a ride on any day,
You'll find an adventure while on your way.

Winter, Spring, Summer, Fall —
I love you so much — I have a ball!

Just so you know the reason for —
the seasons is really clear

Earth's rotation makes them grow
Earth's axis tilts and away they go!

Earth spins around just like a top
The sun sits still and watches nonstop.

Summer Lewis, Grade 5
PA Leadership Charter School, PA

Amid Vines of Lush Green

I walk into a concealed wonderland.
The setting is far from bland.
I smell the brisk, cool air that soothes some pain,
Like scents of fall's mist and rain.
Birds, pleased like newlyweds, sit atop trees,
Chirping at the humming bees.
Green pine bristles reach out to feel the air.
There were no signs of despair.
Apt trees sway like partiers in the night.
The breeze picks up pace in fright.
Walking on, I see a protected tree;
A tree yet to be set free.
The tree: the youngster in this world of green.
Caring is yet to be seen.
Its protective, close relatives stand near,
The tall ones having no fear.
Their branches creeping out from the tree trunks.
Home to a million chipmunks.
And the sun still awaits its turn to shine
Amongst tree, bristles of pine.

Shana Blatt, Grade 6
East Shore Middle School, CT

Freedom

The river rolls on
Through waterfalls and trees
But until dawn
Water runs freely and mysteriously
For on it rolls
Until it has reached the end of its final journey.

Jordan Psimas, Grade 6
Blue Ridge Middle School, VA

The Barn Owl

A rundown barn is where I live.
People think I'm provocative.
So here I stay, just out of sight,
A silent stalker in the night.

For hunting at night, I'm the best.
I save this barn from every pest,
Like mice and bugs and snakes and rats.
Here I stay among the bats.

I'm ready to pounce and attack.
I just hope my prey won't fight back.
I am ready, so I spring,
Into the air with my wings.

I pounce on my unwary prey.
Like a deer in headlights, there it'll stay.
I finish it like a knife through butter.
I thank God for my mouse all aflutter.

I then fly up to my dark beam,
Away from the treacherous gleam.
A mouse who's life has been claimed by a fowl,
Me, sitting up here, the barn owl.

Stephen Senderoff, Grade 6
East Shore Middle School, CT

This Is Baseball

I walk up to the plate,
For my chance with fate.
The pitcher stares me down,
But I don't even frown.
The adrenaline kicks in,
And I start to grin.
As I prepare for the pitch,
I feel a slight twitch.
I let the ball go by,
But it was the pitch I wanted to send sailing into the sky.
I calm myself down,
And dig my foot into the ground.
The pitcher throws the ball to me,
And I hit it farther than anyone can see.
I watch the ball soar,
And I hear the crowd roar.
We just won the game.
This is baseball.

Alex Kovacs, Grade 6
St Stephen's School, NY

Polar Bears

Polar bears float on melting ice
Stranded, alone, deserted, no lie
We can make a difference that would be nice
We need to help before they die.

Jessica Manion, Grade 6
Kelly Lane Intermediate School, CT

Ice Cream

Ice cream is delicious
It feels cold in your mouth

It's creamy and rich
Such a tasty treat

I would eat it all day
At each and every meal

Ice cream is so sweet
It makes you feel happy

Ice cream is good on a hot day
Or even on a chilly day

Cotton candy flavor is
The very best

Vanilla is a favorite
Chocolate is too
Brittany Wilkerson, Grade 6
Chickahominy Middle School, VA

Thunderbird

My wings expand over my earth,
making nights even darker.
My drift swirls the seven seas
with waves upon heavy waves.
I reign over all of the earth,
stalking my weaklings and prey.
Horror scars those who have seen me,
terror yet to come of those who seek me,
for I am king of the world.

My name is Thunderbird,
who was, is, and will always be.
Noah Masimore, Grade 6
Pine Crest School, FL

My Escape

You bring my escape
I wish to see you daily
Ever changing you…
Helps me discover a new,
Large vast universe beyond.
Isiah Botelho, Grade 6
Normandin Middle School, MA

How the Bunny Changed

There once was a beautiful bunny,
who thought of himself as funny,
but when the morning came,
he didn't feel the same,
he found out he stole a lot of money.
Ryan Wilson, Grade 5
Avon Grove Intermediate School, PA

Baxter Outside

He lay
So still
Like time
Had paused
Peaceful, Calm, Tranquil
The light shone
Down on him
Like he
Was in
The spotlight
Peaceful, Calm, Tranquil
Sun shining
Birds chirping
Time paused
Lying still
Peaceful, Calm, Tranquil
Shannon Daine, Grade 4
Riverside School, CT

Macaws

Resting on a cliff
Colorful like a rainbow
Relaxing like me.
Moria Giahn, Grade 4
Bnos Malka Academy, NY

Nature

Leaves sprinkling
down
like falling snow.

The small stream
glides
like a snake
through the woods.

The bright sun
is hidden
behind the tall trees
around.

The peacefulness
makes everything
become
all right.
Emily Winterich-Knox, Grade 5
New Garden Friends School, NC

Writer's Block

My mind is now under lock
Like a store that is out of stock
There's nothing to do
But cry "boo-hoo"
For I have writer's block
Claire Glover, Grade 5
Bancroft Elementary School, MA

War/Peace

War
Violent, gory
Fighting, killing, dying
Stupid, dreadful, quiet, good
Living, agreeing, respecting
Nice, great
Peace
Will Zeigler, Grade 4
Hanahan Elementary School, SC

Untitled

Its feathers shine bright
Swiftly flies from tree to tree
Loud squawking macaw
Ryan Cole, Grade 4
Stackpole Elementary School, PA

Water

Water in the ocean

How did you get there?
Why are you so filled with life?
Why are you that color?

Oh, dear swimmer in my waves
I'm glad you enjoy me.

I cannot say,
God made me this way.
Jake Sonsini, Grade 6
Kelly Lane Intermediate School, CT

A Special Wish

I see all stars and it's very dark
I'm laying on the grass
At the park.
I make a wish
On the first one I see
I watch it twinkle
And I am very sleepy.
Then all of a sudden
A shooting star passes by
It was really yellow
But it was actually a firefly
My mom calls me in
And tells me it's bedtime.
When I start to go in my house
I look at all the stars
I see the moon right next to them
But they are actually far apart.
Then I wake up in the morning
And the sun starts to shine really bright
Then I noticed my wish came true
And I wished for there to be light.
Elena Di Bona, Grade 5
Public School 128 Juniper Valley, NY

My 5th Grade Year

My favorite subject is math
All I remember in math is multiplying and dividing.
Doing shapes like equal lateral triangles.

Maybe some social studies is my favorite
I like to study the wars
But it could be science
Because we did lots of experiments

Now that I think about it
I don't like English what so ever.
I didn't like writing the tall tales
And I didn't like writing anything!

But I can remember P.E.
We played "Poison Ball"
And we did "Capture the Flag."
So my favorite thing about this 5th grade school year is P.E.

Mac Winter, Grade 5
Waccamaw Intermediate School, SC

Spring Time

Spring is a wondrous time of year,
Sitting on the dark oak bench watching the white tailed deer,
Kicking the soccer ball all around,
Hearing all my fans in the crowd,
Taking the winter jacket off,
Putting on a T-shirt made of light blue cloth,
The end of the light fluffy snow,
Time to watch the multicolor flowers grow,
Spring is a happy time of year,
So let's all give a spring time cheer.

Kenidie Kalbach, Grade 5
L Ray Appleman Elementary School, PA

Always a Tree

It was as sturdy as a table
With all roots implanted in the ground
But still a tree

It was a monster with arms
Extending out of it
But it was still a tree

It was a jigsaw puzzle with all
The fragmented pieces of bark fitting together
Still a tree

It was like a dog shedding its fur
But still a tree

It was home to many animals
Keeping lives with precious protection
But still, a tree

Spencer Baxter, Grade 4
Riverside School, CT

Cucumbers

Straight from the fridge,
As cold as an icy drawbridge.
Crunchy as a dog bone,
I love when they are homegrown.
But for me to eat them,
They must be full-grown!
I like them more than an ice cream cone!

Erica Keim, Grade 4
Watsontown Elementary School, PA

Shade

Shade, it comes and goes
Depending on where you are
In and out it comes and goes
Where ever you are it is with you

Listening to bees buzz and birds chirp
It's still there with you right beside you
Walking
    down
        steps
            it's
                still
                    there
                        with
                            you

Following you around where you are
It's still there with you right beside you
A smaller, simpler version of you with you.
And yet, it never leaves you alone.

Matt Payne, Grade 6
Blue Ridge Middle School, VA

I…

As I walk down a street,
My heart with no beat,
My mind in the clouds,
My dreams, are to drown.
The two paths that seek
In front of me
One black and one green,
One seen to be wrong
To make a change for who
Someone wants me to be.
The other is my choice,
For me to stay me
For me to stay stainless and
Flawless in my imperfections
I chose a path, but for I will not tell.
With you should be you, and me should be me.
Destined to be, salient,
I will choose to be
I will…

Amira Hodzic, Grade 6
David R. Cawley Middle School, NH

Half Dome

The sun
was shining brightly
the wind
was very fast
the mountain
was shiny.
Shiny
shiny
shiny
birds were chirping
the trees were rustling
by the breeze
I wonder
what it would look
and feel like
on the top?

Chelsea Bernheim, Grade 4
Grace Lutheran School, FL

Rock 'N Roll

R ock 4 life
O ld guitars
C ome on turn it up
K ids are allowed

N othing but fun

R ock out loud
O ff the walls
L oud, louder, loudest
L et's rock!!

Jonathan Hynes, Grade 5
St John Catholic School, MD

Wonders of the Ocean

The ocean is full of wonders
It shimmers like crystals
It gives you a sense of calmness
You can hear the seagulls

The ocean shimmers a light blue
Whoosh, you can hear the waves crash
You'll feel a cool mist on your skin
Together the waves smash

You see the water overlapping
The brilliant shine blinds you
It stuns, you have to catch your breath
You breathe in the sea air too.

The sizzling sun beats down on your skin
You feel a bead of sweat
Then you take in the scenery
Now you're all soaking wet!

Victoria Botelho, Grade 6
Blue Ridge Middle School, VA

Genesis Guadalupe

Genesis
flexible, talkative, talented
Sibling of Emmanuel, Jeremiah, Jonas, Jorgito, Sofia, Andrea
Lover of Hannah Montana, beach, pool, food, shelter, family
Who feels happy, loving, scared at night, grumpy when alarm rings
Who needs education, food, shelter, family, gymnastics, pool
Who gives friendship, trust
Who fears spiders, bulls, snakes, strangers, scary books and movies
Who would like to see Disney Channel stars, especially Hannah Montana
Guadalupe

Genesis Guadalupe, Grade 4
Harmony Community School, FL

A Younger Brother to Black

Brown is known as a younger brother to black,
The ultimate partner that rainbows lack.
It can be found coloring some people's hair,
And is the brownish-type shade of the great lion's mare.
Brown may be used to describe western folk,
And may be hiding in fizzy Diet Coke.
Brown lives with the ocean off the coast,
And is the color, smell, and taste of BBQ roast.
Brown is the hard, tough bark of a tree,
Which we must preserve if the Earth is to be green.
In the morning, brown is bad especially when you're really mad.
Brown makes the delicious chocolate bar,
And you'll find him resting on the rim of a worn-out car.
If you cut brown onions that are nearby,
You feel the sudden, strong urge to cry.
Most importantly, brown is the color of my skin.
The same goes for the rest of my kin!

Siddarth Narayan, Grade 6
Marshall Middle School, PA

Fireworks!

The golf course starts to fill with people young and old
As the sun goes down after a long day of excitement
People talk and chatter as the anticipation builds
Everyone is waiting waiting for a show of surprise

I lie back on the blanket ready for the show to begin
I look up at the stars and I feel the rain on my skin
People cry out and huddle under blankets
But the show still goes on and the sky fills with rockets

Gold red purple orange all colors dark and light
The sky is filled with rain and explosions the colors mix with sparkling stars
Oooos and Aaaaas fill the air I watch in amazement
As the fireworks twist and twirl jump and leap through the air

There are spirals and squares smiles and bursts
Ovals triangles whistles and chains the night is full of noise and sparks
With bursts and bangs the show comes to a close
Everybody cheers and claps after that wonderful show

Caitlin Porrazzo, Grade 6
Garrison Forest School, MD

Morning

The immense red cracks through the evening
It is the secret of the morning
It blossoms like flowers at springtime
It pronounces to the world work is here,
Day has come.

Emma Huckestein, Grade 5
Edgeworth Elementary School, PA

Final Days

Old people
Most go soon,
Some stay young.

Some are still energetic
Others fight,
For each breath.

When they go, they leave
Items for the young.
But bring with them,

Time
Memories
And the keys to an exciting life.

Josh Pierce, Grade 6
E T Richardson Middle School, PA

If I Were in Charge of the World*

If I were in charge of the world,
I'd cancel boring plays,
The Home and Garden channel,
Chick flicks, and also
Golf

If I were in charge of the world,
There'd be more baseball games,
More dogs, and
Less storms

If I were in charge of the world,
You wouldn't have sick,
You wouldn't have sleep,
You wouldn't have wars,
Or school

If I were in charge of the world,
An ice cream sandwich would be an entrée,
All *Rocky* movies would be PG,
And a person who sometimes forgot to lock the door,
And sometimes fell on the floor,
Would still be allowed to be
In charge of the world.

Trevor Hammonds, Grade 6
Morton Middle School, KY
*Patterned after "If I Were in Charge of the World"
by Judith Viorst

I Wonder Why

I wonder why my nose has two holes.
Only one would have been good I suppose.
I wonder why my eyes blink.
Maybe they don't think.
I wonder why my head has so much hair.
How would it look bare?
I wonder why my ears hear.
Maybe they have no fear.
I wonder why I have two legs to walk.
I few more would have been the town talk.
I wonder why I have one mouth.
Two, three or four would be good to shout loud.
I wonder why I have ten fingers.
They are even not odd I wonder.
I wonder why sometimes my stomach grumbles.
Maybe it loves to play rumble and tumble.

Zainab Shah, Grade 5
Floris Elementary School, VA

John Michael Nowak

John Michael Nowak,
Tall, funny, big feet,
Son of Karen and John,
Who loves life, bikes, and music,
Who feels weary about technology,
Who needs food, water, and sleep,
Who gives advice, clothes, and toys,
Who fears little kids, snakes, and awkward moments,
Who'd like to see world peace,
Who dreams of safe computers,
A student of Mr. Cronin's,
Homer

John Michael Nowak, Grade 6
Lake Noxen Elementary School, PA

Summer Fun

When summer is here,
Everyone is excited!
You can go to the swimming pool,
Or have fun at the beach!

You can do sport activities,
By playing soccer,
Having fun with a jump rope,
Or playing tennis with a friend!

Basketball and canoeing,
Are also really fun!
Everything is perfect,
Since summer has just begun!

Have fun during summer,
And remember,
All activities are fun!

Briana Dincher, Grade 6
Intermediate School 239 Mark Twain, NY

Untitled
The butterfly goes
off in the wind, free again
From its tight cocoon.
Jasmine Vanscoy, Grade 6
New Garden Friends School, NC

Peace
Peace
It keeps the world safe
It keeps things united and together
It keeps the world in harmony
It makes the world a better place
A safe peaceful world would be nice
Life would be better
If there was peace
Maybe the Earth would look better
No war, no more bombs
The world would be better with peace
Cordell McCloskey, Grade 5
Jamestown Elementary School, PA

Untitled
Jamaica's beauty,
Jamaica's wonderful sea,
The lush green palm trees,
The soft sand on the seashore,
The green seaweed on the sea.
Sophia Akopov, Grade 4
Stackpole Elementary School, PA

In My Heart
Why did you go?
I know you watch over me.
I will never forget you.
The special dolls and necklace,
I will treasure for a lifetime.
You're in my heart forever.
I love you and in 100 years from now,
I will see you again.
You're in my heart always.
Madison Hanley, Grade 5
Melville School, RI

Tree of Tranquility
The goddess is gone
Rainbows are lost forever
When will she come back
Kyndal Paige, Grade 6
Linkhorne Middle School, VA

Winter
When the snow comes down
It looks like pretty sparkles
That dance through winter
Christopher Horton, Grade 4
Public School 207 Rockwood Park, NY

Sad Day
Oh sad day
Oh sad day
When nothing goes my way.

Then my mother said
Do anything but play.

I cried boo hoo
When I looked up to the moon

And that night,
When I went to bed,
I couldn't wait
Till the day would end

Oh sad day
Oh sad day
When nothing goes my way.
Hayley Wasson, Grade 5
Salisbury Elementary School, PA

Puffer Fish
Prickly blue body
Puffs itself up in a ball
Like a porcupine
Rivka Zalmanov, Grade 4
Bnos Malka Academy, NY

Rain
The rain is falling down
Down to the ground
Put on your raincoat and hat
And go step in the puddles
Calista Heath, Grade 5
Avon Grove Intermediate School, PA

Three Little White Mice!
I spotted three little white mice,
Oh, wow they looked kind of nice.
How they were so, so white,
They lit up the house during the night.
Erin Conolly, Grade 6
Warrenton Middle School, VA

Seasons
The changing of the seasons
for many different reasons
emerald leaves you and I meet
to the scorching summer's heat
down to the leaves of fiery color
around in a pattern
with the beauty of saturn
got to go
it's about to snow
Kyle Skillman, Grade 5
Tropic Isles Elementary School, FL

The Dragon
A dragon who developed strep throat,
was cold when he swam in the moat.
It scratched and tore,
grew very sore,
so next time he'll put on a coat.
Lauren Diehl, Grade 6
Bedford Middle School, PA

Cat in a Tub
There was an old cat in a tub
who was dirty and needed to scrub.
the water was hot
because he forgot
to turn on the cold in the bathtub.
Meara McCarty, Grade 6
Bedford Middle School, PA

Me
I come from my parents
Who love and cherish me
I come from my friends
Who have been there for me
I come from football
And my brother's teaching
I come from ETR
Where teachers are fantastic
I come from Springfield
And all the great years of my life
I come from having fun at parties
I come from
Me
Tyler Staud, Grade 6
E T Richardson Middle School, PA

Life and Death
Life
Wonderful, beautiful
Moving, talking, playing
Birth, beginning, sad, end
Sleeping, dying, not breathing
Darkness, peaceful
Death
Ryan Pantoja, Grade 6
St Agatha School, NY

The Light
In a dark alley,
Down by the "Galley"
With a light,
As dark as night.
There was a mouse,
Who made his house,
Out of the light,
As dark as night.
Emily Stowe, Grade 5
Calvary Chapel Christian School, PA

Kittens

Small kittens wobble around trying to catch their balance.
Their mother softly meows and licks the smallest one
    encouraging it to stand up.
She lifts herself up on unstable legs,
    only to fall back down.

By now, the kittens are tumbling and playing.
The little kitten blinks slowly
    watching her brothers and sisters play,
    too weak and tired to try anymore.
Her mother won't let her give up though
With one last attempt she uses all her might to stand up
    and walk out of the little wooden bed.

The other kittens are soon by her side
    coaxing her to walk forward.
She tumbles and falls many times
    before walking in a straight line.

The kittens all walk back in victory.
They curl up and snuggle close to their mother.
She purrs softly
    with satisfaction.

Clairese Rogula, Grade 6
Gulfview Middle School, FL

I Love Virginia Beach

I love Virginia Beach
It's also time when I put my sister on a leash

The beach is really hot
But the cool Atlantic ocean is not

I really need sun block
When the sun give me a shock

After I get out of the ocean
I rub on suntan lotion

When I went on the boardwalk
I saw a big brown rock

At the aqua water parks
There are so many fake sharks

I love Virginia Beach
I love Virginia Beach

Precious Gilbert, Grade 6
Linkhorne Middle School, VA

Carpe Diem

When you come to the end of the road
and the sun has set for you,
there is no going back and doing what you didn't do.

Megan Wochoski, Grade 6
Captain Nathan Hale Middle School, CT

Penguins

Penguins waddle
Penguins dive
Penguins swim
Penguins can't fly
Penguins are black
Penguins are white
I love penguins

Grace Lundvall, Grade 4 and Molly Walter, Grade 3
Fishing Creek Elementary School, PA

The Sweet Sound of Spring

As the air moves swiftly across the sky,
I hear the sweet sound of spring.
From the birds who sing like angels,
To the wind who listens amazingly.
All the children outside playing and laughing.
When I'm outside I can smell the beautiful sun,
When I do the sun winks at me in a smile.
The sound of a swingset means to me,
The sweet sound of spring.

Alyssa Rustic, Grade 6
Captain Nathan Hale Middle School, CT

Strange Magic

Some magic cannot be explained.
That magic is considered strange.
But if you travel to the smoke,
And dangerous creatures you provoke,
Strange is not what you'll call,
The magic that protects us all.
And if you do not know the way,
And your luck has gone a stray.
Then magic is the only wall.
The magic that protects us all.
Elves and Sprits, do you know?
Those fools for mortals never go,
Past the place where end is near,
Past the place where all your fear,
Is bottled up, about to boom!
You are nearing sudden doom.
Then believers all us be,
When the only thing between death and me.
When you truly see the rage,
You'll rely on magic strange.

Adam LaPorte, Grade 6
Discovery School @ Reeves Rogers, TN

Storm Coming

The ocean is brushing against the shore, gently
The wind whistles a sad soft tune
The seagulls cry, storm coming, storm coming
The children on the beach are returning home
For there is a storm coming.

Katie Ip, Grade 5
P.S. 4, NY

Mickey Mouse

M ickey is funny
I ntelligent
C ool
K ids' favorite mouse
E verybody loves him
Y awns from a very long day

M ickey loves children
O utstanding
U ses his ears to listen to you
S nakes make him run
E ating is his favorite thing to do

Mickayla Abrial, Grade 4
West Frankfort Elementary School, NY

Snowy Winter

The snow is white
Puffy smothering
Land and regions
Leaves schools closed
Roads jammed
Kids having joyous fun
Building snowmen and igloos.
Sledding
Throwing snowballs
Wearing boots
Gloves for warmth
Drinking hot chocolate
With marshmallows
Sun sparkling on snow
Until it goes away.

Then summer comes again.

Grace Guyre, Grade 6
Blue Ridge Middle School, VA

Chickens

Chickens
Yellow, fluffy
Pecking, eating, thriving
Rosters, hens, birds, and geese
Diving, fishing, catching
Black, white
Penguin

Joshua Kugel, Grade 6
Freedom Area Middle School, PA

Summer

S ome fun
U nusually boring
M aking waves
M ostly sunny
E agles flying high
R eally fun

Cristina Runza, Grade 6
Haviland Middle School, NY

Sandy Toes

Over the plethora of grains my feet sweep
Through the salty water I swim
In my relaxation zone
Out of harm's way
In our daylight source's rays
Around and around my toes go as I engrave my name
In the midst of children having fun
Next to a crab I lay
On top, my tongue rests on my ice cream delight that has nearly melted away
On the outside, my skin sizzles
Inside, I am delighted
Kids make castles out of purchased buckets
In which kings and queens come to stay

Bryn Warren, Grade 6
Berry Middle School, AL

Colors

The blackest black I have seen was the black of the winter night.
The black was cold and dark.
Much like the coldest of the winter snow, only darker and far colder.
The black lasted only a short while but put a forever mark in my memory.
To this day I still have not seen such a black again.

Cam Walton, Grade 6
Morton Middle School, KY

Grandmother

It's one thing to be pretty and
It's one thing to be smart and
It's one thing to be witty or to have a happy heart
It's one thing to be likable and kind
But here's to you Grandmother 'cause you're all of these things combined.

Katelyn Glancy, Grade 5
Glancy Home School, KY

Poems

People say it's hard to write poems
Poems just begin and end with words
Sometimes it can just be about flying birds
For all those people who say it's hard to write poems I'll show 'em.

Here I'll tell you a poem right off the top of my head
Roses are red violets are blue
If you can't write a poem you need to get a clue
See it's easy but not all poems can be spoon fed.

Poems make you feel
Some poems make you cry or just make you want to yell
This may be too hard for you — you may just fail
Oh well you just have to deal.

Some poems make you sad
Some poems make you happy
Some poems are just plain sappy
But no poems at all — just make me MAD.

James Michael Sapp, Grade 6
Charles D Owen Middle School, NC

A Hot Spring Day

It is late spring
We feel the really hot weather
We decide to jump in the pool
It feels nice and cool on our hot bodies
We play water games
Like, "who can hold their breath the longest"
Mom brings in the pool toys
After swimming we played soccer
It was a tough game
We sweated through the whole game
We stopped to have a water break
We all knew the summer was coming
People were setting up their pools
Buying new clothes
And best of all getting ready for sports
It turned dark
Mom brought us out popsicles
We all took showers
It was a beautiful day

Michael Bobak, Grade 6
St Stephen's School, NY

All We Know of Heaven

Memories are all you have when you're alone
But still they can be good company.
Yet when my memories shift to you
They are fuzzy and vague.
Your beautiful face never clear.
Your irreplaceable voice muffled.
I don't know why all the birds leave in the fall.
I don't know if I would be recognizable,
You might not even remember.
I don't know where in the sky is heaven,
All I know of heaven is that I'll see you there.
Tears wash away the joy you held.
They whisper "She's not coming home now."
They leave me to face my fears alone.
You left me with no one to save me.
I'm still writing songs
For they remind me of you.
All I know is that I'll be able to sing them to you
Once we're in heaven.

Ana Maeve O'Donnell, Grade 6
Holy Name of Jesus School, FL

Pool

I love to swim all day.
It is where kids can play.
Splash, drip, drop!

The cool water gives me lots of joy.
I like it because I am a boy.
Drip, drop, plop!

Billy O'Connell, Grade 5
Our Lady of Grace Elementary School, PA

Disney World

Orlando, Florida
Going to the parks
Waiting for an hour to get on a ride
Buying turkey legs
Watching the amazing fireworks
Walking into Magic Kingdom
Seeing the castle
A magical place
Going into Epcot
Seeing the big golf ball
Place of the future
Visiting Hollywood Studios
Going on the new, fun ride
The ride was so fun
Going to the water parks
Cooling down from the hot sun
Slipping and sliding down the water slides
There are many places to visit in Disney
Having a blast
I cannot wait to go back
The founder is Walt Disney

Robb Nappo, Grade 6
St Stephen's School, NY

Simple Things

Tall
Home to many.
A spider,
On its twigs.
A squirrel,
In her hollowed out trunk.
Bees in a hive,
On its thickest branch.
Beetles in her roots.
Home to many.
Birds, in the highest branches.
Worms, in her dead fallen nuts.
The smallest aphid on the greenest leaves.
Sun rains down between her branches.
Brings beauty to the forest.
Tree.
Home for some.
Joy for all.

Sammy Iliff, Grade 6
Blue Ridge Middle School, VA

Colors

R ed is like juicy radishes in my garden,
O range is like tart oranges that I eat for a snack,
Y ellow is like a banana in a basket in my kitchen,
G reen is like fresh cut grass in my yard,
B lue is like a big splash from a waterfall,
I ndigo is like pickled eggs in a jar in my fridge,
V iolet is like a fragrant lilac bush outside.

Rena Shively, Grade 4
Watsontown Elementary School, PA

Shy Green

Green is the grass.
Green likes to match with black.
He is shy.
His favorite subject is math.
He likes to sing and dance.
Green is the best friend you can have.
He likes to eat juicy green grapes.
He likes to laugh and play.
Green doesn't like to share.
Green is the leaves blowing in the wind.
He likes to study sharks.
He has a pet dog his name is Brown.
His favorite animal is a tiger.
He likes to play with fire.
Green likes to color.
Green likes to tell jokes.
He likes to ride his bike.
His favorite sport is kickball.
Green likes a lot of money.
Green likes to help people out.
He always makes a new friend each day.
Alex Galaviz, Grade 4
Youngsville Elementary School, NC

Yellow

Yellow is the color of the sky at dawn
or the sound of a early morning yawn.

Yellow is the color of a new pencil
that sparks an author's creativity.
Yellow is the feeling of being happy
which all people wish to be.

Yellow is like lemons
made into juice.
Yellow is the feeling of comfort
when fighting countries sign a truce.

Yellow sounds like bells
ringing in town
or a canary's song
as you lay down.

Yellow is being cozy
as you lay under the stars
or being warm
while riding through a storm in a car.
Cheyenne Curling, Grade 5
Old Bridge Elementary School, VA

Untitled

Thunderstorms roaring
Drip drop blowing in the rain
Poor little blossom
Brady Stengel, Grade 4
Stackpole Elementary School, PA

Lemonade

Crunchy, refreshing
A summer iced lemon drink
Sweet, yummy, joy, love
Kristin Putman, Grade 5
Fairfax Collegiate School, VA

Untitled

Lovely cherry tree,
blowing in the wind nicely,
opening blossoms.
Rebecca Bonar, Grade 4
Stackpole Elementary School, PA

Memorial Day Pride!

Family coming over
Having a barbeque outside
Celebrating the holiday
Memorial Day Pride

Marching in the parade
Wearing red, white, and blue
Throwing out candy
A lot of bags you go through

Taking family pictures
Standing side by side
Looking at each other
Memorial Day Pride

A moment you will never forget
It really is a beautiful day
In the warm sun
Celebrating Memorial Day

Taking a moment
Thinking of the people who died
Our flag is still waving
Memorial Day Pride
Catherine Harvey, Grade 5
Hamagrael Elementary School, NY

Heartbroken

I wake up
I can't believe
I didn't want to hear
I have my chances to say goodbye
I'm sorry to say
But my mom has died

Worried and scared
Upset and heartbroken
My mom is gone
Dead and lifeless
Forever
Emily Mosenson, Grade 6
E T Richardson Middle School, PA

Doused

A
great big
bucket
full to the
brim
water
sloshes
over the edge
as it comes
towards
me.
Just about to
douse me
soak me to the
bone
why is my one
thought
"What is the Dow's* closing score?"

*Dow's: The Dow Jones Industrial
Allie Corcoran, Grade 6
New Garden Friends School, NC

The Ocean

Its blue comes from you,
Waves crash to shore hitting sand,
Crabs and shellfish swim.
Randy Godoy, Grade 4
Meadow Park Elementary School, FL

Baseball

POW! DING!
The bat bullseyed the ball
hitting homers hulling holes
Boo! Ya! Hooray! Whoooo!
The bat is a weapon
swinging at me
I'm a ball of torture
coming at it. POW!
The ball back in black
bouncing from the hit
this field is a battlefield
the ball screamed its cover off.
Richard Barkhimer, Grade 6
Harmony Grove Elementary School, AR

Music Goes in All Directions

Music goes in all directions,
High notes and low notes.
Even slow and fast.
The instruments, also, big and small.
Some songs are long,
Some are short.
What's *your* favorite?
Corinne Kauermann, Grade 6
Hillcrest Elementary School, PA

Dancing the Story of the Old Red Chair and the Girl Dressed in Black

The old, chipped red chair.
The steady beat of the Cuban music. Center stage.
The girl sitting there, confined to this chair, dressed in black with her back talking to the audience.
Her moves are sharp always on the chair.
The deep and majestic strings play and the girl's motions are now smooth.
For the first time, her eyes, serious yet mysterious strike.
She is off the chair! But is quickly forced back.
And it seems like she is destined there forever.
But then she has broken free! Up on her feet, high on her Pointe shoes, she is still smooth,
Mysterious and her eyes are slowly and softly staring you down.
She moves to the upper corner of the stage.
The steady slow, beautiful music is now more UPBEAT and happy!
She is smiling, jumping across the floor!
Gently touches the chair, but only uses it to give her a push.
She is center stage again, her leg high, high up in a developé.
Smiling so, so happy and her heart and soul smiling too.
The music slows…yet she's still stepping…slowly…closer and closer to the chair…
Final pose…and she is thrust on the chair!
With the music trailing…trailing…away…
She has not only danced, but she has spoken the language.
And has expressed herself and told a story through the art of *dance*.

Sophia Millares, Grade 6
Norton School, CT

You

You, who stood before your father's eyes and deepened your mother's soul
You, who followed the path of least resistance and forgave what you have done, just like you were told
You, who traveled the Earth with love as your compass

I, who stood before my father's eyes and deepened my mother's soul
I, who followed the path of least resistance and forgave what I have done, just like I was told.
I, who traveled the Earth with love as my compass
I, the lady of ladies who created more possibilities.

Laine Thelian, Grade 5
R. J. Lockhart Elementary School, NY

Rainbow

One afternoon at lunchtime in the spring I looked outside my window. I saw a rainbow over the water and some clouds and around the water there were trees, grass, and bushes. I started to eat my lunch but then I heard rain. I walked outside and saw rain hitting the water. The trees were dripping and the grass was squashy. There was mud, water, wet trees, and wet grass everywhere. The colors I saw were rainbow colors. The rainbow was so bright I had to put sunglasses on. Lakes and rainbows are beautiful together. I was really happy to see the rainbow in the sky. Will the rainbow go away?

Megan Tvrdik, Grade 4
Honeoye Falls-Lima Manor School, NY

Mythical Creatures

Mythical creatures in my imagination the phoenix of fire flying with the wind. The griffin souring in the sky with the dragons.
Mythical creatures in my imagination greater than all the animals in the world. The great Cyclops's with their huge beastly clubs.
The mythical creatures in my imagination fly high in the sky and live deep below the ground.
The animals that are real here today compare nothing to mythology.
Wizards and witches using magic to fight for good and evil.
In mythology beast ruled man man fought for freedom but we were weak.
Happy in the real world I am.
Freedom is what makes man a man.

Clifton Matuszewski, Grade 6
Discovery School @ Reeves Rogers, TN

Hope

Hope is a renewable resource
Hope is the strength that helps us to be able to get up when we fall and achieve our dreams.
Hope is the light that shines when we need it the most.
Hope is the key to open the gates to success.
Hope is the positive pathway.
Hope is happiness.
Hope is the reassurance putting its hand on your shoulder and helping you build a confidence that you need in life.
We can't live without hope.

Lindsey Anderson, Grade 5
Jamestown Elementary School, PA

What Christmas Is All About

Christmas is about singing carols, eating cinnamon swirls, and teasing girls.
It's not about being good or bad. So cheer up don't be sad
Christmas isn't only about putting lights on your Christmas tree and wearing Christmas colors — red, white and green.
It's also about giving, caring, and sharing
So that love can be seen.

The sweet smell of yams and Honey Nut Cheerios are what Sherifa likes.
I would just like someone to fix my bike.
I love the smell of pies cooking
And Mom's mouthwatering homemade stuffing.

Hey! What can I give Ari? One of the most coolest cars — a Ferrari.
We can give Jada a pink light saber.
I know what we should give Isaac — a basketball.
Just don't play with it in the hall.
Look! He is beating Kobe Bryant and the rest of them all.
Emil will break the seal on the cookie jar. For him it's joy.
Brian, Brian, a plane will be your toy.
Luis I will give things with a lot of spice
He is so quiet and nice.
Ms. Andrea, how about a trip to Jamaica?
Or this poem, which I am about to give to ya.

Samuel Dixon, Grade 6
Poughkeepsie SDA School, NY

Bowling

Life is bowling
Each game is a brand new game
Each game is a game that permits you to improve
Sometimes you do the wrong thing and throw a gutter ball and have a bad game
Sometimes you choose the right thing and throw strikes perfectly down the middle
You could mess up but redeem yourself and get a spare
You could do the right thing and then change your mind and the pins will move around but stay up
It sometimes comes down to the big decision at the end as to where you will throw the ball and where it will land
If you are not careful, you could do something wrong and everything is over
You lose the big game and everyone turns on you
Everything you used to have is gone
Everyone you used to be friendly with is gone
Now you are at the bottom, beneath everyone
Trying to win and make your way back to the top
Trying to gain it all back
And reclaim everything you used to have in the past.

Alec Berenbaum, Grade 6
Hillcrest Elementary School, PA

Flowers

Round purple petals long curved stems
In the warm sunlight looks like a gem

Chorus
Springtime is when they come around
Those beautiful flowers that sprout out of the ground

She planted a rose it was beautiful and red
In her garden it grows in her new flower bed

Chorus

Oh those flowers as pretty as can be
White, yellow, pink just like me

Chorus

How many are there I don't know
But they don't live when it snows

Chorus
Gianna Romanelli, Grade 5
Lockhart Elementary School, NY

A Magical Autumn Night

In the woods,
Somewhere dark,
A livelihood,
Is about to take part
Late at night,
The fairies take flight,
There are buckets of paint; yellow, orange, and red,
In less than a minute the color will spread
Autumn leaves change color fast,
That's because the fairies will leave last
Obdurate little creatures,
With the tiniest, most perfect features
Their mellifluous chatter never ceases 'til dawn,
But by then all of the fairies will be long gone…
Sunny Drescher, Grade 6
Hinesburg Community School, VT

Book

In a book
You can get lost
In a world of fantasy,
That is made by your imagination.
You'll see so many wonderful things,
So you won't ever want to stop exploring.
A book
     Hooks
          You
               Right
                    Inside.

Christine Roe, Grade 4
Public School 78, NY

Playful Purple

Purple fills people's hearts with joy
She is always playful but not when she is tired
She loves people
Purple is always trying to make people happy
She is never sad, mad, moody, pushy, mean, or crazy
She is always calm, nice, and friendly
She loves to eat purple grapes
She loves multiplication
She has two friends named Lavender and Orange
All three friends love to drink orange soda
Purple and Lavender love roller skating
Orange is better at ice skating
Purple loves to go to the beach
Wow what a lot of stuff!
Purple must have had fun
But now it's good night Purple
Alaina Jaclyn Burbank, Grade 4
Youngsville Elementary School, NC

Helicopter

Above the flying bird, waits the fluffy clouds
For the chopping propeller to reach them in a moment
Over the rainbow a new world to discover
Before the propellers start turning it rolls
To the H pad
After the door slams shut it glides
Into the air
Beneath the soaring bird a city lies there
Inside the big bird a commander flies it to its destination
Until tomorrow the bird sleeps in its anchor
Carson Culton, Grade 6
Berry Middle School, AL

The Love of Nature

The amazingly florescent sun
shines overhead like a light bulb
guiding your way.
Green scenery fills the shining Earth
with the life it owns.
Birds are chirping happily,
while the wind whistles through the land.
Sweet flowers fill the air
mixing with the unique aroma
of minty pine trees.
Soft luscious grass
cushions my thudding feet.
Wshhh, the wind slowly
cautiously fades beyond the horizon,
telling everyone this day is gone
and another one is coming.
This celebration, known as Earth Day,
is a special creation, that brings our world together
as one.
Dakota Kuharich, Grade 6
Litchfield Intermediate School, CT

Testing!

Testing! Testing! Testing!
Oh how I *don't* love testing!
Testing! Testing! Testing!
Instead I could be resting!
Testing! Testing! Testing!
My pencil breaks —
My hands start to shake —
Seriously I'd rather have an earthquake!
Testing! Testing! Testing!
Testing is the worst!
Testing! Testing! Testing!
I think I'm gonna burst!
Ryan Tager, Grade 5
Melville School, RI

Makayla's Eyes

Hazel,
Blue,
Green eyes
How can they be the same pair?
Changing with her mood,
Love and tears
Glisten in her eyes
Those pretty eyes I know

Her eyes will change every day
But all of them are
Hers
Rose McManus, Grade 6
E T Richardson Middle School, PA

Summer

S ome people swim at the beach,
U nder water fish bite,
M aking lemonade,
M owing the lawn,
E ating peach cobbler,
R ain falling in June.
Jessica Manning, Grade 4
Meadow Park Elementary School, FL

Oceans

Though it is filled with danger
It is a masterpiece of Earth.
Among the colorful reefs
Are amazing animals.
Even in the great white
Is a friendly fish.
With the global warming
The ocean is getting bigger.
But the black and white figures
Are losing homes on ice.
Just as the time of life
Slips away.
Christina Mattei, Grade 5
Avon Grove Intermediate School, PA

Carnival

"Look at all this money!"
It's almost as sweet as honey!
We have to use all this dough.
Just in time for the show.
All these lights…
What a wonderful sight!
I show them the green
To see the scene
The performers are fine
I might go blind
It's a very good carnival
I truly think it's the best of them all
Duron Tucker, Grade 6
Linkhorne Middle School, VA

Scary Storms

Storms can be scary
and they look very mean.
If you don't watch out
they will make you scream.
You could hear thunder
that sounds like a drum.
Or you could hear wind
that sounds like a hum.
Karsen Lee, Grade 4
Bethesda Christian Academy, NC

Trees

When you cut down a tree,
You might kill a bee,
If you kill a tree,
You will lose some of me,

Without trees I will die.
So then people will cry.
You make a lot of paper.
You lose oxygen vapor.

They are in lots of places.
Even in really cold spaces.
Stop killing trees so we can live.
If you don't we cannot give.
Dylan Hatch, Grade 6
Captain Nathan Hale Middle School, CT

Candy

I love candy
It tastes so good
So sticky
And great.
Just staring at the jar
Full of Jolly Ranchers
Just wanting to eat
Every little piece.
Brent Griffin, Grade 5
Avon Grove Intermediate School, PA

So Fast

Wobble
Wobble
Clack
Clack
Crushing through the snow
Slip,
Slap,
s
l
i
d
e
s
on her belly to the
cold,
icy,
water
So fast but quiet!
Kelly Paige Hall, Grade 6
New Garden Friends School, NC

I Wish

The sky is gray on bad days,
The gray sky makes you lazy,
Sitting inside, doing nothing.

The sky is sunny on good days,
The sunny sky makes you,
Want to go outside,
Run around and play.

The sun makes you feel free,
No worries, with warmth on your face.

I wish every day could be a good day.
And sun would shine every day.
That's what I wish for today.
Melissa Leavitt, Grade 5
Melville School, RI

Money

Money
Hard, cold, green
Buying, spending, getting
I love money
Cash.
Michael C. Soliday Jr., Grade 4
Lincoln Elementary School, PA

Bill

Bill takes a couple spills
When he runs up the hills
he thinks he's oh so fast
but he always comes in dead last
Dylan Ashelman, Grade 5
L. R. Appleman Elementary School, PA

Baseball Championship

Here I am having to wait
For the ball to be thrown down the plate
Finally here comes the ball
I thought I'd have to wait till fall
It is in the middle of spring
And of course that has to bring
The baseball championship
Which involves good sportsmanship

The ball goes into center field
Like a bird that won't yield
Turning on first base
I head towards second with a fast pace
My team winning by two
Just waiting for the right cue

I hear the bat cling
A bird ready to sing
The ball goes through the air
Getting ready to share
It brings me in
Which results in a win!

Christian Secher, Grade 5
Foxborough Regional Charter School, MA

A Box of Chocolates

"My life is like a box of chocolates,
You never know which one you're gonna get!"
My life is expressed in macaroni.
My life is good like apples and cinnamon!
    My life! My life!

I express myself in my own ways,
Most ways random.
I think my life is awesome like monkeys
Even more than delicious mac and cheese.

My life may be sad at times like a movie that makes me cry,
My life is also good at times like when I laugh so hard I cry.
Things don't always work out my way,
But I get through it like the rest of my life.

I went through hard times.
They were like mac and cheese without the cheese.

Virginia Payton, Grade 6
Haynes Academy for Advanced Studies, LA

Who? What? When? Where? Why?

Edwin, Pedro, Katherine, Dominick, and Nancy
went to reading class
at 10:40 A.M.
on the third floor
to be better readers.

Pedro Fortoso, Grade 4
St Agatha School, NY

Nature

Birds flying, soaring through a bright blue sky
Ants crawling everywhere! Oh no!
Don't get in my hair!
Tweet, tweet, tweet!
New chicks are born.
They're as white as clouds above.
Trees wave as I walk by.
I hope their branches won't poke my eye.
Spring and summer pass by quickly
And now it starts to flurry.
Slipping, sliding everywhere.
Hopefully the snow won't get in my hair.
As I fall and slip on hard ice,
I turn more into an ice cube every time.
Winter passes by, yet again,
And spring starts all over again.

Allie Garden, Grade 6
Litchfield Intermediate School, CT

Found

Sleeps on the pillows in my house
Skinny as a stuffed animal that has lost its stomach
They found her outside the rave
Do you think she's a Hollywood cat?
In a pet store
I was so excited to see the kitten
I saw her
I feed and love her
My best buddy.

Riley Stover, Grade 6
Berry Middle School, AL

The Non Moving Man

He's been beaten up over the years
By storms, by wind, and by children
That have climbed up his green cloak
From babies to kids, kids to teens, teens to adults
After all those years of exploring
His amazingly large arms
And after all that beating
His arms fall off then his cloak
And after the cloak goes he'll finally collapse
Under his very feet
And after decades and decades
Of being stuck into the wretched cement
He is finally free and so happy with glee
That he invites animals in for shelter
Plants to live
And water to drink from
After all that
He finally sinks into the ground
And then a small little child
With his feet already cemented into the ground
Is about to go through his own father's footsteps

Anton Bystedt, Grade 4
Riverside School, CT

Love

Love
is
in
the
air
as
the
couple
walks
off
in
different
directions
screaming
at
each
other
into
the
night
Karishma Desai, Grade 6
J E Holmes Middle School, NC

Joy

Nightly visitor
Loved a lot
Miniature bundle from afar
Little enough to take along
Blue eyes like Dad
Enjoyed longer than anything
Doll
Angela Epplett, Grade 5
Whitinsville Christian School, MA

Marine Life

Marine life is so fantastic
No I am not being sarcastic
Most of these creatures are prey

Spiky, slimy and squishy
Look at the little blue fishy
They live in the brilliant bay

Red crabs pinch
And lobsters clinch
Be careful in the seaside clay

The anenomes squish
With little clown fish
And the seaweed sways in the bay

I love marine life to death
They make me out of breath
"Let me see more," I say.
Mindy Gosselin, Grade 6
Captain Nathan Hale Middle School, CT

Carpe Diem

Oh I grieve for those who despaired through their life only to find they have none left
Oh I smile at those who truly live until that breath's last draw
And I glance at you, all you who still have time to live until tomorrow
Nicole Gadzik, Grade 6
Captain Nathan Hale Middle School, CT

Winter

Fluffy white snow floats down from the sky
It blankets the ground, making it look like a pristine white rug a queen might own
It looks untouchable
But that doesn't stop me.

I clamber out into the snowy wonderland
Winter's cold breath makes my teeth chatter and my hands go numb
I exhale and see my breath floating in front of me
It soon disappears.

Trees are barren of leaves
But are dusted with white powdered sugar
Inside them, animals hide in their homes
Cuddling with each other to produce heat.

I shiver, deciding to return to my own home
I tread to my door, then go inside.
I heat up tasty hot cocoa
And stare outside to enjoy winter.
Erin Sadowski, Grade 6
Gulfview Middle School, FL

Hike of Beauty

We stared off our journey at the beginning of the trail.
The first thing we saw was a white pine tree as tall as a sail.
We traveled to a nearby pond.
We heard the birds chirping beyond.

The pond was a clear mirror, so still and clear.
I looked left and saw a deer that paused in fear.
The cool and humid forest air around us tingled upon my face.
We saw a turtle in the pond, but it soon vanished without a trace.

The skunk cabbage was as vile smelling as an overflowed septic tank.
We saw a little frog leap out of the pond and onto the river bank.
I cautiously approached and tasted a spice bush leaf.
It was both critic and spicy beyond belief.

We saw an old monumental stone colonial wall,
And a tree that was struck by lightning 'cause it was so tall.
My teacher picked up a baby newt.
It looked like an orange plastic fruit.

The beautiful red-winged black bird was singing its beautiful song.
We were nearing the end of our tour, so we hurried along.
The tree teaches us that no matter the difficulties we went through, to keep living.
Nature is a gift to everyone on Earth from the God who is constantly giving.
Dana Xu, Grade 6
East Shore Middle School, CT

The End

The only one who could make me laugh.
A pleasant smile,
Once in a while,
Oh Richard!
It would get my heart beating,
Fill me up with joy.
The day, one day, changed everything.
Like an eclipse.
Everything went dark.
Being sealed in a black darkness forever.
When you left, I was grieving for you back,
But an angel told me to move on.
I'll be with you soon.
The world didn't stop spinning.
The sun, didn't stop shining.
So now I know,
It's not, and will never be,
The End.

Jennifer Orr, Grade 6
Gardnertown Fundamental Magnet School, NY

Jordan's/Shaq's

Jordan's
Expensive, cool
Running, jumping, jogging
New school, da bomb, old school, whack
Walking, pacing, strutting
Old and rusty
Shaq's

Messiah Moore, Grade 4
Olde Providence Elementary School, NC

Pickles

Tickle, tickle
I'm a pickle,
See me in my jar,
With a sticker, that's a star,
I don't know if it means clearance,
And I don't know where I am
Now I know I'm in someone's hand
Now I'm in a buggy rolling round and round
It's kind of disturbing because it's shaking me
I'm in her hand again
Now I'm on something that I don't know but I do now
I'm moving very, very slow
Now the side of my jar
With a sticker is on a weird screen
Now I'm in a buggy
It's so not my thing
Now I'm in a cupboard with many, many cans
Now I'm being moved once again
Now she's taking me apart
She's opening her mouth and
Crunch, crunch, crunch!

Destiny Kennedy, Grade 5
Southern Pines Elementary School, NC

Hot Hot Hot Red

I'm the stitches on a baseball.
I'm the petals on a rose.
I live in your body I come out when you fall
I rush to your head when you turn upside down.
I fly out of a volcano.
I'm really really hot
I am red.
I'm the lipstick on your lips
Whenever you kiss something I rub off on it in the shape of lips.
I'm the red yarn your kitty plays with.
I am red.
I'm a dark color if you lighten me up I turn pink.
I love mac and cheese.
I turn purple when I'm sad.
Your face turns me when mad or jealous.
I'm a great friend to have.

William Rees, Grade 4
Youngsville Elementary School, NC

Expressions of Blue

Blue is the gigantic sphere
revolving in the dark endless space
surrounded by millions of twinkling wonders
displaying the art work of God.
Blue are the soothing peaceful waves
crashing against the hard jagged rocks
washing away all the pains
of a sorrowful past.
Blue is a modest sapphire locket
hooked to a yellow golden chain
containing the memory
of a lost child.
Blue are the tears of a little girl
flowing down her cheek
as her mom tells her dad goodbye
and slams the door.
Blue are the dazzling fire works
erupting in the black night sky
leaving a cloud of smoke
and smiling faces.
Blue is all around.

Skyler Leach, Grade 4
Waynesburg Elementary School, KY

Summertime in Alaska

Where the midnight sun comes out,
And the cool wind whistles through the air,
The forget-me-nots are ready to blossom,
Under the bridge near the tree trunk
Moving its branches waving at them
Across the magenta hydrant.
Yes, Yes, Yes!
It's definitely the time of summer.

Fatima Qutab, Grade 4
Naquag Elementary School, MA

Winter

Snow tapping on the bumpy roof
Calling all creatures that it's winter
Animals begin to hide
While the grass gets buried by snow
Winter grows on all of us.
Lexi Kulik, Grade 6
Kelly Lane Intermediate School, CT

Raccoon

I had a cage with a raccoon
But it ran away
And left me a very nice shiny spoon
Amber Cazeault, Grade 6
Warrenton Middle School, VA

A Day at the Beach

School is out and it's time to play!
The beach is busy,
And all kids are having a race.
Everyone has a smile on their face,
It's a day at the beach!

The waves are big,
And surfers are here.
Fish swim away
When kids come near.
Children count — one, two, three!
Then jump in for a swim.
It's a day at the beach!
Natalie Ronty, Grade 6
Gulfview Middle School, FL

Liberty

Liberty I sight
The most wanted sign in life
Liberty means free.
Devora Zalmanov, Grade 4
Bnos Malka Academy, NY

Opposites

What is the opposite of play?
Perhaps it is work in the midst of the day
This work is so tiring
I should start hiring

What is the opposite of sure?
I might not endure
I must find the cure
This wasn't on the brochure

What is the opposite of a lie?
It's as beautiful as you may try
It's the truth
You don't have to be a sleuth.
Ryan Kaufman, Grade 6
Freedom Area Middle School, PA

The Attacking Hams!

There once was a girl named Sam
Who got into a traffic jam
She had a scary dream
Then started to scream
It was all about attacking hams!
Samantha Varney, Grade 6
Captain Nathan Hale Middle School, CT

Spring Is Coming

Birds are singing,
Plants are sprouting,
It is warm and raining.
Good-bye cold winter,
Spring is coming!
Mindy Li, Grade 6
Sacred Heart Elementary School, PA

Cheetah and Turtle

Cheetah
Fast, quick
Jogging, sprinting, bolting
Spots, cat, shell, green
Plodding, trudging, walking
Slow, reptile
Turtle
Juliana Owens, Grade 4
Pike Creek Christian School, DE

The Olympics

Torches blazing
Crowd shrieking
Hearts galloping
People hurtling
Tears streaming
Winners coronated
Prejudice remised
Happiness triumphing
Sports dominating
World uniting
A world of dreams.
Alexandra (Ali) Maloney, Grade 5
Hamilton Avenue School, CT

Beware the Alligator Gar

If you go down to a river shore,
you better beware.
An alligator gar is sure to be there.
It will chomp ya
and thromp ya
and really womp ya.
So remember…
if you go down to a river shore,
you better beware.
An alligator gar is sure to be there.
Kevin Marchioni, Grade 4
Pike Creek Christian School, DE

Forgotten

Twinkling in the sky
Shooting for nowhere
The stars danced playfully
Seemingly without care
Thinking of my childhood
Wishing upon these stars
The thought bringing back memories
That for a while seemed distant and far
Abigail Lewis, Grade 6
Canterbury School, FL

Dragonfly

Fast and fluttering,
Near swamps, lakes, or dirty ponds,
A majestic bug.
Helen Rodriguez, Grade 4
Meadow Park Elementary School, FL

Crab Cakes

Crab cakes, crab cakes
Taste so delicious.
Made of crab meat
They're so nutritious.
Crab cakes, crab cakes
I hope they don't overheat.
They taste better full, than incomplete.
I can eat them with two left feet.
Crab cakes, crab cakes
Oh man, they taste so great.
Oh fish on top can't be beat.
I could eat a full crate.
Noah Klingler, Grade 4
Watsontown Elementary School, PA

Eraser

An eraser is like a bed,
When you lay on it,
It erases, erases your thoughts.

When erasing, erasing,
It makes a sound.
A sound as if it is singing.

When you erase, erase,
It simply drifts your hand
Away from your work.

It seems as if it is
Floating
On a river.

The eraser, eraser,
Goes across the board,
As if it is running through a valley.
Rachel Harmon, Grade 5
New Garden Friends School, NC

The Wind

The wind blows in a certain direction,
It skims across the mountaintop,
Soars over the valley
And flies into the ocean making a big crash.

It blows against children's laughter,
Carrying it far, far, away.
As it goes over the water it crashes into the fisherman's ears,
Bringing him joy to his heart as he smiles.

The laughter echo's leading him to his children.

He hugs them and says,
"I'm Home."

Katherine Vasta, Grade 5
Brooker Creek Elementary School, FL

Summer Nights

I love summer nights.
I listen to the bullfrogs in my pond.
It is much cooler at night than during the day.
The grass is much cooler too.
Sometimes my family and I have a campfire,
And sit on our chairs next to it.
The flames are hot near my legs,
But my back stays cool.
I make smores on the fire.
They taste so yummy!
In the distance, I hear a coyote
Calling to its family.
And an owl hooting in a tree.
I love to use my senses on a cool summer night.

Emma Grace Maggiolo, Grade 4
E J Russell Elementary School, NY

The Cheetah's Cry

The cheetah cub looks back in awe,
At what the family left to rot,
The little city's lot.
The cheetah's home was gone at last,
But the worst hasn't come to pass.
The cheetahs make their way through the grass,
And there the cub cries his last.

Cahil Carey, Grade 6
Lake Noxen Elementary School, PA

Your Nature's Eye

Your eyes as brown as the earth you live on.
Your nose as wet as the river you drink from.
Your fur as soft as the leaf you eat.
Your fur as dark as the forest you live in.
Your nature's eye, your nature's eye,
You're the rabbit that stole all our eyes.

Melina Molinare, Grade 6
Jorge Mas Canosa Middle School, FL

Homemade

I searched through my lunch to see what I had.
I wasn't sure whether or not to be glad.
In front of me was a pile of glop,
There was even a bucket of slop.
I found moldy raw chicken,
With a scent that makes your stomach sicken.
I had five fried ferrets,
With a side of slobbered on carrots.
And last but not least was roasted frog,
With a small topping of sprinkled hog.
To decide if it was any good, I took a few munches —
Man, I love my mom's homemade lunches!

Emily Jennings, Grade 6
Captain Nathan Hale Middle School, CT

Nature's Wonders

Nature is beautiful with all its trees,
They cover the Earth and provide the breeze.
Sometimes trees are pretty and small,
Other living trees are giant and tall.
Some plants stink like skunk in your face.
Sure, it's not mace, but from natural base.
Creatures live on our Earth today;
Some live in caves; some live in hay.
There are many creatures that live today,
Some furry creatures want to play.
Other animals eat all day.
Some live in woods where there's no room to play.
Some animals roar and quake,
They keep everyone who's sleeping awake.
Some have a hard, rock like shell;
Which they use like a block,
So birds won't mock.
Most people take the world for granted,
But I think life is greatly enchanted.
For people who don't heed this rule,
You should not think life is so cruel.

Chris Forgette, Grade 6
East Shore Middle School, CT

I Think I'm Going Crazy

You've got to be kidding me.
I don't know how to write a poem.
My hands are sweaty, I've got a headache,
My desk is wobbly, I'm hungry, I don't even have a pencil.
You've got to be kidding, me write a poem.
You're crazy.
Time's up? Uh oh!
All I have is this list of excuses.
Wait you like it? I should get it published you say.
Too bad that was only me talking to myself.
Oh gee look now I'm going crazy talking to myself.
You've got to be kidding, me write a poem.
Never in one million years.

Jake Anthony, Grade 5
Jamestown Elementary School, PA

Lacrosse

Lacrosse is my favorite thing to play
Always trying my hardest
I could play any day
Always going for the win

Scoop the ball
Shoot the ball
Score the goal
That's the game

The score is tied
I'm running down the field
There is no place to hide
I shoot it in the goal and we win

Scoop the ball
Shoot the ball
Score the goal
That's the game
Casey Sheehan, Grade 5
Lockhart Elementary School, NY

A Ode to Sassy My Kitten

An ode to Sassy my kitten
with whom I am quite smitten
she is unbelievably sweet

She likes to run and play
and lay in the sun all day
and for dinner she loves to eat meat

She likes to cuddle
and play in puddles
but at hide and seek — she'll cheat!!
Jennifer Robert, Grade 6
Captain Nathan Hale Middle School, CT

Flip-Flops and Sneakers

Flip-flops
Open, comfortable
Walking, skipping, slipping
At the beach, at the park
Playing, biking, jogging
Closed, sporty
Sneakers
Monique Beltre, Grade 6
St Agatha School, NY

Sam

There once was a man named Sam.
He loved to eat country ham.
He lived in an old shack.
He had a humped back.
For a living he sold grape jam.
Will Ebling, Grade 6
Linkhorne Middle School, VA

My Dog Buster

Buster
Cuddly dog
Licking your nose
Barking, loving, smiling creature
Funny
Victoria Becker, Grade 4
Public School 207 Rockwood Park, NY

Animals

Animals are very cool
Some of them swim in a pool

My favorite animal is a bear
And it has long furry hair

The fastest animal is a cheetah
It hunts a certain zebra
Daniel Scott, Grade 5
Avon Grove Intermediate School, PA

Marshmallows

Marshmallows, marshmallows,
Oh, wonderful marshmallows.
Fluffy, sugary, and sticky like clouds,
Brown and crispy over the fire,
Marshmallows, marshmallows,
That I admire.
Marshmallows, marshmallows,
They're so great!
I would like them on my plate.
Rachel Ritner, Grade 4
Watsontown Elementary School, PA

S'mores

Chocolate with,
graham cracker crust
marshmallow tastes
so much!

Tastes so sweet
In my mouth
just like I'm
at my house!

By the fireplace
and the fires so
bright these s'mores
are more than
a delight!

This is a wonderful
night to have these
wonderful s'mores
delight!
Luciey Garland, Grade 5
A D Owens Elementary School, KY

Lady Bug

When I go to the park
In the summer,
On my nose I see something,
Red and black.
I named it Lady,
Because it was a Lady Bug.
I took it off my nose and it,
Landed in my hand.
Then my father told me that,
We are leaving.
So I took Lady,
Out of my hand.
And told her, "fly home,"
Because I am going now.
You are beautiful and small,
And I wish I could stay long.
Jessica Zovich, Grade 5
Public School 128 Juniper Valley, NY

Who? What? When? Where? Why?

Edwin
fell out a window
at 9:00 P.M.
in his house
because he was playing a game.
Edwin Duran, Grade 4
St Agatha School, NY

Dreams or Reality

Dreams
Scared, happy
Flying, soaring, loving
Everywhere, imagination, cruelty, life
Never-ending, feeling, touching
Hard, truth
Reality
Hannah Bini, Grade 5
Avon Grove Intermediate School, PA

Inferno Cake

A guy was baking a cake,
but he didn't know how to bake.
The cake got burned,
and so he learned,
how not to bake a cake.
Vincent Taylor, Grade 4
Stackpole Elementary School, PA

Fridays

Fridays
We wait for the
Bell to signal the end
Of the school week and freedom from
Homework.
Tyler Sprigg, Grade 6
Bedford Middle School, PA

The Ballpark
The Ballpark,
It's a place of unmeasured greatness,
From the red and blue uniforms
To the grass stained pants ripped with holes.
With the parents cheering from the stands
Watching their kids' team through good and bad.

The Ballpark,
The bonds the teammates make
That only players know about,
Friendships that are made for a lifetime.

The Ballpark,
From the sacrifice bunts to the pinch hitters.
The home runs! The great hits!
The curve ball, the fastball, and the nasty knuckle.

The Ballpark,
The banging of bats
The rivalries shown
The last hit on the game
Strike one, Strike two, Ping!
HOME RUN!
Baseball the players, the game, the ballpark.
Christopher Ryan Costa, Grade 5
Melville School, RI

Fights
Friends fight over boys
Like they are toys

Friends fight over dumb things
Like they don't share rings

Friends fight over clothes
And always say "so's"

Friends fight over pearls
And make fun of their curls

Friends make up and apologize to each other
And they be nice to one another
Morgan Carroll, Grade 6
Freedom Area Middle School, PA

Father "O" Father
Father "O" father you think you're not special,
Father "O" father but you really are.
Father "O" father if I could, I would buy you a brand new car,
Father "O" father you think you're under-appreciated.
Father "O" father but we love you so,
Father "O" father I love you so much.
Father "O" father let me say Happy Father's Day,
Love, your daughter Mae.
Maegan Daly, Grade 4
Nelson Place Elementary School, MA

Softball
I am up to bat
My palms are sweating

I'm standing there with knots in my stomach
What if I do not hit the ball?
I am so nervous with those smiling faces staring at me

The ball is coming at me
Finally I hit it
I am running
First, second, third,
HOME RUN!
Jordyn Riley, Grade 5
Melville School, RI

Lost Fishy
Once I had a little fishy;
My fishy was very fat.
He was a whale of a fish;
"GULP, GULP, GULP," he said all day.

One year of living with me —
He is getting older and so carefree.
He became as slow as a turtle.
The only things he does all day is swim and eat;
It looks as if he was free.

That day, that horrible day,
That's the day he passed away.
I was scared, I was shocked,
All I could do was cry.

My mom said, "He has to go,"
I said, "NO, please don't!"
I brought the fishbowl to the bathroom;
I heard the toilet go "SWOOSH, SWISH!"

That's the day I lost my fish.
Trisha Murphy, Grade 5
Foxborough Regional Charter School, MA

Turtles
Despite my speed, it's better safe than sorry
Across a log to sun myself
Outside in a swamp or pond
Into my shell I retreat from predators
Toward the nice cool water
As well as green, I'm also brown
Among the tall grass, I look for food
Along the log I see my other shelled friends
Without my sharp beak, I couldn't open nuts
Instead of being outgoing, I'm very shy
Who am I?
Mackenzie Mullins, Grade 6
Berry Middle School, AL

Lucky

My dog Lucky tastes like trouble,
he sounds like a shredder
and smells like dirt.
My dog Lucky is an eating machine
and he makes me feel all right.

Ahmon Watkins, Grade 4
Black Fox Elementary School, TN

The Fish

There once was a fish called cat.
He lived in the sea on a mat.
Though he was quite fun,
He was cooked on a bun,
And fed to a rat named bat.

Kayla Greer, Grade 5
Avon Grove Intermediate School, PA

Florida

I lie there
in the hammock
so far off the ground.
It seems so peaceful
nothing makes a sound.
I can hear the ocean
about a mile away.
It seems so far, yet so close.
If I lay
perfectly still,
a cardinal will perch above.
If I speak
a soft word,
a mockingbird will sound an alarm.
Oranges grow above me,
very orange indeed.
This place is Florida,
the BEST place for me.

Brittany Jean Welch, Grade 6
Gulfview Middle School, FL

Kitchen Fun

I really like
fresh garden tomatoes,
But I would much rather
have a big baked potato.

Meghan Wille, Grade 6
Warrenton Middle School, VA

The Owl

As night falls upon my face,
The owl wakes from his slumber
Asking who who disturbs me.
The stars begin to rise,
As the owl asks who who wakes me
For night has just begun to fall.

Kayley Stallings, Grade 6
Discovery School @ Reeves Rogers, TN

Wonder Dog

I always sleep safe and sound
Knowing that you are around

You roll your big, heavy ball
Down the long, narrow hall

You always loved the park
And when you see a squirrel you bark

I love it when you squirm
You look just like the worm

Even though you're such a hog
You'll always be my wonder dog

Racheli Platt, Grade 6
Arthur I Meyer Jewish Academy, FL

Revealing Red

Red are beautiful delicate roses
swaying gently from side to side
in the warm summer breeze
whispering, go away, go away!

Red are the round smooth tomatoes
hanging on green tangled vines
in the burning noon day sun
begging, pick me, pick me

Red are dazzling cut rubies
embedded in the royal crown
of the wise old king
summoning, come forth, come forth.

Red is the precious soul saving blood
dripping from His tortured flesh
on the cross of Calvary
pleading, trust in me, trust in me!

Clay Grant, Grade 4
Waynesburg Elementary School, KY

Skiing Trip

Calm and peaceful
Shoe resting on the smooth white floor
Cat creeping across carpet
She leaps

A second later
She's skidding across the floor
On a blue and black shoe
Hissing with shock

Crashes into the couch
Then runs to an empty room
Planning her revenge…

Mary Coates, Grade 6
Chickahominy Middle School, VA

A Tiger's Prayer

In forest hidden
Deep and protective
Tiger hides
I pray not the hunter
Become the hunted

Tess Borsecnik, Grade 6
Kelly Lane Intermediate School, CT

Nature

Rivers flow lightly
Deer run wild in the woods
Trees are red in fall

Lucas Valdes, Grade 5
Fairfax Collegiate School, VA

The Ocean

Beyond the sand
Underneath the moon's gravitational pull
Over the corals and animals
By the rusty, wooden dock
Against the shore it sits
Across from the condos
Among the hidden unknown
Down hundreds of feet
As cool as refreshing
Despite the harsh waves
Without much sound it dances

Sneha Peri, Grade 6
Berry Middle School, AL

Winter

Frozen, blue, liquid
Trees falling down on plain white
Frost is everywhere

Rupali Dhumne, Grade 5
Fairfax Collegiate School, VA

My Present

My present
For Mom
For Mother's Day
This year

A clay ornament
Made in art class

A great ornament
For a great
Mom

A
Mom
Like
Mine

Jonah Levin, Grade 6
E T Richardson Middle School, PA

An Outdoor Stroll

sunny day
walk in the forest
watch the birds fly
walk between the trees
wind rustles through the leaves
branches sway back and forth
music of tweetering birds
ribbiting of frogs
coldness of the creek ripples through my bones
rocks form shadows of human shapes
shadows growing larger as the sun sets
creating beautiful colors on the horizon
I must gather sticks
for a fire before dark
for warmth and a great desire
for a good night's sleep.

Ryan Bartel, Grade 6
Blue Ridge Middle School, VA

The Hot Dry Wind Pursued Us

We dragged on across the scorching hot desert,
the hot dry wind pursued us
Our throats were as dry as the sand that our feet walked upon,
the hot dry wind pursued us
Our skin cooked under the burning hot sun hovering over us,
the hot dry wind pursued us

Alaina Bisson, Grade 6
Kelly Lane Intermediate School, CT

My Deepest Fear

My deepest is the darkness inside us.
It reproduces for each dark deed.
No one is proud of the dark.

The darkness never goes away.
It's a neverending scream.
It haunts everyone.

It turns you into a monster
The monster will keep coming
The darkness drives us all mad.

Ratnajirao Mylavarapu, Grade 6
City of Pembroke Pines Charter Central Middle School, FL

Vacuum Cleaner

My vacuum cleaner is a dinosaur
Cleaning anything in its way
It makes noise and roars all throughout the day
Very heavy and big.
Its cord like a twig, pounding down on the rug
With a quick tug it goes around the corner.
Onto the ground that it has recently cleaned,
This dinosaur is an eating dirt machine.

Alexandra Caselli, Grade 6
Woodbury Middle School, CT

Birds

Birds oh birds
How do you fly?
With your wings glistening in the bright and sunny sky
I wish I could fly among the clouds with you.

Jeremy Marshall, Grade 4
H Austin Snyder Elementary School, PA

The Lightning

The moon was a glowing orb in the sky
The thunder rumbled as if singing a lullaby

I stand still — so still
In the pouring rain

And feel the darkness
Closing around me
As if I'm alone.

People surround me
With voices and laughter
But I can't hear them
It's just me and the sky

Then the clouds flash
I wake from my daydream
The wind is howling in my ears
The lightning is near

Just then my mother drives up
Beckoning, "Come here!"
I run to the car
But I can't forget
The lightning.

Katelyn Dalton, Grade 6
Chickahominy Middle School, VA

Finding My Coat

You'll never believe what I found in my locker,
It truly was a huge shocker.

I found a gigantic colorful peacock,
It was choking on a dirty gym sock.

I also found some moldy cheese,
My friend asked me for it please.

I found an African elephant,
It was very stubborn yet elegant.

There was a crushed up soda bottle,
In it was a tiny pirate ship model.

Then out fell a wooden row boat,
Finally I could go home in my coat.

Tucker Bedard, Grade 6
Captain Nathan Hale Middle School, CT

Thailand Water Fear

Thailand waves
Blue but dark
When you go near
You're sure to find
A blaze of water
Just full of fear
Tumbling down
And wiping the sand
You'll be terrified
Of the thundering
Blaze of water
Just waiting for
Just one person
To
Hug around
Like a long
Blue but dark
Blanket.

Connor Weigold, Grade 4
Riverside School, CT

Nature

Swans making shadows
The branches of willows curve
The world is peaceful

Chris Jo, Grade 6
Fairfax Collegiate School, VA

My Race Car

My race car is so fast that…
I beat Speed Racer.
It's faster than the Millennium Falcon.
It's faster than a laser.

I crushed Tony Stewart
And creamed Dale Earnhardt.
I smoked Darrel Waltrip
Like he had a go-cart.

I whipped Rusty Wallace —
His car took quite a fall,
And I beat his son Steve
In the biggest race of all!

Hayden Desmond, Grade 5
Hilltop Montessori School, AL

Silent Tear

As the silent tear fell into the abyss,
Alice walked through the mist;
The woeful rabbit followed to and fro;
The mouse wiping sweat from his brow;
When that silent tear fell,
I know we will be;
All safe with glee.

Sydney Seif, Grade 6
Canterbury School, FL

The World in My Eyes

The world so big with many places to go
Big and green with areas of blue
To me the world used to have no light
But when I was born it became so bright
Everybody thinking in every way
Nobody can control the problems of today
There is hope in my eyes
For me the world will never be despised
I hope that someday there will be peace
Maybe the hope of everybody will increase
Someday people will think what I am thinking and help make a change
Peace will spread to a far away range
All the pollution; the destruction will stop
It will be like a huge bubble that will pop
Then there will be peace
Everywhere there will be peace
Someday no hate will be around
No hate in any mind
Good thoughts will combine
Together we will make peace

Raeven Waters, Grade 5
Moyock Elementary School, NC

Black

If I were black I would be a midnight sky with stars in me.
I would be darkness all alone.
I could be a blazing fire's ash.
I would be a stinky skunk or a rotting piece of fruit.
I would be a sweatshirt on a gothic child.
If I were black I would be paint on a wall or paper to be written on.
If only I were black.

Savannah Densley, Grade 4
Howard W Hathaway Elementary School, RI

Life in 1933

There were Nazis, guns, terror, screaming and weeping.
Jews were despised by Germans.

But not all Germans.
Only a few, like the resistance or the ones hiding Jews.

The people that did hate them were the ones on Hitler's side.
Concentration camps were filled.

All the Jews felt and looked the same way.
It was like a black hole to them. People died.

Hundreds died some all at once.
There were gas chambers and lineups
that they just went down the line and killed them.

Couple years passed and finally Germans got defeated by the Americans
and the Americans came to liberate them.
Nazis lost their chance.

Maya Wales, Grade 5
Shafer Elementary School, PA

The Field Trip

Walking through the woods is a lot of fun,
But our journey has only just begun.
The grass is soaking wet and icy cold,
Good thing my sneakers are extremely old.
The pond has many eye-catching features,
Because it's home to many cool creatures.
Spotted turtles, croaking frogs, swamp snakes too,
Don't worry; I'm not even halfway through.
There's black fish, calm deer, mean gnats, and rabbits;
All with such beautifully unique habits.
But while most animals are free to roam,
The hopeless barn owls are losing their homes.
They're like snow lightly falling to the ground,
Their heads go almost completely around.
Animals don't only live in this space;
There are also plants living in this place.
Spice leaves would be loved by my picky dad;
He won't think lemon and basil smell bad.
The hike's a roller coaster ride for me;
This trip was like a vacation but free.
But unfortunately, it's time to flee.

Kathleen Grisier, Grade 6
East Shore Middle School, CT

The Cat

A cat is the walking form of curiosity,
It's two round, jade eyes take in everything it sees
Ready to explore yet cautious, you see
It's long slender body and mind can fool many.
For a cat is a trickster, a wonderer, and adventurous.

Shannon Williams, Grade 6
Kelly Lane Intermediate School, CT

The Deep Blue

Crashing through
The cold waves of the ocean
Slowly falling
Through the clear deep waters
Softly landing
On the bottom of the life filled sea
Fish swimming all around
Filled with colors glowing
Reveling the beauties of the water
Lighting the way
To discover treasures beyond
Your
Wildest dreams
Answering the questions of the sea
The rush of the water running
Through your veins
Feeling
Seeing
Knowing
The deep blue

Nathan Melcher, Grade 4
Goshen Elementary School at Hillcrest, KY

My Coffee

I am coffee so sweet and bitter
I am a great morning wake-up call
In the morning you take me to work with you
But remember to drink me all

Annie Nelson, Grade 4
West Frankfort Elementary School, NY

Summer

Summer is when I go to the pool.
Oh fine summer, so mild and cool.
Put on your bathing suit and come on.
Let's ride to the beach and teach.
Why don't you put on your flip flops and plop.
Oh the sun is so hot.
"Let's go swimming," someone said.
Why don't we go watch the sunset?
Oh summer, so mild and hot.
What a pretty day at the beach.
I can't wait to go to the beach.

Jessica Andrews, Grade 6
Linkhorne Middle School, VA

Old Wooden Stool

Cracked, broken, and streaked light brown.

The old wooden stool in the classroom.

If it is sat upon,
it wobbles and creaks,
leaving you unsteady.

It has lasted many years
of being sat and stood upon,
yet it still stands tall,
waiting to aid you
when you fall.

Natalie Gaiotti, Grade 6
Currier Memorial School, VT

Summer

When school is over we yell "Hooray!"
Because our summer vacation begins that day
In the morning we are woken by the song of cicadas
And at night by the bonfire the fireflies float
Every day we play with our friends
We go to the park and we see more of them
We search through the creek to find tadpoles and frogs
We also can hike across forests and bogs
We ride our bikes
We play kickball too
Soccer, baseball, or swimming will do
At the end of the day we fall asleep at 12 or later
Every summer gets greater and greater

Jacob Frosolone, Grade 6
St Stephen's School, NY

Sunday Walk

Running, running and running
I am slowing down and starting to stop and stopping
Hesitating and hesitating, breathing heavy
For a second I relax and listen to the tune of the wind whistling in my ear
Then starting to run again
Trying to reach a specific street to turn around
But then realizing how wonderful and peaceful this moment is
I suddenly saw the street sign to turn back the other way
As I walk back I feel the cool breeze whipping across my face
I see millions of vibrant colors and trees with bright green leaves
I hear another tune, the chirping song of birds
Then there was a silence
All I could hear was the tapping of my feet on the pitch-black pavement
I see that the sun has almost disappeared along the mountains
The sky has beautiful shades of color starting from the horizon
It turns from red, orange, yellow, green, blue and a light shade of purple at the top of the sky
I feel focused on my running
I feel lively, brave and free
I feel like I can do anything
I feel alive

Lucinda Mileto, Grade 4
Sacred Heart of Jesus School, PA

If I Were in Charge of the World*

If I were in charge of the world I'd cancel Twizzlers, Monday mornings, *Leo Little's Big Show*, and Chicken Pox shots.
There would be less trash, more precious polar bears, and cleaner gas station restrooms.
You wouldn't be lonely, you would have later bedtimes, you would have better healthcare, you would all have flat screen TVs.
A brownie with whipped cream on top would be a Brussels sprout, all ages would be allowed to see PG-13 movies without adult supervision and a person who forgot to flush or say "Thank You" would still be allowed to be in charge of the world.

Alexandra Estep, Grade 6
Morton Middle School, KY
*Patterned after "If I Were in Charge of the World" by Judith Viorst

The White One

As I walk down the marble floors, the open skies seem to hug me through the windows.
The oil paintings on the walls seem to stare at me, and on the side of the domed walls
Of this place I recognize as my old home sit the lonely benches that my sister and I used to play on years ago.

The misty fog comes; it tires to squiggle through the walls. Then, the moon shines, it shines under the same sky.
Under it, the stars never seemed to have changed. The moon lets out a glow. A welcoming one!

The tapping on the walls from other wanderers gets louder. The wind howls outside and the tree branches whirl in a vortex.
I am safe inside, but I am aware I hear evil chuckling away.

Why am I here?
What has become of my sister?
Is that the light?

The light shines not too far from where I am. It is brighter than the sun but does not hurt my eyes.
It is inviting and it gives me a warm, fuzzy feeling.

Going into the light…
Going into the light…
Going into the light…

Jordan Liptak, Grade 5
Melville School, RI

Our Deepest Fear

Our deepest fear is not that of homework, lizards,
Or even death
It is that of not measuring up to the rest
Feeling like you aren't good enough
Living up to parent's expectations
People constantly saying
Be like your mom,
Dad, brother, or sister
Feeling like you can't be you if you want to fit in
People getting mad if you are you
Living life without being heard
Getting judged without a say
People bringing you down so they can feel powerful
Our deepest fear is not that of spiders, darkness,
Or ghosts
It is that of emotion

Sarah Zaharako, Grade 6
City of Pembroke Pines Charter Central Middle School, FL

Mystery Soup

Quick!
Call the ambulance!
Somebody ate mystery soup!
I tell the student named Mark to hang on.
He says that it isn't so bad at all.
Then he eats the whole thing!
Maybe it isn't so bad.

Minsu Kim, Grade 4
White Oaks Elementary School, VA

Silver Is All I Know

Silver is the color
Of my Christmas bells
Silver is the feeling
Of wanting to say, "Hello!"

Silver is the shine of gold
When the one who is right for me
Bends on one knee and asks
The question, "Will you marry me?"

Silver is the sequence on my dress
Silver is the color of my knight and shining armor
Silver is the color that shines down from heaven
Silver reminds me of a rifle at war

Silver is the color of my sword
That I swing to and fro
To protect myself from
The evil dragon in my dreams

Silver makes me feel myself
And that is all I know!

Valentina Faulisi, Grade 5
Public School 128 Juniper Valley, NY

The Farm

The farm is a great place.
You can do whatever you want there.
You could ride horses, play on the playground,
Pet cats and everything imaginable.
My favorite thing to do at the farm is
Ride horses or go on a golf cart ride.
Other things that people like to do are go golfing,
And go down to the creek,
Where you find all sorts of things such as,
Salamanders, minnows, snakes, and even cray fish.
This is what you can do at the farm.
This is also the best place to play.

Rhodora Moore, Grade 6
Christ the Divine Teacher Catholic Academy, PA

Snow Is Here!!!

As the woods get covered in snow
Leaves fall off, from Paris to Rome
Dog and cat prints dent the snow
Leading to which way they go.

As the night goes on
You don't hear a peep
For all you know everything is asleep.

As children are asleep in bed
They are soon to wake up to the morning ahead.

As the children get up from their pillow
They run to the living room to look out the window
For what they see, snow is covering the willow tree.

Austyn Krecicki, Grade 6
Gulfview Middle School, FL

Winter

I see a reflection of a mountain, trees on water.
There is no movement.
The water is still.
The plants and trees aren't in.
The movement of life.

I hear complete silence.
There is no chirping of birds.

I touch the cold lake water and I am frozen still.

Renée Liporace, Grade 6
Suffern Middle School, NY

Your Eyes

I was walking with my dog,
and we seen men doing construction,
but all my ears heard was some mass destruction,
I put the radio on and it was doing a production,
oh why do I see and hear all this corruption.

Lakeijonay Hamilton, Grade 4
Black Fox Elementary School, TN

Round Sound

A man was playing all around
town, waiting for a loud, round sound.
When he heard the sound,
He fell to the ground.
He got hit by something round.
Austin Jones, Grade 5
Avon Grove Intermediate School, PA

The Pearl

There once was a girl
Who wore a pearl
She found it on the beach
Laying next to a peach
And so she did a twirl
Lauren Poletti, Grade 6
Linkhorne Middle School, VA

My Mini Dog

beautiful and loyal
jumping to play with me
like a cheetah jumping
if only he could still be with me
Fernando Rosales, Grade 4
Black Fox Elementary School, TN

Crazy Daisy

I have a chihuahua named Daisy,
Who loves to run around like crazy.
Tail down and ears back,
She hasn't time for a snack.
I hope no one dares call her lazy!
Victoria Banks, Grade 6
Newport Middle School, NC

Deer

Deer are
in the forest
munching on leaves and twigs
and gracefully jumping over
huge logs.
Victoria Rosser, Grade 6
Bedford Middle School, PA

Polar Bear

Large with sharp white teeth,
It can survive the harsh cold,
Cubs are hungry ones.
Geralyn Moore, Grade 4
Meadow Park Elementary School, FL

The Mouse

Little desert mouse,
Scurrying through the tall grass,
Entering its hole.
Sarah Zhou, Grade 5
Fairfax Collegiate School, VA

Heaven

Jump from cloud to cloud,
Where no tears come out of eyes,
Happiness is there.
Ivy Fox, Grade 4
Meadow Park Elementary School, FL

Fireworks

Purple, green, orange.
Fireworks of all colors.
Colors splattering.
Gila Max, Grade 4
Bnos Malka Academy, NY

Summer

Everyone likes summer,
It is meant for you to have fun,
There are plenty of things to do,
Like sit and relax in the sun.

Summer is a time for vacation,
It is a time to get a tan,
If you want to take a scenic route,
You should drive there in your van.

You can take a trip to the beach,
Sit back and relax in the sand,
Never go on vacation,
Without getting suntanned.

Summer is for family,
Aunts and cousins and all,
But don't get caught up in summer,
Because next thing you know it's fall.
Eddie Helmich, Grade 6
Hillcrest Elementary School, PA

Hockey

From scoring a
Puck.
To wristshooting a
Puck.
To slapshooting a
Puck.
From controlling a
Puck.
Practice leads to
Perfect.
Perfect leads to
Scoring a
Goal.
I will always
Have to chase a…

Puck.
Josh Biondi, Grade 6
E T Richardson Middle School, PA

Day

Underneath the fluffy clouds
The blue birds fly
Up and down all around
The brilliant blue sky
Jessica Wrightington, Grade 6
Normandin Middle School, MA

Water

I wander around the park,
The storm clouds gather,
My water gun ready to fire.
I throw a water balloon,
Twelve marks noon,
My friend's team stops hiding,
And some are bike riding.
I start to fire,
I give the signal,
And my team charges with me.
It starts pouring,
Our water balloons are soaring.
We fire, Splish! Splash!
We all get soaked.
One o' clock, Tick! Tock!
We are all drenched,
We head home and warm up.
Freddy Rodriguez-Sawao, Grade 5
Public School 128 Juniper Valley, NY

The Gold Glow

I stared out the window
Everything I saw,
I saw in black and white

When I saw her
Nan
In that funeral bed
She was glowing
Gold

Her shirt
Pink
Her blanket
Pink
Her memories
Unforgettable

It's scary
To see her right there
In front of me
Lifeless
Helpless
Not talking

Dead
Ava Lambert, Grade 6
E T Richardson Middle School, PA

Cheeseburgers

I can see the smoke rising, it's getting hot.
I can hear it sizzling in the center spot.
I can just see it brown, juicy, and oily.
I can taste the chopped lettuce in my mouth.
It's greasy, it's delicious, and it's great.
It's sitting in front of me on my plate.
I can feel it spicy and round.
It's tasty, it's ovally.
You know I could cook it on the ground.
Cheeseburgers, cheeseburgers all over the world.
Cheeseburgers, cheeseburgers for every boy and girl!

Hali Newman, Grade 4
Watsontown Elementary School, PA

Smoking

Worthless
Pointless
Careless
Darkness
A white worthless, pointless stick of flame.
The darkness and careless shows the shame.

Skye Green, Grade 5
Princeton Elementary School, ME

Remember

Remember to wash the dishes, clean up the house,
bake some more cookies, and check for a mouse!
Remember to clean the litter box, sweep the floor,
clean up my room, and do many many more!

Isabelle Pascucci, Grade 5
Thoreau Elementary School, MA

It's a Dream to Be Free

I would love to go away from this place.
So that species can see my nice, soft face.
I see other animals just like me.
All they say is "go away from me please."
I want to spread my wings like a big fly.
I know I will be able to survive.
My species are like tigers stalking their prey.
I hope that goes for me in the same way.
I know I am tinier than others.
I'm just as good as all my owl brothers.
People say I am amazingly cute.
I want to talk to them, but I am mute.
I love to have fun with bird games and play.
My mind is set now, I will never stay.
I cough up pellets with rats fur and bones.
They might look like some nasty human scones.
My colors are brown, white, and lastly tan.
I have a humongous three foot wingspan.
I am a species that is endangered.
I can also put a mouse in danger.
Can you guess what I am? Answer: barn owl!

Alekhya Vankayala, Grade 6
East Shore Middle School, CT

The Special Friend

When you're lost and confused and feeling down,
You need somebody to turn your mood around,
Someone to catch you when you fall,
To laugh and cry with you through it all,
A friend that you can tell everything to,
They are special in a way that comforts you,
Just like a sister, there is a sweet connection,
Always helpful, providing loving protection,
Like your own angel right from above,
It's great to have a special friend, one that you love.

Erin Swierczewski, Grade 6
Chickahominy Middle School, VA

Timeline

I come from Lisa and Jeff,
A doctor who works 2 days a week
And an engineer who works 5 days a week
And still have time for their 4 boys

I come from the middle of 3 boys,
Jim, Jeff, and Josh,
Who annoy the heck out of me
But saved me from being a boring old only child

I come from E.T. Richardson Middle School,
Where I'm currently serving the rest of an important grade
6th grade

I come from Springfield, Pennsylvania,
Where I've been living happily for the past 12 years.
I come from my friends
Who stood by my side whenever I was in need

I come from my mistakes,
If I didn't learn from them
I would be so lost
I come from my life,
The best life
Ever

Jared Kilgallen, Grade 6
E T Richardson Middle School, PA

What I Like About Dogs!

Dogs are cute!
   Dogs are funny!
      Dogs are family!
         Dogs are soft!
            Dogs are fluffy!
               Dogs sometimes don't have hair!
               I WILL NEVER HATE DOGS!!!!
               I LOVE DOGS!!
Dogs are my best friend!
   Dogs are my FAMILY!!!!!!!

Joey Swanson, Grade 4
Crestwood Elementary School, KY

My Dog

I have a blog.
It is about my dog.
His name is Tike.
He's fast as a bike.
He has lots of hair.
I think he is fair.

Marcus Velasco, Grade 6
Warrenton Middle School, VA

I Am a Swimmer

I am a swimmer.
I wonder how to work even harder,
I hear my team cheering,
I see the water droplets,
I want the gold medals,
I pretend to swim with the top regions,
I am a swimmer.

I touch the block,
I worry about getting disqualified,
I cry on occasion,
I am a swimmer.

I understand the joy in swimming,
I say, "You did really well!" to others,
I dream of beating old times,
I try to go faster and faster,
I hope to go to the Olympics,
I am a swimmer.

Jena Pisani, Grade 4
Meadow Park Elementary School, FL

Summer

S pecial
U nder the sun
M eeting new friends
M aking sandcastles
E lla helps
R ain

Gabriella Belknap, Grade 4
Bayshore Christian School, FL

Lady Luna's Tears

Silent screams
fading quietly
gloved fingers
catching silver tears
which glimmer in moonlight
Lady Luna's sorrow
in the palm of your hand.
Her voice echoing
through valleys and forests
to be heard by you only
capture her tears.

Lindy "Lu" Ramsey, Grade 6
Linkhorne Middle School, VA

Transformers

T ransform
R obots that are disguised
A utobots
N ever harm humans
S trong
F un
O ptimus Prime
R evenge of Megatron
M ore than meets your eye
E vil forces
R otate
S ome protect us and some destroy us

Benjamin Dessecker, Grade 5
St John Catholic School, MD

Spring Has Come

Spring has come
Trees giggle in the breeze,
Flowers bloom in the spring,
I'm glad spring came finally.

Ibana Smith, Grade 4
Ridgeway Elementary School, MD

Winter

White strong and fearful
Cold and dark as the night is
When red leaves fall off

Sam Allison, Grade 6
Blue Ridge Middle School, VA

In an Instant

Blood is like a river of red
Flowing in your veins

When it receives oxygen
It takes on a whole new appearance

Sometimes it's good
Sometimes it turns on you

Sometimes it keeps you alive,
And other times it ends your life
In an instant.

Robert Paynter, Grade 6
E T Richardson Middle School, PA

Biking

Biking
Climbing, stopping,
Speeding, coasting, resting,
Races, jumps, leisure, rest,
Working, sleeping, playing,
Fun, delightful,
Freedom

Brendan Flanigan, Grade 6
Kelly Lane Intermediate School, CT

Pier

On a pier
It is so clear
I like to hear
The waves
JUMPING
BUMPING
Near my ear

I see the seagulls fly
I see beagles run
I see the sand blow
I see the water flow

The fisherman sits
On a cooler filled with bait
Patiently waiting
For the fish that will never be late
Then the fish will be caught
And BOUGHT!!!

Tamer Tamer, Grade 5
Public School 128 Juniper Valley, NY

Rain

Pitter patter drip,
Precipitation is here,
Close your eyes…listen.

Macy Mazzola, Grade 4
Meadow Park Elementary School, FL

Jack's Jellybeans

Joseph jaguar
jacked Jack's
jolly jellybeans.

Israel Garcia, Grade 5
Tucker School, AR

Music

Music is the voice of the soul.
It heals the hole
Of the heart.
But that is only part.
Music is the voice of the soul.

It becomes bandages from a fight,
And voyages with light.
Helping you through life,
Without a strife.
Music is the voice of the soul.

The feel of rhythm in my soul,
Is not a ghoul,
But an angelic feeling,
And excitement peeling.
Music is the voice of the soul.

Libby Rodriguez, Grade 6
Queen of Peace Catholic Academy, FL

Broken Wings

He lied there dying
his vibrant orange wings
torn in places
his dying wish
was to fly one last time
that wish could not happen
for these were broken wings
there he was;
dead, no life left
his wings faded
to a brown color
the wind began to blow
that carry him on
to get that dying wish
but there's nothing left to him
except the broken wings

Madeleine LeBoeuf, Grade 6
Haynes Academy for Advanced Studies, LA

Under the Sea

Under the sea new life is sprouting just like buds
beginning to grow upon the fresh spring trees.

Under the sea, sand is surfacing under the crashing waves
that sound like a soothing heart beat, a drum.

Under the sea, seaweed is swaying like a feather
blowing in the midday breeze.

Under the sea clams are singing high notes,
and low notes that would soothe a soul.

Under the sea dolphins are leaping over the surface,
just like a butterfly flapping its wings in the wind.

Tiffany Coble, Grade 5
Quidnessett Elementary School, RI

Excitement

Excitement is like puppies running on an open field
Being free from an evil ruler's way
Being able to choose their own path
Following their own, wonderful minds
Eating, swimming, having fun
Playing with each other before it is time to go to bed
Chewing on anything in front of them
Playful, playful exciting puppies
Stopping to eat their puppy chow
Eating faster and faster each bite
Starving, exciting puppies
Swallowing on big gulps of water
To wash all food down their small throats
Laying down in their puppy beds, sleeping
Tired, warn out, exciting puppies

Brittany Garcia, Grade 6
Haynes Academy for Advanced Studies, LA

Rain

I was lying down in the rain,
And realized I had no more pain

Calm and quiet I lie
I no longer had to cry

'Cause when I'm lying in that rain
Nothing matters, it's not the same

So if you understand me dear,
Realize that the rain is clear

Just like my head when I am standing there
Everything is simply fair.

Caitlin Gaine, Grade 5
Public School 128 Juniper Valley, NY

Ordinarily Orange

Orange are the firm unripe persimmons
drawing my mouth
to a tight pucker.
Orange are the tall graceful tiger lilies
their fragrance,
whispering in the cool night breeze.
Orange is the furious flaming fire
engulfing the forest,
tree by tree.
Orange are the beautiful autumn leaves
tottering slowly,
to the cold crunchy ground.
Orange is the exquisite Albatross butterfly
fluttering back and forth,
from flower to flower.
Orange is the lazy striped tiger
snoozing peacefully,
with her cubs in the African bush.
Taking a look at the world
with orange.

Ally Salyers, Grade 4
Waynesburg Elementary School, KY

Just Because I'm Different

Doesn't mean you have to be mean to me.
Doesn't mean you have to make fun of me.
Doesn't mean you have to laugh at me all the time.
Just because I'm different…
Doesn't mean I can't play sports.
Doesn't mean you have to be rude or selfish.
Doesn't mean that I'm a girlie girl.
Just because I'm different…
Doesn't mean I am different from you.
Doesn't mean I mess up all the time.
Doesn't mean you have to bully me all the time.
Just because I'm different, just give me a chance.

Rebecca Morris, Grade 6
Freedom Area Middle School, PA

Preschool to High School
Preschool
toddlers, cubbies
crying, whining, pooping
crayons, toys, pens, textbooks
fighting, achieving, learning
teenagers, lockers
High school

Shemaiah Slaughter, Grade 6
Linkhorne Middle School, VA

The Lizard
Its thick, long tail,
with patterns on its back,
and little black
feet
feet
feet.
Dark tree shadows,
and a light wind.
I hear giggles,
birds chirping
and stomping of feet.
I wish that the lizard was bigger,
it could get stepped on.
And all I wonder is,
how does it move so fast?

Carson Hall, Grade 4
Grace Lutheran School, FL

White Tiger
Slowly creeping, silently peeping.
White tiger pounces toward the ceiling.
Slowly reeling in a mouse.
Me watching from my house.

Shelby Kayga, Grade 4
Pike Creek Christian School, DE

New York
Busy quiet people
Rapidly rush
To their awaiting jobs.
Sluggish impatient cars
Angrily honk
At the annoying traffic.
Dirty crowded streets
Shine in the light
Of the sun.
Tall impressive buildings
Scarcely scrape
The white clouds.
Gigantic neon signs
Continually "blink…blink…blink"
In the day and night sky
Of New York

Sam Talley, Grade 4
Beechwood Elementary School, KY

Where I'm From
I'm from a baseball team who sweats 'til they melt like molten lava
I'm from a house that cheers during football season
I'm from a family who's relatives recently pasted away
I'm from a team who might make it to the Little League World Series
I'm me and you can't take that away.

Daniel M. Combs, Grade 5
Hamilton Avenue School, CT

Tommy
Yes! Tommy's home and I bet you can't guess what that means.
Well, it means that we can relax and have fun in the sun just he and I.
Sweat running down our face from playing at the beach all day
And we smell like fish from swimming in the water, ewww!
What a fun time we have together!
When we watch the sunset we can hear the seagulls squawking
And the water crashing onto the sandy shore.
We see kids flying kites and dolphins taking their last dip for the day.
What a fun time we have together!

Shannon Scanlon, Grade 6
Gulfview Middle School, FL

Sitting in My Apple Tree
I sit in my apple tree
I swing my legs,
Sing with the birds.
I look down
And when I see how high I am,
I start to believe I am flying
Higher,
Higher,
And higher, until I am able to lift up my hands and touch the sky.
I look up,
To see that what I am actually touching is the rich green leaves.
The leaves feel smooth in my hands.
As I look down on to the brown and crunchy bark I find a small caterpillar
With green skin and little hairs sticking out of its back.
It gets dark
Therefore, I go inside and lie down to sleep.
And when it's morning I go back outside and sit in
My best friend.

Samantha McClure, Grade 6
Currier Memorial School, VT

John Columbia
John
Friendly, shy, sensitive and outgoing
Sibling of Maria and Savannah
Love of Lake Cumberland, history, and family
Who feels sad when I leave Lake Cumberland, bored at school and
angry when my sisters cause trouble
Who fears homework, anger, and heights
Who would like to be a teacher, live a happy life, and be successful
Resident of Lexington, Kentucky
Columbia

John Columbia, Grade 6
Morton Middle School, KY

Ode to My Dog Peanut

Peanut you will be in my heart forever.
You have been my puppy since I was 2 years old.

You have been there through thick and thin
When I was sad you were there

You make me laugh by tickling me, by licking my face
And that always makes me feel better and makes me laugh to.

Peanut you are the best
When you die you will still be in my heart.

Jayda Owejan, Grade 5
Melville School, RI

Horse

A
horse
is an amazing
animal. Of all shapes
and sizes.
Always
brushed.
Loves attention and playing
in the mud. Loyal and caring.
There to care for you. Never
wants to be alone. Friend for
life as you know. Let's ride!

Saddle	Pad
Sugar	Cube
Stirrups	Carrots
Water	Saddle
Girth	Grain
Reins	Bit
Barn	Hay

Kierra Ashlyn Kimble, Grade 6
Lake Noxen Elementary School, PA

Sliders

I see the sign that says Sliders in Allentown, Pennsylvania.
The strong smell of BBQ sauce makes my mouth water.
The hot plate hits the wooden table with a tingling sound.
I taste the tangy sauce on the wings as I bite into them.
The hot slimy sauce coats my fingers, and I lick it off.
The waiter comes up to the table and hands us the bill.
Wait, I'm ready for some more BBQ wings please!

Austin Coup, Grade 4
Watsontown Elementary School, PA

Romeo

My little cousin Romeo is so much fun
He loves when we play in the blazing hot sun
And he really likes to run
He loves to say the word ton
He likes when I tickle him and blow on his stomach

Princess McAllister, Grade 5
Southern Pines Elementary School, NC

Polio Boy

The poor boy…
He was just playing with his toys.
He never saw it coming.
It felt like a bombing.
It attacked fiercely at him.
His life was on a limb.
It looked bad.
I felt so very sad.
I saw the boy that night.
As his brother it gave me a fright.
In the ambulance, I cried.
But then I saw an angel by his side.
Then he went to Heaven.
I'm going to miss you, Devon.
I hate Polio.
It must of felt like being attacked by a bull in a rodeo.
Now he's looking down.
Straight at my frown.
I have a hole in my heart.
Now that my brother and I are apart.

Christion McMillan, Grade 6
Linkhorne Middle School, VA

Spring

The leaves are growing, it's spring!
The sky is cold and blue.
You wear a lighter coat now,
There's no more snow to plow.
(Remember winter, with white monster piles taller than you!)

Part of the season, Easter's in spring.
In your Easter basket, there's a puppet on a string,
But don't dance it out the door;
Clouds are gathering, the rain starts to pour!

By May more plants and flowers have sprouted
1, 2, 3 give the petals a count,
See tiny traveling parades of busy ants.
You wear shorts, not just long pants,
And play outside, run and shout!

Hurrah! When June has begun,
You can swim in a pool, the weight of a ton.
Look at that, school is almost over;
(Oh, no, it starts again around September!)

Danielle Nicholson, Grade 5
Foxborough Regional Charter School, MA

A Kangaroo Named Moose

I like to watch kangaroos hop.
Have you read the book *Hop on Pop*?
Hop on Pop is by Dr. Seuss.
Does my pal Jen have a pet moose?

Peter Trouba, Grade 5
Avon Grove Intermediate School, PA

Shooting Star
Shooting through the sky at night,
A bright star you wish upon,
In the sky at night.
Kendall Kisamore, Grade 4
Harmony Community School, FL

Smile
Maybe if you would smile
Even just for a while.
We wouldn't be so sad
So we wouldn't get mad.

Maybe if you would smile
Even just for a while.
We wouldn't have a clue
That we wouldn't ever be blue.

Maybe if you would smile
Even just for a while.
There wouldn't be war
There'd be peace ever more.

It would change the course of this nation
To a future of historic celebration.
Maybe if you would just smile
Even just for a while.
Adrianna C. Hargus, Grade 6
Charles D Owen Middle School, NC

Changes in Time
Many things have changed,
Many days have passed,
Many leaves have fallen,
Many weights have been lifted,
Many birds have flown,
Many logs have drifted,
Through your beauty and grace,
My love for you will remain the same,
For nothing can be changed in love
Though technology will grow,
And our age will increase,
Many things will change,
But I will always be yours,
And you will always be mine,
For nothing can be changed in love.
Cintia Samaha, Grade 5
Westlawn Elementary School, VA

Who? What? When? Where? Why?
Ashley
wanted to sing
in the afternoon
in the park
because she wanted to make a song.
Nancy Quizhpi, Grade 4
St Agatha School, NY

My Feelings
I'm happy
which makes me more happy.

Sometimes I get sad.
Then, also I feel bad.

Why do I have all these feelings?
What are the meanings?

I want to go away
so I can play.

Then, I see red
Which makes me fumble on my bed.

It's just too much
It puts me in a bunch.

Please let me
be free.
Daniella Aboagye, Grade 4
Nelson Place Elementary School, MA

Smart Black
Black is like a tire
He likes to play sports
If you make him mad he will yell at you
Black is a slimy slug
When he is scared he starts to shake
His favorite food is chicken

His favorite color is blue
He likes to spy on people
He likes fishing, hunting, and NASCAR
Black is my favorite friend

He sings with me
He sleeps with me
He plays baseball with me
His favorite sport is baseball
My fishing poles are black

I caught a black fish
Black catches everything
We play tag
We like swimming together
We like watching TV together
Malik Braxton Wellman, Grade 4
Youngsville Elementary School, NC

The Statue of Liberty
Behind the water
Standing high in the tall sky
Welcoming all boats
Esther Shira Chait, Grade 4
Bnos Malka Academy, NY

Snow Angel
The tiny snowflakes
Brush against my cheek
As light as a bluebell

I stomp in the snow,
Then take a leap
Onto the white blanket of Earth

I'm lying on my back,
The ice soaking through to my skin
Moving my arms and legs

The stars in the sky
Look like a pack
Of little snow angels

Glistening
Shining
Watching over me
In the sky
Caroline Lurz, Grade 6
Norton School, CT

What Is Wind?
Wind can be nice
Wind can be mean
Who knows what the wind is going to be?

Wind is fearless
Wind is a monster
Will it attack or will it not bother?

What does it do?
What does it have?
Why does it make that ghostly laugh?

Wind is a menace on cold winter days
But, in summer it cools us while we play.
Courtney Sturgeon, Grade 6
E T Richardson Middle School, PA

Spring
The grass is green
The sky is blue
Spring is fun
And so are you.
The sun is yellow
The moon is gray
Spring makes
A very fun day.
The clouds are white
The water is clear
I know this is going to be
A fun year.
Kadie Hummel, Grade 5
L Ray Appleman Elementary School, PA

Summer

In the summer, the sun is hot.
It's as hot as a burning pot.
Sizzle, sizzle, pop!

I like to go to the pool.
It is nice cause it's so cool.
Brr, brr, ah!

Justin Brandwein, Grade 5
Our Lady of Grace Elementary School, PA

Mardi Gras

Purple,
Green,
And gold!
Masks, king cake
Beads, and parades
Revelers in disguise
People yelling throw me something Mr.
So they can get the colorful prize
From the people on the float,
People have a delicious
Mardi Gras cake to celebrate!
People on floats in parades dress up
From jesters to wild animals.
Mardi Gras is a colorful
And wonderful holiday.

Erin Andrus, Grade 6
Haynes Academy for Advanced Studies, LA

Leading His Team to Victory

The eager crowd eating the scrumptious popcorn
while screaming like angry babies
hoping their team can win the championship game

A frustrated and nervous Tubby Smith
pacing across the hard, shiny floor
watching and attempting to lead his team to victory

An anxious but confident Jeff Sheppard
shooting a jump-shot to take the lead
hoping he can steer his team to victory

A worried defender
trying to block Jeff Sheppard so he can try
and lead his team to victory

Both teams playing hard,
their sweat dripping,
so their team can win the championship game

Tied up with only seconds left,
the concerned Jeff Sheppard shoots a three at the buzzer
he is successful at leading his team to victory.

Brandon Castle, Grade 6
Edythe Jones Hayes Middle School, KY

The Sneeze

An elephant started to sneeze,
it sounded a lot like a wheeze.
Something's caught in his trunk,
wound up being a skunk,
the skunk yelled "Will you sneeze please?!"

Samuel Huslin, Grade 4
Stackpole Elementary School, PA

Rainforests

Birds calling
Large brown crickets creeping everywhere.
As I walk, sticks crackle,
Water rushing down rocks.

Rough, bumpy leaves against my legs;
Fresh water spray,
Like a shower of sparkles, hit me.
The amazing tropical toucans can't hide!
Green leafy tropical plants
Soak up the sun.

Heavy humid August air all around;
It's almost a dream.

Finally I get where
I'm going;
I can't wait
To enter the wondrous rainforests again.

It was a long journey
Through exotic colors and meander trails,
And exhausting trip but worth it.
I can't wait to enter the wondrous
Rainforests again!

Tasha Phillips, Grade 5
Foxborough Regional Charter School, MA

Summer

Summer is here
Get out our shorts, tops, and flip-flops
Get in the pool
Take a dip
Get nails done
It is time to shop
So we have to hop, hop, hop
Stay up late
Ride your go-cart
Jump on your trampoline 'till night
Go out to eat so you will have a bite
Go on boat rides
Play on the playground
Relax and enjoy your summer light
Until you have to go to sleep and it flies right by
So that is what you can do in the summer day and night

Amber Fealy, Grade 6
Buckhannon-Upshur Middle School, WV

April

April
Tricks, fun
Jumping, exercising, playing
It's my birthday
Raining
Julia Keohane, Grade 5
St Agatha School, NY

My Hand

Waves hello
Waves goodbye
My hand can reach the butterfly
It can climb on a tree and
Can touch a bee
My hand can write
And it can also bite
My hand can hold many things
And can wear many rings
Julia Vinnytska, Grade 6
Hillcrest Elementary School, PA

Streams

Muddy bottom, leaves ruffle.
Green leaves waving all around.

Like a castle's moat.
Deep
Mulch bottom.

Roots on the edges,
Like vines,
Trees, like towers.

The old bridge,
Looking,
Like it could break at any moment.
Endless woods…   High.
Above the stream,
I'm sitting.
Victoria LeBaron, Grade 5
New Garden Friends School, NC

Birds

Wafting like a breeze
Gliding through the tallest trees
Flapping wings all day
Will Baker, Grade 5
The Cathedral School, AR

Midnight Tiger

A tiger stalks with his eagle eye,
As he silently says goodbye.
Through the jungle he is creeping,
By his prey who is still sleeping.
Cassie Billig, Grade 5
Avon Grove Intermediate School, PA

When Will This End?

Profanity in every dark alley. Graffiti cakes the cities.
Crooks breaking and entering. Tabloids bearing false witness and jabbering.
Poor with no houses. Rich with five spouses.
Racism. Plagiarism.
Lows that are broken. Lies in the open.
Drugs and thugs rule the US as cops cannot make the arrest.
Hungry and helpless are some. And others rather be full than say they are done.
Injured by a drunk driver truck. Government running a muck.
Illegal. Unreal. Ideal for a criminal.
These problems will never end. I guess we just have to pretend.
A late night killing spree. I hate you. You hate me.
Abusing our freedom is plain dumb. It's all un-fun.
Money runs our nation. And money in some countries is rationed.
Suicide bombers. Mean thoughts on computer monitors.
When will this end. We have no friends.
Rumors spat from a "trusting tongue."
Animal abuse. Child abuse. Can we just cut loose.
Environmentalists trying to save dead meat. Terrorists with a gigantic fleet.
Who can change us? Who knows the name?
We must step up this is not pretend.
Drew Schwarz, Grade 6
Norton School, CT

Sky Reign

A strong wind rips through the fresh, crisp, smooth air creating sky ripples
This is not painful, but awakens you like a bat at night.
You dare to look down, seeing everything as if watching a slide show
Floating freely through the dense clouds, feeling lighter than a pin.
Driving forward powerfully, yet at a relaxing pace for you.
It is magnificent; cool, calming, and it leaves you speechless.
The enormous golden sun filtering rays of light upon your face
A smile shows across your face, knowing not where to go but what to do.
Soar; soar up, soar down, sideways, left to right, anywhere you choose
And realizing how free it is without restraints, barriers, nothing but blue sky.
Shortly, you pass over an orange grove, the citrus fruit a tantalizing smell
Now, passing over an expansive turquoise ocean, a salty smell reaches you.
For a while, you fly above bushy green woodlands, with a collected mind.
Suddenly, dark gray clouds chase you, looking as dangerous as a razor blade
A rumble of deafening thunder and blinding bolt of lightning quicken your pulse.
Rain soaking you, dragging you heavily, and making you weak and terrified.
A strong gust of wind sends you out of control, spiraling towards the ground
You shut your eyes tightly, ready to be smashed on the ground.
Thud! you bolt upright sweaty, all this but a crazy dream.
Neil Joyce, Grade 6
Dr Kevin M Hurley Middle School, MA

My Mom, Alethea

A lways there when I need you.
L uvs me more than enough
E verything I need and want, you get it for me
T he prettiest and sweetest mom ever!
H elps me with homework, transporting, cleaning, and studies
E xamples of stuff I should do to be a great role model for my lil' cousins.
A lways loves, helps, hopes, suggests, and asks that I listen and stay in school
Kaleigh Byrd, Grade 4
East Jones Elementary School, MS

Chaser My Long Lost Pet

Swimming gracefully and elegantly in his bowl
His mouth midway open
As he timidly and carefully pecks at his food
His gill slits sucking and blowing
As he inhales and exhales
His scales shimmering in the soft light like a knight in shining armor
As his eyes peek out at the outside world from his own
But always keeping watch of his surroundings and whereabouts as he swims
In case he has to make a quick dart for the comforting darkness of his mini mountain
Then there's a whip of his tail and a flash of red
As his body glides through the world of water that he wisps through all day long
Then the darkness inside his mini mountain swallows him as he swims through it
But now sadly he is not with us anymore
But I am always thinking of him
And the tears I shed when he passed on
As he is thinking of me
I will never forget him as he will never forget me
Chaser

Greyson Warfield, Grade 4
Goshen Elementary School at Hillcrest, KY

What Is Love?*

Love is warm as a campfire.
It is a good feeling inside of you.
God shows His love through the world around us.
Love might be a gift that makes you feel better.
When people support each other they show how much they love and care for each other.
Maybe a kiss or a hug from somebody you know is love.
Love can be soft as fluff or hard as steel.
Everything and everywhere is love.
Without love everything would be a disaster because it is important.
But love doesn't mean fights and hatred.

Abril Rosales, Grade 4
Youngsville Elementary School, NC
*Inspired by John Denver's, "Perhaps Love…"

Months

January is a start of a thrilling new year everybody screams and cheers.
February is a time of love filled with life and flying doves.

March is when color is coming back green and bright it is such a beautiful sight.
April is when the flowers bloom that means summer is coming soon.

May brings grass and leaves to the trees every second is a gentle breeze.
June is when we get out of school we laugh, have fun and play in the pool

July is when fire crackers boom they make lots of shadows loom
August I hear waves crash so I jump in and make a big splash.

September is when the leaves change green and yellow everything begins to feel real mellow
October is for screams and scares people are ghouls, goblins and bears

November is when we have Thanksgiving dinner the sad thing is, it's almost winter
December means here comes Santa's sleigh his reindeer Rudolph will lead the way.

Katie Hayes, Grade 6
Captain Nathan Hale Middle School, CT

Sun Setting

The sun was setting
Like a flare
Getting darker
And darker
By the minute
The sun was setting
Like a flare
Turning the snow to darkness
The sun was setting
Like a flare
Saying goodbye
For now

Peyton Larkin, Grade 4
Riverside School, CT

Horses

Gallop around you
Police on huge, brown horses
Clippety clop clop

Shira Strauss, Grade 4
Bnos Malka Academy, NY

I Am a Skateboarder

I am a skateboarder.
I wonder if I will be a pro,
I hear the snap of the breaking board,
I see big air,
I want to land hard tricks,
I pretend I am a professional,
I am a skateboarder.

I touch my skateboard,
I worry when I fall,
I cry when I break my bones,
I am a skateboarder.

I understand when I fall,
I say, "Get up" to myself,
I dream of being in the X-Games,
I hope to make my dreams come true,
I am a skateboarder.

Joseph Williams, Grade 4
Meadow Park Elementary School, FL

Glasses

Glasses,
You always help me see
Especially the letter "D!"
You sit on my nose
In the perfect pose,
Your lenses are oval,
When I wear you, I feel
Noble!

Jonathon Johnson, Grade 5
Public School 128 Juniper Valley, NY

Red

Red is a sunset
Red is blood
Red is lipstick
Red is a stop sign
Red smells like a rose
Red tastes like Twizzlers
Red sounds like a kiss
Red looks like a heart
Red feels like hot fire
Red makes me mad
Red is an apple

Emily Coblentz, Grade 4
Lincoln Elementary School, PA

Candy

Tasty, sweet full of goodness
Eat it in the morning
Eat it at night
Candy is good full of greatness
Candy is bad for your teeth
But brush, brush, brush
Different kinds Starburst
Jolly Ranchers, and many more,
Candy, candy, candy all so good!

Aquilla Obare, Grade 5
Avon Grove Intermediate School, PA

Foal to a Horse

Foal
New, wobbly
Struggling, falling, hovering
Strong, soft, sturdy, lean
Prancing, neighing, running
Tall, old
Horse

Brianna Marriage, Grade 4
Harmony Community School, FL

Sunrise

Look up!
Out of the vast darkness
Watch the sunrise appear.

Lauren Nalley, Grade 6
Charles D Owen Middle School, NC

PB & J

Peanut butter
Brown, chunky
Sticking, spreading, getting eaten
Salty, thick, fruity, sweet
Jiggling, wiggling, wobbling
Purple, shiny
Jelly

Ben Bowers, Grade 6
Chickahominy Middle School, VA

Morning

The Japanese maple
though a small tree
stands majestically over the garden
its leaves rubies
studded with tiny raindrop diamonds
the magnolias
their leaves like dark green emeralds
their flowers spun of pink silk
and diamonds
diamonds glitter everywhere
on the oaks and pines
on the grass and ground
as I look down the street
I see that it is not just beauty
it is magic
this bustling world
turned to a world of happiness
majesty
silk
nature

Shira Abramovich, Grade 5
Zervas Elementary School, MA

Coed

Coed is her name.
Bobbing is her game.

She puts her food in the wrong bowl.
After it's soggy, she swallows it whole.

She thought she was funny,
Killing that poor bunny.

She attacks and sleeps on our chair.
Now it's covered in her black hair.

We got her all skinny.
Her best friend is Vinnie.

I call her a tick hotel,
But she's really a motel.

They stick and they stay,
Until I pull them away.

Chance Rogers, Grade 6
Captain Nathan Hale Middle School, CT

Sour Flower

There once was a beautiful flower.
It was so disgustingly sour.
All of the bees
Who lived in the trees
Almost tried it but decided to cower.

Madelynn Crawford, Grade 5
Tucker School, AR

Winter

Tis to be the first of the year
Though we thought it would never come back
White fluffy down
Floating from the heaven above
An even blanket soft as the duckl'n's feathers
As we saunter in the winter's white rain
For this will be the perfect moment
As we came upon an open field
The blanket felt moist under our feet
The last sight of down
Slowly vanished in the
Muddy earth
Who dares to destroy the Earth's heavenly snow
The brightness upon the horizon
Appeared high in the sky
Like a beautiful goddess
The harmonious sound
Ringed in our ears
Beautiful specks of color appear before our eyes
It is spring.

Phyllis Lee, Grade 6
Canterbury School, FL

Lights

Lights.
They flicker in the darkest nights,
While being very bright.
Yet mysterious and lurking,
They are secret and secluding.
In neon oranges, reds, blues,
Lights come in many hues.
Joy, comfort, and warmth is what they bring,
To you and your offspring.
Lights are whimsical,
And fantasy-like.
Twittering, flickering, flitting, flashing,
Almost taking flight.
They light up your mind,
With thoughts from the inside.
Lights.

Ysabella Ramirez, Grade 6
Haynes Academy for Advanced Studies, LA

First Day

I walk down the unfamiliar hallway,
The big kids pass me by,
I am only a kindergartner,
Innocent and scared.
I arrive at my classroom,
Staring at the large door before me,
Before I know it the door clicks open,
My teacher stands in the doorway
And greets me with a *smile*,
Right then I decided I would stay in kindergarten for a while.

Sara Bertuccio, Grade 5
Melville School, RI

My Deepest Fear

I am not afraid of the monsters that can give me a fright
Or the darkness that engulfs me at night
I'm not afraid that I won't be good enough
But I know when she leaves times will get rough

Twelve days won't leave enough time
For everyone to say their goodbyes
I'm afraid that our bond of friendship won't be the same
What if she doesn't remember my name?

We will all miss Carmela so so much
I hope that we make sure to keep in touch
I know my life won't ever be the same
But I know that I am not the one to blame

It feels as if our bond of friendship will fall apart
She was the bond, the rock, the heart
When she leaves what if we forget each other
And all the fun times we shared together

Everything started the first day in kinder
We both got along and I became a bestie with her
We vowed we'd always stick together
But now that she's moving can we still stay friends forever?

Joanna Papastavros, Grade 6
City of Pembroke Pines Charter Central Middle School, FL

Darkness

A blank mind stares at a canvas
A gray cityscape all around them
Darkness surrounding them like a wall
The curtains are pulled back to reveal endless gloom
Wind wails in the distance
When will the light come back?
When will joy be regained?

Rowan O'Connell, Grade 4
John Lyman School, CT

My Deepest Fear

My deepest fear is losing the ones I love and care about
Being alone in the world
Nobody to see or hear.

Never seeing my friends and family
Everybody is gone
I am alone.

I am afraid of never seeing anybody ever again
I am alone
I can't see anybody
Are they dead
I am alone
My deepest fear is losing the ones I love and care about.

Kristen Rodriguez, Grade 6
City of Pembroke Pines Charter Central Middle School, FL

Crystal Flower

Beautiful crystal flower comes in day time. Comes in early spring. When you go near it you hear bells ringing. You can smell the greatest things like sugar, lollipops, and the smell of bubbles! The texture is cool and damp. The colors you see are pink, blue, white, purple, tad of mustered yellow, light red and last orange. Bubbles fall on leaves some have color. The leaves now have bubbles all over. It's happy because it looks happy and cheerful. Will the flower ever die down?

Bailey Hoy, Grade 4
Honeoye Falls-Lima Manor School, NY

River of Words

Listen quiet, it whispers…the small creek at sunset
It seems like there is nothing there, but it is alive
In the morning the sun makes the water reflect like a lamp
In the night the moon reflects off the water and makes it seem like an angel is in the water

Matthew Cully, Grade 4
Pleasant Valley Elementary School, PA

I'm From

I'm from the computer and Wii games I thought I would never like. I'm from the sticky gum under a few fast-food tables, and the recycled water bottles (Poland Spring) spilling all over the kitchen table. I'm from sewing the last stitch to Hershey Kisses in tiny bags, and pencils without erasers at the end.

I'm from my favorite hide and seek spot, behind the garbage can and in the garbage can's cabinet, the overlapping shirts in a tiny drawer, my pool parties and water balloons. I'm from cartwheels and somersaults to roasting marshmallows over an old fireplace.

I'm from lasting memories in pictures, or just in my head. I'm from many places, many things, but I am really from me.

Abbey Norton, Grade 4
Abraham Pierson School, CT

Fall Through Ice

Don't go, stay away, it is scalding cold. You won't be able to come up, you won't be able to feel warm again. Don't step on for you may never be able to turn back. Stay away or the dark night might swallow you whole. The ice won't hold up forever. Already coated with a thin layer of snow that has been falling for days. No it's a bad choice, don't step foot, for your clothes will be pulling you down. Don't go like this. For if you do all I will be able to do is suffer and stare. Stay away from the cold scalding ice.

Ana Chew, Grade 6
Avon Grove Intermediate School, PA

The Hidden Truth

A lone candle flickers, threatening my very soul to take leave of my being but yet, in the midst of that lingering emblem of enlightenment, lies a hidden truth
The truth is such that if man could only open his eyes and delight in this, all of the sufferings of our species would be burnt to dust.
The Dead would rise, babbling and bubbling in utter joy at seeing life restored to their families again
What is this reality you ask me, this life-giving nectar we have yet to realize?
Rather than exerting myself in trying to bestow upon you the essence by which the gods survive, I have chosen to show your souls a glimpse of this reality instead
An unearthly atmosphere submerges me, laden with the blossoms of warmth and the fruits of bliss.
The bitter sweet scent of fresh pine envelopes my spirit in elation, takes me by the hand and swings me around in pure ecstasy.
Suddenly, a child reaches for his mother's soft pale palm, slides his hand into hers and the truth shines. Pure Love.

Pooja Chandrashekar, Grade 6
Nysmith School for the Gifted, VA

God

I am running. All I can hear is the sound of the wind. All I can see is the trees and birds. With the sun shining on my face, I am blinded. I know that even though the sun is blocking my vision God will be there to guide me the right way on the right path and He will keep me from going on to the wrong path and getting myself in trouble.

Kara Hibler, Grade 6
Concordia Lutheran School, MD

American Flag

High up in the sky
I can see something fly.
Then I know it's the American Flag,
I know that it's true.
Because I see all of the colors —
Red, white, and blue.

American Flag, standing up so tall,
We know that you won't let our country fall.
This flag represents our hard work,
So every American is free,
Even Americans from sea to shining sea.

If you're black or you're white,
If you're short or you're tall,
It doesn't really matter —
The American Flag welcomes all.

High up in the sky
I can see something fly.
Then I know it's the American Flag,
I know that it's true.
Because I see all of the colors —
Red, white, and blue.

Amanda Lattanzi, Grade 5
Forest Avenue Elementary School, MA

Winter Break

Summer goes, winter comes
Winter break is so much fun
Ten days off you can go somewhere nice
Or stay at home with the cold, cold ice
But the snow starts to melt and winter's going away
Bye, bye winter come back another day!

Dina Mor, Grade 4
South Area Solomon Schechter Day School, MA

God's Wonders

The gentle breeze and the softening sky
Drift as if by song
The sun sets in an array of colors
Blue, purple, orange, then red.

Soon the sun drifts away and the shining moon comes out
The marshlands echo into light darkness
And cattail sway in the gentle breeze.

About a mile away sits a girl reading her Bible tonight
And is thinking of this in her mind:
God is amazing, God really knows
So look out your window to the world below.
Because everything you see and far beyond your eye
Is part of God's wonders far and wide.

Ashley Brown, Grade 6
First Baptist Christian School, LA

Soccer

My favorite sport
My golden shoes pull
me into the soft cushiony leather
The grass scrunches down beneath my shoes
and pops up after every careful step I take
The mud tries to make me fall
I stand sturdy and firm
I take control of the ball
Not letting it take me over
I am the sport
Soccer

Nick Laforme, Grade 4
Garrison Jones Elementary School, FL

George Custer

There was a brave man named George Custer
He led all the troops that he could muster
He attacked at the Bighorn Battle
But was shot right off his saddle.

August Lutkehus, Grade 6
Warrenton Middle School, VA

Setting Stars

Isn't it unfair,
How all the stars out there,
Dim their lights away,
To make room for day?

But happily, they come back every night,
To once again share their light,
But still I wish they were always in the sky,
So I never have to say goodbye.

Jenna Mortenson, Grade 6
Lake Noxen Elementary School, PA

Me

Me.
Can you describe me?

I cannot.
I am afraid I will say something about me
That you will say is wrong.

We do have different opinions,
But what if they're not respected?

Will we be in a fight?
What will we do then?

Will we move on,
Or hold onto the past?

I guess we will never know,
Right?

Alexis Dubovick, Grade 4
Naquag Elementary School, MA

Wolves in the Forest

Whispers
Of
Longing,
Very soon the men will come.
Everything will be destroyed.
Soon, we hear them.
Insisting on destroying our forest.
Never will it be the same again.
Tonight, our
Howls
Ease.
Frightening humans cut down
Our trees,
Ruin our rivers.
Even the sky is gray with
Smoke.
Tonight, our howls ease.

Grace Keating, Grade 6
Canterbury School, FL

Precious One*

She came into my life
One cold February morn
All wrinkled and pink
But glad to be born

I am a big sister!
Happy am I to be one
Then she turned two
And all joy was gone

Autism, oh no!
Not my precious one
How can this be?
Take this pain far from me

God, won't you heal her?
My little sister, my girl
Will she call my name?
Will she ease my pain?

I woke with a start
"Ecky Becky," a tiny voice said.
My little sister, so smart
Said my name and filled my heart

Rebecca Ramnauth, Grade 4
The UFT Elementary Charter School, NY
*Dedicated to my baby sister Regina.

Otter

Beautiful creatures,
Harmed by many chemicals,
Rivers are their homes.

Samantha Lampi, Grade 4
Meadow Park Elementary School, FL

Stars

In the night,
The stars are bright,
And never leave 'til morning's light.
The stars are like
White birds at night.
They always fly
In the dark, dark sky.
When midnight strikes,
The moon's alight
With tiny, tiny craters.
There's a girl out there
With reddish hair,
Wearing a navy blue dress.
The stars of white
Are alight
On that beautiful navy blue dress.

Adriana Romano, Grade 4
H Austin Snyder Elementary School, PA

Maxy

There once was a man named Maxy
Who was as fast as a taxi
He slid on the floor
Crashed through the door
All because the floor was too waxy.

Greg Traver, Grade 6
Blue Ridge Middle School, VA

Summer

On a summer day,
Splashing in the hose water,
Cooling in the sun.

Teyla Dawson, Grade 4
Ridgeway Elementary School, MD

If I Could Talk to God

If I could talk to God
I would say good job
If I met God
I would say I'm sorry
For what I have done
I have used violence
I have used words
However, I have never used peace
If God was listening I would say,
I hope you save people
If God heard my voice
I would say
I hope you save my family
And my future family
If I could talk to God
I would say please help anyone
Who really needs your help

Daniel Quintana, Grade 6
South Middle School, NY

Why War?

I understand going to war
But it doesn't seem right.
People dying
For no reason.
Why war?

I don't get
Why they last so long.
If countries are mad,
Talk to each other.

I just don't want people
To die for nothing.
Why war?

Why invent bombs and guns
For the public or military?
All they hurt
I'm just so mad.

I just can't take
Everyone dying
While I live
A happy life.
Why war?

Cody Maid, Grade 6
Captain Nathan Hale Middle School, CT

The Bright Road Ahead!

The bright road ahead,
Has more than just delight.
Your burdens taken away,
In the resting place of light.

The bright road ahead,
Has no more sadness,
With tears left behind,
In the cold night of darkness.

The bright road ahead,
Will guide you the way,
Of goodness and kindness,
Even when you're astray.

The bright road ahead,
Will be the best road you've taken.
Even though it's narrow,
You'll find it like a sparrow.

I've found that bright road,
The one that leads to life.
I'm on its paths to the Promised Land,
And I'm looking for you in delight.

Jordan Reynolds, Grade 6
Discovery School @ Reeves Rogers, TN

My Deepest Fear

My deepest fear is not of success or failure.
But of death and its effects.
Forever lying in my grave with no soul.
Never seeing loved ones again.
My heart would bear an everlasting hole.

The day God puts his arms around me.
The day I wish I could control.
The day I hope will never come.
The day I go to heaven or hell.
The day my era comes to a close.

How will my life come to an end?
Hopefully because of natural causes.
Will my death be short and sweet?
Or will it be a long and painful one?
In which I cannot enjoy my last breaths.

Peter Dourvetakis, Grade 6
City of Pembroke Pines Charter Central Middle School, FL

Shadows

Your companion for life;
they'll never leave your side,
but when it gets dark or rainy,
they decide to stay inside.
A silhouette so perfect,
a painting so precise,
an exact replica;
your companion for life.

Addisyn Kendall, Grade 5
George R Austin Intermediate School, MA

Nazi

Evil, mean
Killing, finding, spying
Guns, weapons, secret newspaper, hiding
Saving, hiding, sabotaging,
Secret, sneaky
Resistance-fighters.

Anthony Lotz, Grade 4
St Joseph School, KY

The Crystal Flower

At night a crystal flower would shine in the moonlight.
In the winter the flower would glow in the snow.
The crystal's color on the flower are clear white,
A sky blue, and a very light pink.
People feel happy when they see the crystal flower.
Also when people see the flower on windy days
The air feels cold and damp on their skin.
Everyone loves the flower just for the beautiful crystals
And its smell of red roses.
On windy days the wind blows the flower and crystals all over.
Will the flower have more crystals when it is bigger?

Alyssa Coates, Grade 4
Honeoye Falls-Lima Manor School, NY

Lance

Lance, Lance,
He's golden like a lion
and rarely is he cryin'.
His fur is super soft,
but his tail is hay in a loft.
He's energetic and fun
while playing in the hot sun.

Lance, Lance,
My dad brought him home all wrapped up,
but back then, in my room, he was only a pup,
and now he's all grown and likes going for walks.
Barking and growling are the only way he talks;
He knows all kinds of tricks and he even fetches sticks.

Lance, Lance,
He eats his food like a hog…
My friends, he is a dog!

Bobby Trudeau, Grade 5
Foxborough Regional Charter School, MA

Pleasure of Snow

Running outside before it stops!
Every step you take is cool as ice.
Milky white color with cream on top!
The pleasure makes you feel with every single drop!
Different sizes and shapes fluttering to the ground!
A way to make your frown upside down!
Frozen water droplets fall from the sky.
There just so beautiful, they make you cry!

Yusra Hafeez, Grade 6
Poe Middle School, VA

My Deepest Fear

My deepest fear is not of sharks,
Nor snakes, nor death
My deepest fear is not of bees,
Nor monsters, nor strangers

I hear that noise, that swirl of wind
The destruction, the terror, the pain
Black clouds filled with rain and hail
Thunder, lightning, and high winds
Tornadoes…my deepest fear

It may sound stupid and I may be a wimp
But tornadoes are scary and
They are whirlwinds of death

I cry and I cry and I want it to stop
I want it to end
I want it to disappear
Tornadoes…my deepest fear

Alexandra Orr, Grade 6
City of Pembroke Pines Charter Central Middle School, FL

The Whisper*

He leaned his weight
On his trusty old hoe
He tried to see his fate
A fate he did not know.

A light hoarse whisper
Coming from over that hill
His pain in his heart grows deeper
And through his spine, a chill.

He sees the late sun
He sees a lone hare
His work will never be done.

The overturned earth
Like a flickering pool
He thought of the birth
A birth that will change his life.

The birth will change his people
A change for the world
And as long as he had his soul
That moment will be pearled.
Adrien Denis, Grade 6
McCall Middle School, MA
**Based on the painting "Man with a
Hoe" by Jean-Francois Millet*

Frogs

Little hop machine,
Once a tadpole in a swamp,
There goes the green frog.
Victoria Suarez, Grade 4
Meadow Park Elementary School, FL

Cheetah

Black spots all over
Glowing eyes when it's pitch black
Running so swiftly
Rivka Dayan, Grade 4
Bnos Malka Academy, NY

Maple Leaf

A battered flag,
its remnants ruffled by the wind,
like a twisted blanket,

A complicated network
of rivers and streams,
weaving its way through hilly terrain,

A great fire,
green at its heat,
blazing 'til autumn falls.
Martin Malotky, Grade 6
New Garden Friends School, NC

My Amazing Friend

My amazing friend Brad is like a brother to me
Because he treats me like I'm part of the family even though I'm not.

My outstanding friend Brad helps me when I'm hurt
Like when I ran into my friend Maurice on my bike by accident.

My excellent friend Brad stands up for me when I'm
In a fight or if someone is about to hit me.

My hilarious friend Brad always makes me laugh
Like when I was sad one day and he said something funny and I laughed.
Abby Hughes, Grade 6
Chickahominy Middle School, VA

What?

What should you do? What should you do, when there's nowhere to turn?
When sickness reaches your family and there's only months to live?
Do you count the tears? Or visit while you can?
What should you do?

What do you do? What do you do when you're flunking your grade?
And you do all you can, and study and study,
And lose sleep at night but that doesn't help.
So what? What do you do?

What will you do? What will you do when there's only one hope?
And that hope is quite hopeless, and there is nothing else left,
Because that hope is at its end?
What will you do?

You smile. You keep your head up high.
You keep doing what you can, and be with your family,
And get extra help, and just continue hoping.
Fight off the bad, it will not empower you.
Be the best that you can, and you know you are.
Somebody out there will be with you.
Helping and hoping right alongside you.
Because you, yes you, a singular, special, wonderful child,
Dear friend, you are loved.

Grace Stingle, Grade 6
Kelly Lane Intermediate School, CT

Silver Cascades

I see the exquisite flora — crimson, golden on the budding trees.
I see the rocks piled on top of each other with leaves scattered chaotically.

I hear water rushing between the rocks and out into the distance.
I hear the trees rocking and swaying and making a beguiling beat.

I smell the aroma of the juicy, scrumptious berries.
I smell the fresh, clean, spanking new fresh air.

I touch the stones as I sit and enjoy the calming waters.
I taste the silver cascade as it slips down my throat.
Carrie Johnson, Grade 6
Suffern Middle School, NY

Cake on My Face

On my first birthday
I had so much fun,
There was cake on my face —
Here's how it had begun…

In front of me Mom put the cake,
For her it was a big mistake.
The squishy frosting made me glad,
Cake on my face is what I had!

The whole family laughed,
Like hyenas, in fact.
The cake was a mud pie,
On me it was packed.

My mom took a picture.
I looked so wild,
With cake on my face,
Such a silly child!

Sydney Rowe, Grade 5
Foxborough Regional Charter School, MA

Sunrise

She crept through the graveyard like a cat on the hunt.
Her tombstone was gray like that of a small child's eyes,
It was worn with age.
Her coffin creaked the sound of that small child's cry.
The child whom would never live again.
She lay down in the old, wooden coffin.
The sun was slowly rising over the horizon.
As her coffin door thumped closed,
That wicked smile spread across her face,
As she waited for the sun to set again.

Krista Hartmann, Grade 6
Linkhorne Middle School, VA

Love for You and Me*

Love is like a rainbow, colorful and bright.
Love is like the ocean, calm and quiet.
It is like the best day of your life.
Most of it is awesome, and some of it is sad.
Love is like a fire, burning in my heart.
Love is like a river, calm and beautiful.
Love is like blankets warm and soft.
Love is like a waterfall, soothing.
Perhaps a hug warm, and tight.
Love is like a building, tall to protect.
Love is like a shadow, staring back.
Love is like speed, it goes by fast.
It is like a car, it comes and goes.
Perhaps a sunset, cool and relaxing.
That is what love is all about.

Brayton Haws, Grade 4
Youngsville Elementary School, NC
*Inspired by John Denver's, "Perhaps Love…"

Sports

Either you're running down the field,
or setting a volleyball,
or you're hitting a grand slam,
you might as well do them all.
Scoring a goal,
or hitting a par.
You can play them anywhere.
Either on grass or on tar.
Penalties and fouls all the same,
score the last touchdown to win a game.
It's all about how you play each sport,
it's not to win or lose.
So just keep practicing with all your might,
next time you just might get it right.

Alexander Barnes, Grade 6
Gulfview Middle School, FL

Seals

Seals use flippers to skip in the water.
They flip and flop.
They're super speedy in the water
Their blubber protects them wherever they go.
If you're lucky,
You will see them in a show.

Kyle Scott, Grade 4
Pike Creek Christian School, DE

Where I'm From

I am from apple trees
From big cities and little towns
I am from swimming pools
From skies and bicycles

I am from Jewish stars and menorahs
From Hebrew school
I am from the torah
From being on my own
From my little shana-punim

I am from swords and daggers
From costumes and pictures
I am from haunted houses, popcorn and cotton candy

I am from those we have lost
From the sad times that have made me strong
I am from the lost faces that I will never forget

I am from someone watching over me
That made me the fearless girl I am today
I am from the purple belt I wear around my waist
And the black belt I wear around my heart

I am from my dreams and no one else's
I am from the choices I make and the chances I take

Genessa Taub, Grade 5
Cherry Lane Elementary School, NY

Love

Love,
an angel fallen from above
a slow mist cloud
a coo of a dove
a fresh breath of air
long locks of hair
the wings of a butterfly

Please don't leave me,
Please don't die.

Sawyer Hurst, Grade 6
Norton School, CT

Spring

Clouds are going, sun is coming.
Baby hummingbirds are humming.
Flowers blooming, animals waking.
Spring is now in the making.
"Spring spring!"
Everything seems to sing.
Baby birds, young deer,
Spring is here!

Erin Newhart, Grade 4
L Ray Appleman Elementary School, PA

Lax

I play so many lacrosse games.
I'm starting to learn the ref's names.
We have a game today.
I really like to play.
I hope we will make it a blowout.
I really do not like to go out.
I run with a team named Wax.
We always play to the max.
I wear number eleven.
My buddy, Brenden, is number seven.
It's always fun to score,
But assists should count as more.
I play middie and attack.
You better not turn your back.
If you're going to play, you got to be fast,
Otherwise, in this game, you'll never last.
I hope I play a solid one,
While having lots of fun.
My teammates would say the same.
That lacrosse is an awesome game.

Luke Hurley, Grade 5
St John Catholic School, MD

Rain

Gray clouds start moving
Showers of mist fill the air
It starts to fall down

Maura Schatz, Grade 5
St John Catholic School, MD

Harry Potter

Harry has two friends
They help him fight Voldemort
And they defeat him

Gabriella Monte, Grade 4
Public School 207 Rockwood Park, NY

Invisible

I lie there in a crowd of people
Waiting for somebody to see
How hurt I am
And how much I need
But people don't see me
I'm invisible
It gets to me some times
Because nobody notices
How I don't have a home
Or a loving family
I'm invisible
I beg for money and I beg for food
But people just stare
And want me to move
I'm invisible
So invisible

Leanne Ellis, Grade 6
Canterbury School, FL

Tornado

You are destructive
You might destroy my bedroom
You spin super fast

Jami Farwell, Grade 4
St Joseph School, KY

Coming Home

The rain is falling
As the night sky takes over
A terrible storm is coming
In the city of Dover.

I listen to the rain *tap tap tap*
As I am sleeping in my bed
Then I hear a *rap rap*
I am scared so I cover my head.

I wake up that morning
And smell the fresh air
I know today won't be boring
Because there's no fear.

I know I said bye bye
But today I couldn't be happier
I love that guy
My Daddy is coming home.

Cammy Sky Holt, Grade 6
Charles D Owen Middle School, NC

Turtles in a Pond

Turtles in a pond
swimming happily ever after
to their very own beach

Griffin Kasch, Grade 4
Ridgeway Elementary School, MD

Blue Forest

At twilight one day, wind whistling,
snow falling from the trees,
will the snowfall ever cease?
The air frigid and cold,
winter taking its toll.
Trees, water, snow,
twirling to and fro.
The forest aqua blue,
nightfall slowly coming to.

Maxwell Kammermeier, Grade 4
Honeoye Falls-Lima Manor School, NY

Star

A glorious star
That hovers
Above
Watching carefully
Over us
Making sure
Nothing
Happens
And when something
Does happen
They open up
And grab
Your
Spirit
Promising
Happiness
To you for all
ETERNITY

Kelly Young, Grade 4
PS 10, NY

Climbing

Climbing higher, higher to the top
No one dares to hop a hop
Climbing, climbing up a peak
I hope it does not take a week

Elizabeth M. Grove, Grade 5
Avon Grove Intermediate School, PA

Recess

I am playing games
I am playing some kick ball
I just caught the ball.

Trevor Breeden, Grade 4
Ridgeway Elementary School, MD

A Question with No Answer

I would've asked her what her favorite color was,
maybe even her favorite animal
or even her favorite music.
But I can't ask her any of that,
she's gone away.
Never to come back again,
I never *really* saw her,
never felt her.
When I imagine her
I can meet her
in my dreams,
in my heart.

Elaine Wehmhoff, Grade 5
Coleytown Elementary School, CT

Seasons

Seasons, people have favorites,
but why don't I?
The weather always changes,
but it always seems dry.

We have winter break and summer vacation,
but I don't see a reason.
Winter, spring, summer, and fall,
feel like one big season.

No snow, no sleet, I must make a fuss,
because seasons don't affect any of us!

I think seasons are a lame excuse
for places to have sales,
because all we get in Florida are
hurricanes and gales.

Marion Truax, Grade 6
Gulfview Middle School, FL

Arts and Crafts

Arts and crafts are so much fun
There are ways to use them well.
Colors like yellow for the sun
And the color blue for a bell.

There is paper for nice, neat stuff
There are kinds that are nice and tough.
My project needs designs and art
So put some supplies in the cart.

Glitter and glue sparkle and shine.
Sparkle and shine for a nice big star.
And some glitter on the paper make lights.
And why don't I buy seven or nine.

Arts and crafts are so much fun.
My project is finally done.

Andrew Tully, Grade 4
Nelson Place Elementary School, MA

Dawn Dances

Dawn dances
Around the sphere
That is the world,
Lending light
To the sky,
Melting the stars away.
Dawn welcomes Morning
And hides,
Watching Morning
Greet young Noon,
Who flitters away.
In trudges Afternoon,
Slowing toward Evening,
Who trips over napping Dusk.
Dusk hugs Night
And —
Dawn gets ready —
Dawn springs out,
Eagerly pushing noiseless Night
Out of the way.

Annie Sherrill, Grade 6
West Woods Upper Elementary School, CT

Black

Black, black, black
"You can have it in any
Color as long as it's black."
It is the sound of cats whining
Or an infant who has seen a ghost
It makes me feel upset, alone, and scared
It's the color that creeps me out the most.
It smells like dead flowers, burnt food,
And someone smoking
It tastes like coffee, sorrow, and something disgusting
It is the color of a biker's jacket and an
Old lady saying, "Stop the racket!"
Black is the color of a haunted house gate.
Turns out it's not a color,
It's a shade!

Petra Udvarhelyi, Grade 5
Public School 128 Juniper Valley, NY

The Hollowed Soul

The hollow soul is nothing but a shell,
Its eyes tell a story that not words can even tell.
Their body cannot move as death bells toll,
People wondering about their everlasting soul.
After the soul is gone and left,
Only hoping he was Heaven kept.
Most people close their eyes,
Darkness swallows their cries.
Gone and off the soul went,
The hollowed soul was Heaven sent.

Rachel Gallardo, Grade 6
J E Holmes Middle School, NC

Kisses

When you were gone, so far away,
your love still reached out here,
and every kiss upon my cheek,
never did smear.

Those little bright red kisses,
covering my cheeks,
dancing like the butterflies,
on the light green leaves.

I'm so glad you're here now,
so you can give me more,
of those bright red kisses,
you're the person I adore!

Noelle Schneider, Grade 6
Home School, FL

Bath Time

There was an old cat in a tub,
who didn't want to scrub.
But he was so dirty
and couldn't be flirty
so he finally started to rub.

Kendra Morningstar, Grade 6
Bedford Middle School, PA

Lincoln's Life

Little Lincoln
was born in 1809
he was forced to move to Indiana
in an early age

When he got to Indiana
he worked in the fields
in 1812 his brother Thomas Jr. died

His friend, Austin
saved him from drowning

When he got older
he became the 16th President
he was the President during
the Civil War
he fought against slavery and won
one horrible night
in Ford's Theater
he was shot

Jarad Vanzant, Grade 5
Edmonton Elementary School, KY

Ireland

A clover is green
Little leprechauns wear tall hats
Irish people dance

Alexia Andre, Grade 4
Pope John Paul II Academy, MA

Animal Cruelty

Their sad eyes
fill me with despair.
Trusting us with all their needs,
betrayed by humankind.

Giving loyalty and companionship;
expecting nothing in return,
except our love and friendship.

Protecting our homes and loved ones.
Working and herding in the field.
Playing with the children,
or lying by our side
when we are ill.

Some get no payment,
no food or warmth or love.
Only beaten, abandoned, or starved
by the ones they love and serve.

No more animal cruelty!
Humanely treat our pets;
helpless and unable to speak for themselves,
they deserve our care and respect.

Hannah Porter, Grade 6
J E Holmes Middle School, NC

The Orange

On the outside I'm as simple as can be
my dimples dapple my soft yet fragrant skin
that protects my juicy insides.
At first peel my tropical-citrus aroma
breaks free and fills the room,
my host gets a humorous squirt of my juice in the eye.
The bite tart yet it fills his mouth with a tropical party almost unleashed.

Rona Randall, Grade 6
Northside Middle School, VA

Boom!

Boom!
The glowing, yellow lightning zigzags out from the terrifying clouds.
Boom!
It starts raining rapidly.
Boom!
My dog dashes under the bed.
Boom!
Boom!
He crawls further.
Boom!
My sister shrieks of fright.
Boom!
The room goes pitch black.
I find myself on the floor of my room with heavy blankets.
I ask myself, "Did it really happen?"

Thomas Kim, Grade 4
White Oaks Elementary School, VA

Animals

A ll kinds of animals are different by their personality
N ice in different ways
I nside, and outside
M ake great pets, and some can help you
A like with some of the same species
L ove one another like humans would
S ome animals are smart and kind

Laura Heilig, Grade 5
St John Catholic School, MD

The Bad News

I've been through a lot of obstacles
in my life.

My mom and dad just had to give me the news;
that I had to give my dog away.

She was my first and only friend.
I loved her dearly.
She was like a daughter to me.

We had so much fun together
we would go on walks together,
play in the backyard, and best of all
take naps together.

Mollie Duesberry, Grade 6
Chickahominy Middle School, VA

We Won!

Swishhh the other team scored.
Now the score is tied.
The coach yells,
DEFENSE! DEFENSE!

My teammate shoots the ball
It hits the backboard,
It was the sound of a rock hitting a brick wall
The other team steals it
DEFENSE! DEFENSE!

The stomp of our feet running
To the other side of the court
Sounds like elephants running across the grass.
As I run down the court I smell
The hotdog machine. I shoot the ball,
The fans scream and my mind I know I scored.
DEFENSE! DEFENSE!

Then the buzzer went off
"We won the game," the coach yelled.
We shake hands with our opponents.
I got the winning basket I thought,
DEFENSE! DEFENSE!

Madison Turner, Grade 5
Foxborough Regional Charter School, MA

Gymnastics

The bars were yelling, "Just do it, just do it!"
Next thing I knew, "Crash!"
I jumped to the high bar; missed,
and fell on my head.

My coach was yelling that she would call the ambulance,
and so I started to shake.
My mom said, "Let's go home and ice it up
and maybe you'll feel better."

Time went by fast,
I entered the championship,
and I felt as stiff as a board,
a scared baby bird.

The bars were yelling, "Just do it, just do it!"
I jumped to the high bar,
the crowd cheered.

Marissa Holske, Grade 5
Foxborough Regional Charter School, MA

The Baseball Game

A player hit the ball
The ball hit the wall
And a player from the other team caught it
I was about to have a fit.

Another kid was up to bat
He hit the baseball mat.

He hit the ball with all of his might
The ball took flight.

He ran and ran, he had scored a run,
I told him the game had just begun.

The batter swung around
Everyone on the team frowned.

The batter missed the ball
The umpire made that call.

He hit the ball so very high
It looked like it was flying.
It was a big home run
That game was very fun.

Nicholas Weaver, Grade 4
Nelson Place Elementary School, MA

Summer

Today is the first day of summer.
When summer ends is such a bummer.
When I go to the beach,
I look in the water and reach, reach, reach.

Alyssa Borcky, Grade 5
Avon Grove Intermediate School, PA

Feel the Wind Blow Free

The sun is shining
Butterflies are flying
Feel the wind blow free
Feel the wind blow free
With sand in your toes
And water up your nose
Feel the wind blow free
Feel the wind blow free

Michaela Costello, Grade 4
West Frankfort Elementary School, NY

A Stray

A stray
Searching for a home
His whole life
In the city
For happiness and joy

Cody Kirschbaum, Grade 6
Kelly Lane Intermediate School, CT

Dogs

Krista
Amusing, kind,
Running, smiling, eating,
White, brown, white, black,
Frowning, begging, vaulting
Humorous, growling
Misty

Ashley Merritt, Grade 5
Avon Grove Intermediate School, PA

Red

The reddest red
I've ever seen was
A barn in Somerset
The reddest red
I've ever seen was
A field full of tomato plants
The reddest red
I've ever seen was
A sunburned man on a beach in Florida
The reddest red
I've ever seen was
A box full of apples in a grocery store

Jacob Collins, Grade 6
Morton Middle School, KY

The Dog

A dog sleeps by me
Gently, calmly, relaxing
The day escapes him
Or maybe he drinks it in
Smarter than we are

Dan Bailey, Grade 6
Canterbury School, FL

Tim

There once was an old boy named Tim
He wanted to go for a swim
He sunk like a rock
Then wanted to talk
And that was the very end of him

Dyllyn Laird, Grade 5
L Ray Appleman Elementary School, PA

White

White is bright
When it rains she is tired
When it is sunny white is bright
White loves to go swimming
White loves to play with her black lab
When she lies she smiles
Her favorite friend is me
She is a great friend you could have.

Kaitlin Oakes, Grade 4
Youngsville Elementary School, NC

Airplanes

Airplanes are very useful
we travel all around
we go to Puerto Rico
but we don't make a sound
then we go to Mexico
I don't want to catch the flu
so we travel south
to the South American Zoo
it got a little wild
so I guess I'll take it mild
we'll go all the way to China
to see the dragons there
I hope I hope I hope
they don't eat my hair
China isn't right for me
so I guess I'll see the sea
all the way in America
that's the place for me

Nicholas Cohen, Grade 4
Public School 42, NY

Lemonade

Lemonade tastes good,
It is very good for you,
It's so refreshing.

Paul Whittington, Grade 6
Fairfax Collegiate School, VA

Bubble Gum

Yummy chewy pink
Too bad if you have braces
Clear away your hair!

Chava Leah Cohen, Grade 4
Bnos Malka Academy, NY

Puzzle

My friends
My family
They are all pieces
Of my puzzle

They make up me
And shape who I am
Losing even one piece
Would change me

I have many pieces
All of them special
I don't know what I would do
Without them

If there were
No pieces
There would be
No me

Becky Neergaard, Grade 6
E T Richardson Middle School, PA

I Am in the Navy

I am in the Navy,
I wonder how it is to fly a helicopter,
I hear my name in history,
I see myself in a battleship,
I want to fly in the sky,
I pretend to be in the navy,
I am in the Navy.

I touch an AK-47,
I worry about going home in peace,
I cry when my teammates are shot down,
I am a veteran.

I understand how to survive in war,
I say I am a survivor,
I dream to be honored with awards,
I try to save my teammates,
I hope to be honored by the President,
I am in the Navy.

Matias Alarcon, Grade 4
Meadow Park Elementary School, FL

The Life of a Butterfly

The fuzzy caterpillar
Crawls up the majestic tree
Feasting on leaves

The beautiful butterfly
Flutters around the vast forest
Landing on bright flowers

Ali Benson, Grade 6
Kelly Lane Intermediate School, CT

Full Pockets

On my way to school
I see a shiny penny.
I pick it up and put it in my pocket.

As I start to walk again
I spot a paper clip, acorn, and a rubber band.
They too go in my pocket.

As I continue to walk I discovered
A giant fifty cent coin, and three flip tops
From soda cans.
I pushed them into my pockets.

I finally got to school
I realized that I couldn't fit through the door.
When I looked down my pockets were HUGE.

That is why I could not get in.

Amber Roberts, Grade 5
Melville School, RI

Nature at Its Highs

I sit in sand
Watching the waves come in
The wind flies by my face
So cool my hair stands up

I hear seagulls yelling at the water
Then they attack
Water splashes like I dropped a rock in a pond
A nice sight to see

When it's gone rainbow appears
Beautiful colors like I've never seen
Red, orange, yellow, green, blue, indigo, purple
Burst in the air illuminating a cloud

Now I see what it means
To see nature
At its highs

Brian Layden, Grade 6
E T Richardson Middle School, PA

Lies

Lies are like cigarettes
It's never the right thing
You will always have the bad taste in your mouth
Every time you light it you realize
That you are doing the wrong thing
Then why do you do it?
It doesn't make sense
Lies and cigarettes will eat you alive
Next time you hang with the pack
Do the right thing.

Michael Agasar, Grade 6
Hillcrest Elementary School, PA

Goats

Goats are soft on their head, ears, and nose
Goats are cuddly because they
Sleep with you, lay down with you,
Curl up with you
Goats constantly smell like farm animal or wet dog
There are 7 different breeds
Alpines, Lamanchas,
Nigerian Dwarfs, Nubians,
Oberhasli, Saanen and
Togganburgs
Goats have a variety of colors
It's pretty easy to clean up after them, you have to
Shovel poop, put down clean shavings, feed grain, hay,
Clean water, and clean outside pen
Goats are pretty funny because they
Jump in the air sideways
They do stuff with their ears and tail
They make MA's for a sound
Goats are a wonderful thing to have!

Caitlyn Verbridge, Grade 6
Captain Nathan Hale Middle School, CT

Holocaust

In the light of dawn.
I see my brothers beaten.
As I wait my turn.

Jacob Euster, Grade 6
Katherine and Jacob Greenfield Hebrew Academy, GA

Pebble

One little pebble sitting like a king on the ground
The pebble is small, oval shaped, smooth
And very gray
Waiting
Sitting 'til someone picks him up
No one comes
The pebbles getting depressed

Raining
The pebbles getting wet
Then when the sun comes out it dries
A kid sees him
Picking him up
Saying "Perfect shape and size."
The pebble is excited
The kid is calling him perfect

Smooth soft hands holding him
Feeling like a fluffy huge cloud
Very happy and excited
Skipping the pebble across the lake
He won't ever see the kid again
But he hopes

Nathan Houfek, Grade 4
Goshen Elementary School at Hillcrest, KY

Monkeys

Climbing and swinging
Vine to vine and tree to tree
Eating bananas.
Shana Neuhauser, Grade 4
Bnos Malka Academy, NY

Buried Went the Bug

One day
I looked at a bug

It buried
It destroyed my garden

I tried to catch it
but it hurried underground

It
  made
    a
      tunnel
        deep
          down
            in
              the
                ground
Nothing can stop that bug!!
Emma Bonner, Grade 5
New Garden Friends School, NC

Red Eft's Story

I run around on the forest floor,
looking for what I'm looking for.
I'm looking for a refreshing mist,
around a lake where I'll exist.
I have to find it soon to evolve;
that is the question I must solve.
My instincts tell me to find it soon,
'Cause I must be there after June.
Smelling skunk cabbage isn't my delight;
it's smelling a skunk at night.

I see some things like the leaves above,
and eat insects I'm in awe of.
I don't see the starry sky at night,
but instead see the city light.
I hope I find what I've been callin' for;
when I find it, my life will restore.
Rebecca Fraleigh, Grade 6
East Shore Middle School, CT

Summer

Summer is awesome.
Summer is awesomely cool.
I love summer time!
Kayla Hill, Grade 6
Jackson Christian School, TN

I Am

I am big hearted and strong minded.
I wonder if I am being watched.
I hear the sounds of life crawling in my ears.
I see everything and I breath it all in.
I want peace on Earth every second of the day.
I am big hearted and strong minded.

I pretend I'm someone I'm not, even when I am.
I feel the feelings of everyday words, actions, and movements.
I touch life in a way no one else does.
I worry if I fall I may never get up.
I cry over sadness and hatred.
I am big hearted and strong minded.

I understand life and death, even when it can't be understood.
I say what I want, what I can, and what I will.
I dream of soaring high above mountains, but low under valleys at the same time.
I try to be the best person I can be and
I hope I will always understand who I am.
I am big hearted and strong minded.
Nora Salo, Grade 5
Hamagrael Elementary School, NY

Softball for Girls

S creaming fans cheering you on
O pposing teams trying to catch you off guard
F eeling your heart beat race as fast as it can
T rying to focus if it is a ball or a strike
B ending down as low as you can so the pitcher throws a ball
A ligning yourself with home plate
L etting your back foot take all the weight
L ifting you back elbow

F eeling the courage to hit the ball
O ptions to hit the ball or let it hit you
R eady to hit the ball, just waiting for a good pitch

G oing to first as fast as you can
I mpressing the other team by hitting a home run
R unning to the dugout to have a group hug
L etting the other team's mouths drop
S howing yourself (and others) that you are a good softball player.
Darby Pfeifer, Grade 6
Canterbury School, FL

Springtime Madness!

Spring is flowers and baby birds hatching and tiny bugs buzzing.
Spring is the taste of the first ice cream,
fresh air and new dirt smells like spring.
Spring is the sound of birds chirping and water splashing.
Spring is playing soccer, fires in the back yard, and frogs croaking.
Kids playing outside is spring.
Small seedlings growing in the garden is also spring.
Spring is fish swimming in shining lakes.
Jillian Chase, Grade 5
Mayfield Elementary School, NY

Lady Liberty

As seen from the eyes of an immigrant…

The shores swept with freedom, dusted with faith
The pride and the hope, opened the golden gate
For reassurance and liberty that swelled in our souls
The happiness and joy for immigrants, young and old

Her eyes hold the fire of every man's dream
The grace and beauty of her torch may seem
Like thousands of fires shining throughout the world
Like millions of angels bowing down to the ground
The heavenly beings…to freedom bound.

Milika Dhru, Grade 5
Stevens Creek Elementary School, GA

Prayer*

The Lord is my coach; I shall not foul out,
He makes me train hard on the field,
He leads me through drills,
He helps me train.
He guides me in the games,
For His namesake.
Even though I foul out,
The other team makes fun of me.
I will fear no evil,
For You are with me,
Your ball and Your team
They comfort me.
You prepare the game before me,
In the presence of the other team.
You anoint my head with glory;
My cup overflows.
Surely, goodness and love will follow me
All the days of my life,
And I will dwell in the house of the Lord
Forever.

Jacob Benn, Grade 6
Park Avenue Christian Academy, FL
*Inspired by Psalm 23.

Red Is My Friend

Red is blood
Red is a feeling I get when I get mad
Red is a scarf wrapped around my neck
Red are the seven stripes on the American flag
Red smells like a rose
Red tastes like a juicy apple
Red sounds like a red colored pencil sketching a picture
Red is a new manufactured brick
Red feels like a cardinal's feathers
Red makes me feel mad
Red is my favorite color

Darick Moran, Grade 4
Lincoln Elementary School, PA

Cubo to Cupcake

Cubo to Cupcake, so sweet in a bound.
Wagging her tail when I come around.
Sleeping soundly at night, okay in the day,
Cubo to Cupcake never runs away.
Trained to sit, lie down, and come up.
No one can catch that little pup,
When under the table she goes away.
Cubo to Cupcake, wanna play?
Up and down goes my little dog.
Happy to play, happy to love.
Spoiled yet sweet and cute as can be.
Cubo to Cupcake, time to go flee,
On the leash and into the grass.
Lurking away from the dogs and the cats.
By day and by night, she's at my side.
Makes life feel good when it isn't my time,
To shine in the spotlight, or feel real good.
Cubo to Cupcake, I love you! "Woof woof!"

Rachel Sendrow, Grade 6
Canterbury School, FL

Rainbow in Nature

Red shouts from the robin's chest.
Orange warms the fire.
Yellow is a radiant dazzling light.
Green is nature's desire.
Blue flings its life at the sky.
Purple enters the sunrise paintings.
Pink whispers across the garden.
I love all these colors that nature is creating.

Lindsey Webb, Grade 6
Discovery School @ Reeves Rogers, TN

Horseback Riding

Pure energy beneath me
Speeding along until…
Boom: flying through the air
Free as a bird
Broken from his chains
Sky-high, the moment seems to last forever
But then down, down
Thud! A smooth impact on the ground,
But not for long, up, up again,
Like riding the wind.

Katie Oakes, Grade 6
Avon Grove Intermediate School, PA

In New York City

In New York City
At the home of my least favorite team in baseball
With people trying to mug you
In a cab stuck in traffic
Near the main terrorist target
It is the worst place for me to visit!

Brett Harvey, Grade 5
Jamestown Elementary School, PA

Where I'm From

I am from the flowers on my table
From the markers that I use
From the pots and pans that I would play with
I am from the chicken coop that I helped my dad make
From the swing I would swing on
From the fence I would climb with my friends
I am from the love my grandma would give
From the happiness and smiles my grandpa gave out to the world
From my parents that helped me learn
I am from the saying "early to bed early to rise makes a man healthy and wise"
From the saying "red skies at night sailors delight red skies at morning sailors warning"
From the saying "an apple a day keeps the doctor away"
I am from the rice krispies I make
From the cake I bake
From the brownies I make with my nanny
I am from the chickens I play with
From the pets I love and the love of my hamster
I am from the picture album I have in my room
From the rabbit I loved
From the tree I climb
I am from the earth

Allysa Dunbar, Grade 6
Meredith-Dunn School, KY

Waiting on the World to Change

We keep waiting, waiting on the world to change, says John Mayer.
I'm not sure what you're waiting for
But I'm not
We've been waiting for the world to change
And we've been slowly watching it pass by
Right in front of us, we see the world change
But none of us say it's always for the better.
Wars, pollution, global warming, gangs, fights, all these horrible things happening?
They're partially our fault.
John Mayer, says that we are the next generation
But our generation is part of all the trouble
We make our own decisions whether we just hang around with the crowd that makes us feel good
Or the people that have a point
The ones, not waiting on the world to change
But changing it themselves.
Making the world better, nicer, stronger
And we; this generation
Are doing it for the next generation, in hopes that they will prove better than us
So I won't sit back and wait on the world to change
I'm gonna change it
So I'm not waiting, waiting on the world to change.

Chanler Harris, Grade 6
Garrison Forest School, MD

Darkness

Splash! Complete darkness. I open my eyes to find shades of black and blue as I sink into what seems to be never ending darkness I see a hand just out of reach I want to grab the hand that is leaving me fast my only speck of hope gone just out of reach I look down, nothing I look to my left, nothing I look to my right, nothing I look up again, nothing! The hand is gone! I think this is the end when I am pulled onto the boat I am safe and lathered with hugs. That was a day I will never forget.

Makayla Kokai, Grade 5
Abraham Pierson School, CT

Perhaps Love!!*

Love is God answering your prayers
Perhaps love is baking a cake
And some say love is just resting
My memories of love will be of you

Love is rainbows filling the sky
Perhaps love is like the ocean full of hearts
And some say love is everything
The memories of love will take you home

Love is like a cloud
And some say love is holding on
The memories of love will see you through

Perhaps love is an open door
Love is wind blowing hearts off the trees
And for some as strong as steel
My memories of love will be for you

Love is like fire when it is cold outside
Perhaps love is like a resting place
And a shelter from the storm
My memories of love will be for you

Arianna Fuller-Bell, Grade 4
Youngsville Elementary School, NC
*Inspired by John Denver's, "Perhaps Love…"

Ode to Puzzles*

Puzzles
mysterious,
mind-bending.
Like a human,
different and
unfinished.

Pieces lead up to
a beautiful picture.
Some easy,
some difficult.

Puzzles,
the ultimate mystery.

Megan Anderson, Grade 6
Martin Avenue School (The Alpha Program), NY
*Inspired by "Ode to the Book"

Family

My dad is lazy.
My house is crazy.
Ouch, bang, crash!

My grandpa's asleep.
Our car goes beep beep.
Snore, boom, bang!

Ellese White, Grade 5
Our Lady of Grace Elementary School, PA

Sunset Rises

I hear the waves *whoosh, whoosh*.
I feel the light breeze
in the sunset air.
I love the strong smell of the sea.
The beach is a relaxed place to be,
though sand keeps blowing in my eyes;
I sit on the soft beach
and I watch the sunset rise.

Beautiful, bright colors,
I love the red and pink, mixed together,
not shinny, but not dull.

I wonder where the bottom half goes,
that orangy color of the sun,
looking like a bright citrus fruit.
Dark red sky, but I still see the pink,
the sun a round glowing gum ball.

I hear the waves, *whoosh, whoosh*.
The wind blows again,
OW, more sand in my eyes!
I walk away, one more glance at the sunset,
and think, "How beautiful!"

Erndie Erase, Grade 5
Foxborough Regional Charter School, MA

The Lonely Picture

Here I sit upon this dusty shelf.
As I watch people come and go.
Here I sit a lonely picture.
Forgotten it makes me sad.

I yell and yell!
But no one cares about me.
They think I am ugly.
They say I am old but I think otherwise.

I am only about 100 years old.
I don't think that is old do you?
Oh well never mind.
So here I sit on this dusty shelf.

My fate to be decided.
Will I be tucked away forever?
Or will I be loved once more?
Til that day I am just a lonely picture on a shelf.

I am so afraid.
What shall happen if my colors fade?
I hope my day comes to be loved again.
But until then I will sit upon this dusty shelf.

Nicholas Manino, Grade 4
West Frankfort Elementary School, NY

Bobby Joe

His hair is coal-black,
his blue eyes shine like the moon.
What a strong face he has.
His smile so sweet,
it makes me melt like chocolate.

His strong arms hold me tight,
he never lets me out of his sight.
Oh, how he loves me so,
he will never let me go.
He is picture perfect.

He is big-hearted,
kind, loving, and caring.
He is everything I ever wanted,
everything to me.
He is my hero!
He is my dad.

Jennifer Stegall, Grade 6
J E Holmes Middle School, NC

Poem

P eople get to write whatever,
O n your own,
E xpress your feelings,
M akes you think.

Madison Buckmaster, Grade 4
Meadow Park Elementary School, FL

Gold Fish

Gold fish make splashes.
Swimming in the sea and lake.
Hearing the wind shake.

Racheli Borohov, Grade 4
Bnos Malka Academy, NY

Staple Remover

A shark
undoing mistakes

an ominous demon
taking the life of one's staple

a simple servant
at one's command

a spring loaded monster
waiting to strike

a set of jaws
too sharp to be real

A slave to one's hand.

Charlie Freedman, Grade 5
New Garden Friends School, NC

The Dark Night

The leaves swirl in the night,
like a tornado in the sky,
don't be afraid the monster's await,
you will be eaten away.

Connor Grant, Grade 6
Gulfview Middle School, FL

Growing Up on Its Own

A panda was born
And it was abandoned
The panda was sad
His tears were dropping on his hands

He proved that he could stand
Without a parent
He's growing up
On its own

He made some nice friends
And he fell on the ground
His tears were all gone
He stood up without any help

He proved that he could stand
Without a parent
He's growing up
On its own

Sydney Lu, Grade 6
River Bend Middle School, VA

The Creek

The creek
runs and water
flows over rocks with fish
swimming to avoid the water
falling.

Evan Hooper, Grade 6
Bedford Middle School, PA

Monkeys

Monkeys swinging from a tree
It makes me happy and filled with glee
As I watch them swing so high
Never want to say goodbye

Amanda C. Hirst, Grade 5
Avon Grove Intermediate School, PA

Peaceful

Peaceful
Beaches are calm
With the sound of the shore
So relaxing I drift away
Asleep.

Megan Moorhead, Grade 6
Bedford Middle School, PA

Karlie

karlie
nice, athletic, kind, outgoing, and funny
sibling of katie
lover of softball and ice skating
feels happy
needs more time to play
gives love
fears spiders and clowns
likes spain, china, and hawaii
tennessee
west

Karlie West, Grade 6
Livingston Middle School, TN

Untitled

Blowing white petals
Beautifully in the wind
Enjoying daisies

Ariel Goldberg, Grade 4
Stackpole Elementary School, PA

River

Flowing through the woods
Travels onto the ocean
Now, part of the waves

Abigail Drennon, Grade 5
Melville School, RI

A Teacher

Someday I will be a teacher
And tell students what to do.
I'll get my own desk, too.
I'll even have my own classroom.
I will be a nice teacher,
Someday in the future.

Noraya Pettiway, Grade 6
North Albany Academy, NY

Autumn to Winter

Autumn
leaves are bright and
colorful when they fall
preparing for the harsh wet white
winter.

McKenzie Coffield, Grade 6
Bedford Middle School, PA

Mickey Mouse/Icon

Mickey Mouse
Captivating, noble
Starring, performing, entertaining
A famous cartoon character
Icon

Davis Kohler, Grade 5
The Cathedral School, AR

Open Book: Bella from "Twilight"

One look, that's all it takes
a glance, a gaze, then you can see what I'm feeling…
Look into my eyes, what do you see?
A tear, a smile, a confused expression?
Well that's what I am, just an open book
for everyone to read.

Siloe Garcia-Elizalde, Grade 6
Avon Grove Intermediate School, PA

Volleyball

As I smack the ball on the court,
    four times before I serve, like always,
I think about how much power
    I need to use to hit the ball over the net.
Maybe a lot,
    Maybe a little,
        It depends on the team.
Are they good?
Are they bad?

As I bend forward,
    ball in my left hand,
        right hand back,
BAM! I send it sailing forward.
It's flying across the net
    right between the middle of two players.
Score! Score! SCORE! our team yells.
I made our first point.

Marina Yergey, Grade 6
Gulfview Middle School, FL

Season Leaves

The summer leaves twitter in the light breeze,
they're waving at me.
I wave back at them.
I look back
the leaves are not on the tree,
they're scattered across the ground,
all different colors.
The leaves that are left on the branch
are struggling to be free.
Summer is gone and autumn takes over.
Soon the leaves turn white with snow
then they shrivel up and die,
they neither were autumn leaves
nor were they summer leaves,
but they are cold winter leaves.
About three months later, the leaves grow back
I greet them,
I welcome them back.
Good-bye winter,
spring has come to take your place.

Kaelyn Beach, Grade 4
Crestwood Elementary School, KY

In the Wind

Grass is a waving
Ocean of green in the wind
Flowing back and forth

Kacey Sharpe, Grade 5
Foxborough Regional Charter School, MA

Things in the Sky

So many things are in the sky
Like an airplane, which flies so high.
You can look down on everything,
Or hear the birds which happily sing.

You can see a bird flying through a cloud
Singing its tune so very loud
With its colorful wings she is so proud
Then you see her fly above the crowd.

Ragin Smith, Grade 5
St John Catholic School, MD

Machu Picchu

It was the mysterious feeling
That made us wonder
What lies beneath the surface
Of this eerie place

Was it treasure?
Was it a curse?
Was it meant to be discovered?
Should we be here?

These were the questions
That hung thick in the air
Like the gloomy fog
That covered the mountains

It was a place filled with surprise,
Or evil, or magic
Which it was, I do not know
And that may be what this place intended.

Hannah Curran, Grade 5
Litchfield Intermediate School, CT

Earth

The Earth is full of land and water.
I pray that it won't get hotter!

We have a lot of animals and trees.
We have to protect what we see.

Fish and flowers make us smile.
Eco-friendly cars go the extra mile.

Chemicals and global warming make me scared.
Solar panels should not be rare!

Molly Cahlink, Grade 4
Rolling Knolls Elementary School, MD

Need You

Hey Lyssie:
I don't know if you're listening
But, I want you to know a few things

I know your death
Really wasn't my fault
But I feel like I could
Have done something to
Keep you with me…

Since I didn't,
I blame myself
For what happened
That painful day

From up above, looking down
I guess you know how
Our once happy family
Was ripped to shreds

As I recover from losing that
I realized
All I really want is
You back in my life
Cara Monastra, Grade 6
E T Richardson Middle School, PA

Animals

Animals are cute
Rabbits, horses and cool snakes
Are some examples
Frank Ding, Grade 4
Fairfax Collegiate School, VA

I Am

I am a boy.
I am a Wickersham student.
I am a very smart person.
I am a very handsome son.
I am a fun kid.
I am a great dancer.
I am a cool person.
I am a great swimmer.
I am a Pokémon trading card collector.
I am a Star Wars watcher.
I am a #1 Star Wars fan.
I am a good fighter.
I am a video game player.
I am a cute boy.
I am an only son.
I am a grandchild.
I am a fearless person.
I am Giovannhy Saint Georges!
Giovannhy Saint Georges, Grade 4
Wickersham Elementary School, PA

Jill

There was a girl named Jill
She had a best friend named Bill
They both wanted fins
They are both like colorful pins
They both have a new friend named Will
Uriel Bernal-Pedroza, Grade 5
Avon Grove Intermediate School, PA

Cleansing Rain

I sit and wonder why
Everyone is so gloomy.
Could it be because
All the rain is falling so smoothly?

I love the fresh smell,
The moist feeling it has,
Looking as if the dark clouds are crying.

Drip, drop, drip, drop
The soothing sound it has.
For if you cannot hear it,
You must sit, ponder and have patience.

For I see the rain
As a great new beginning,
Starting out fresh and renewed.
Madison Sherman, Grade 5
Blessings Christian School, NC

A Sunny Day at the Pool

It was a very sunny day
at the pool
it was so hot
you could bake an egg
on the sidewalk.
I could hear
kids jumping in the pool,
having fun.
I wonder if it's someone's birthday?
Danielle Peterson, Grade 4
Grace Lutheran School, FL

Trapped

Underneath the stone
With thy name
Among the living
But with the dead
Under the natural lights of earth
Instead of laughter I hear grief
Away from a love forever
Upon my brothers
In sealed unforgiving brown walls
Apart from others my heart still walks
Asia Rodriguez, Grade 6
Berry Middle School, AL

Months

April rain is falling now
down down to the ground.
April is over
and May flowers are found.

October is here
and I want a treat.
November dinner, coming soon
my new cousin I'm going to meet.
Nathan Clark, Grade 4
Harmony Community School, FL

Summer

Having the heat rush against my face
Trying to embrace
Drinking lemonade
Just to catch a wave
Seating in the pool
Acting like you're so cool
In the heat rays
Do you have those hot days
Myra Richardson, Grade 4
Delmont Elementary School, LA

My Little Friend

Black like a Goodyear tire,
Fuzzy like a big fur coat,
Cute like a newborn baby,
Fast like a cheetah,
And small like a ball.
She runs, she plays, she hides,
She lives, she loves, she dies.
But still twelve years to go,
With fast, with medium, with slow.
I'll just simply call her, my little friend.
Cedar Hittle, Grade 4
Abraham Pierson School, CT

The Beach

Riding in the car,
it is not far.
We're almost to the beach,
it's just out of reach.
I yell, yes,
it's time to make a mess!
I like to ride a wave,
no need to behave.
My cousins and I aren't afraid,
to walk and get a fresh lemonade.
Now we make a castle,
and the grownups don't hassle.
Because we are at the beach,
and happiness is now within reach.
Ben Hartman, Grade 6
Memorial Elementary School, MA

God's Tears

I sit, look out the window at the rain.
Thousands, even *millions* of tiny droplets.
For God is crying.
Or, are we doing good
Is He happy or sad?
Does He want His people to do better?
Representing kindness?
I follow one tear
Till it gets lost on the ground.
I look up, follow another drop
Till it gets lost on a tree,
One of God's creations.
Maybe God is sad
About what we are doing to Earth.
Wrecking and poisoning
Innocent creations and creatures.
Or is God happy?
Happy about the people who are
Trying to do good.
I follow another drop,
Another tear, another symbol of God's feelings.

Jane Powers, Grade 5
Hamagrael Elementary School, NY

Christmas

Snow falling in the white winter wonderland,
Bells ringing on every corner of town,
Turkey cooking in the oven,
Candy in every stocking,
Tummy aching after a big Christmas dinner,
Christmas

Fallyn Yonish, Grade 5
Claysville Elementary School, PA

Fall

F alling from trees bright colors spin and twist
A pples that are bright and juicy are picked from trees
L aughing children run and jump into a pile of crunchy leaves
L oudly kids run inside for their hungry bellies

Shannon Ryan, Grade 6
Kelly Lane Intermediate School, CT

School

Math, reading, writing, art
They say it's supposed to make you smart

But does it really
Maybe it just makes you silly

Science, social studies, read aloud
It all makes quite a sound

PE, music, lunch and tests
We all need one big rest

Rose Russell, Grade 4
Naquag Elementary School, MA

Rainbow

Drip Drop, Drip Drop,
The rain falls gently on the window pane,
It is frigid outside,
But I feel cozy and warm inside my house.

The roar of the down pouring rain,
Makes it,
Become harder and harder to hear,
Until finally the rain stops.

And what I find,
Is extraordinary,
A single rainbow with all of its colors,
RED, ORANGE, YELLOW, GREEN, BLUE, PURPLE.

All of them glistening in the sun,
Everything turns bright again,
Like a newly lit light bulb,
And I feel better.

Allison Smith, Grade 6
Norton School, CT

Rain Drops on My Window

The rain is scary
In the night
While people fill taxies
With yellow light.

It seems that the rain will never end
In the ocean, waves
Break and bend.

The children feel the raindrops
Hit their tongues,
The taxies' wipers go swoosh, swoosh,
The rain goes drop, drop.

Yellow raincoats all around
The children stomp their wet boots on the ground.
Rain, rain go away
Please come again another day.

Michael DiTommaso, Grade 5
Public School 128 Juniper Valley, NY

Summer

In the summer it is scorching hot
The sun shines as bright as a blazing fire
But the grass is a carpet of granny smith apples
The forest is as crowded as a New York City highway
The sky is a ceiling of blue ocean water
Summer is full of wondrous sights
See what you can find on a hot summer day

Natasha Austin, Grade 4
Naquag Elementary School, MA

A Dream

You have a dream
but only once
if only you could dream
that same dream
every night
your whole world
would fall into place
as your head fell into your pillow
in the blink of an eye
that person's dream came true
everyone would see
who she really wants to be
if only that person
could be
ME.

Taylor DeBello, Grade 6
E T Richardson Middle School, PA

Color

Color is never dull
Color color everywhere
Grab a crayon and bam
Color here color there color everywhere
Color is never dull
On the wall at the mall
Color color everywhere
Color in cloth
Color in different shades
Black blue green and all
Look around you'll find them all
If there was no color life would be dull
But with color life is not dull at all.

Matthew Williams, Grade 4
H Austin Snyder Elementary School, PA

Earth

My Earth is green and so serene
And very blue and true
But that's not all
That makes it awe
It's also very cool
There's tons of pools
And oceans too
But it all ends with you
So today be green
And be true to OUR big blue

Laurel Tipps, Grade 6
Discovery School @ Reeves Rogers, TN

The Rain

I hate the rain
It is such a pain
But the rain is helpful
When the plants are dying.

Patrick Connacher, Grade 5
Calvary Chapel Christian School, PA

I Feel

Sometimes I feel happy but sometimes I feel sad.
When I feel happy, it's like being in a world where there is no such thing as despair.
When I feel sad, it's like I have this deep dark feeling inside of me.
Sometimes I can have a smile on my face but be hurting inside.
I can have a frown on my face, but be jumping with joy inside.
But all that I know is I feel.

Tomari Parks, Grade 5
Jumoke Academy, CT

Now That He Is Gone*

My dad was the best; he always stood by me.
Through thick and thin, he was always beside me.

His voice was like the sounds of crickets in the morning — brave, bold, and strong.
A ringing in your head which is never stopping.

His looks were like a wall — strong, mighty, and tall, always staring down at me —
an arm around my shoulder — always by me.

My dad was my favorite person to be with.
Whether in a boat or in a blind, or maybe even a camp; he was the best.

Without him here, I feel so different —
the kid without a dad; the kid with a step-dad.

I miss him so much, but I am thankful
he's healed by taking a trip to the big pair of gates.

I know I will see him again as long as I go to church
and believe in the One always watching me.

I will never forget his last words he said to me,
"Always be a good Christian, and we'll meet up again."

Zachary Israel, Grade 6
Vidrine Elementary School, LA
*Dedicated to Scott Israel.

Head in the Clouds

If I could have a perfect day that would be fun in every way.
I think that I would try
To imagine places far and near to think of sounds you'd never hear,
And I cannot explain why.
It's something I have always dreamed to rip apart my imagination's seams
And let my logic fly away,
So this is how and why in a blink of an eye
I would organize my day.
I'd visit the ocean's deepest seas, I'd go in the ground, where no gentle breeze
Would ever dare to go.
So if you want me to stay awake, and put my imagination at stake,
I would always say no.
Therefore when I drift to deepest sleep watching stars, or counting sheep
I'd dreams of things this way,
And this is how, when, and why, when I go to close my eye
I live my perfect day.

Dillon Schetley, Grade 6
Christ the Divine Teacher Catholic Academy, PA

Wind

Windy gales, flying by
Through the blue and open sky.
Snow, thunder, lightning, rain
The pleasure of wind, they'll never obtain.
Going past your face and through your hair,
Floating through the fresh sweet air.
And on the ever more green grass
The scene is like a picture in glass.
But when a window is closed, the wind is done
So don't be afraid to let wind come.

Jeffrey Gao, Grade 4
H Austin Snyder Elementary School, PA

A Cave in the Distance

Following the pack leader through the trees,
Through the fog and thickets the wolf cannot see.
As the thunder got louder the pack sped up,
And that didn't help the little cub pup.

As the journey continued to a cave in the distance,
The little wolf began to slip and slide.
As the lightning danced an endless dance,
The pack leader led the pack with endless pride.

As the cave came into the little wolf's sight,
The leaves swirled in the air like mini kites.
With a yelp of joy the wolf hopped right in,
The little cub was happy because now he was with his kin.

Shawn Kidd, Grade 6
Lake Noxen Elementary School, PA

A Walk Through the Wilderness

As I walked through the moist, thick heavy cream-like air,
I kept getting stickier than I could bare.
The first thing we came upon was a huge white pine.
I counted five needles, and that was the sign.
We then spotted the green heron with its long beak.
He looked very regal but not very chic.
Then came the cabbage, like a skunk it was smelly.
It would not soon fill a predator's belly.
Next was the marsh with its tall grass, cattails, and reeds.
There I heard the songs from frogs of different breeds.
Then came the struck tree with its beautiful features,
Whose wide trunk was the home to many creatures.
Dividing the farmland there was a low rock wall
The sheep couldn't cross, though it wasn't too tall.
The herb lemon basil has an orangey smell
Many animals ate it; I could just tell.
At the end of the walk, Mr. Hribko scared all,
With his very talented quon-ko-ree call.
A lovely walk like that is very hard to find,
That's why it's like a snowflake, one of a kind.

Olivia Corvino, Grade 6
East Shore Middle School, CT

Summer

Summer, summer
It's no bummer.
Watermelons, lemonade,
It's your backyard on parade.

Trips to the pool,
No more school.
Go to the park,
Stay up till dark.

A sunset for all,
Climb a tree 50 feet tall.
Oh, summer summer,
You're no bummer.
A wonderful time for all.

Piotr Sowulewski, Grade 6
Manchester Elementary/Middle School, VT

Wait, Wait, Wait

I can't wait for summer to go to the beach
Visit my relatives that live in Ohio
I go to many parks and places my family has a lot of fun
But I can't wait for school to see all my friends
Say our hellos and do our homework
But at the end of the year we say our goodbyes

Bailey Woodfin, Grade 6
Warrenton Middle School, VA

Winter Trees

Trees covered in snow,
Like powdered sugar on pancakes,
Sun setting sky reflects on the snow,
Making it florescent pink, purple, and blue.

Trees covered in snow,
Covered in new fallen snow,
Feet marks from kids playing,
Looking like fun.

Trees covered in snow,
Birds chirping,
Kids playing.

Trees covered in snow,
Looking like powdered sugar on pancakes.

Morgan DiChiacchio, Grade 6
E T Richardson Middle School, PA

Nature

When you go outside and look around
and look up at the sky the sun is there and smiling at you.
Birds fly free. Seeing the airplanes fly around.
See the clouds float around. Try to see what they look like.
Just think rain and snow comes from the clouds.

Kayla Broad, Grade 6
Slippery Rock Area Middle School, PA

Magnificent Forest

A lush
green
land
with flowers,
animals
and a blue sky.
The sunny forest
with a beautiful breeze,
spaded shrubs
by the darkness
of the shadows.
Birds chirp,
woodpeckers pecking.
I yearn to discover
their secret: how did the trees
get so big?
Feelings of serenity,
peace of mind
and happiness
fill me.

Keegan Gallite, Grade 4
Grace Lutheran School, FL

Friendship

Friendship is caring for one another,
To be there in a time of need.
To lend your hand as you speak,
And show that you're not weak.
Friendship is trusting, keeping dear.
I just want to make that clear!

Ileeanna Trinidad, Grade 4
PS 10, NY

Mangroves

The waves
were flowing
through the mangroves
with trout jumping
out of the water.
The sun was
glistening
glistening
glistening
on the water.
The rustling leaves
made a beautiful sound.
I wanted to catch
a trout,
shark,
snook,
or tarpon.
Where were the fish?
How far in were the fish?

Philip Peterson, Grade 4
Grace Lutheran School, FL

Rose

A girl's name
A flower of fame
Also a present
And really quite pleasant
Red, yellow, and more
Commonly sold in a store
Placed in a vase
Or tied in pink lace
Rose

Laura Wisniewski, Grade 6
Linkhorne Middle School, VA

The World

The World the World
Nobody saves it
And all the things on it
We just crave it
The help the help
We could have gave it

The World the World
We basically hate it
But wait just wait
Only God can recreate it

Dylan Foskey, Grade 5
Southern Pines Elementary School, NC

Dodge Challenger

D odge
O ut of gears to go faster
D odging other cars
G ranted license to drive
E xciting to ride in

C hallenging other racers
H igh speed racing
A lot of horse power
L eading the race
L eading car in dealers
E xtremely fast
N eutral, park, drive
G reat car to drive in
E ngineered in a factory
R acing other people

Joseph Streeter, Grade 4
West Frankfort Elementary School, NY

Spring

Sunny
It is very sunny
It's almost funny
I see a bunny
Come here funny, bunny honey

Katelyn Fahnestock, Grade 5
Fishing Creek Elementary School, PA

Flying

Egg
fragile, smooth
hatching, breaking, shacking
Turtle, Platypus, Robin, Blue Jay
feeding, flying, chirping
feathery, colorful
Birds

Connor Madsen, Grade 6
Captain Nathan Hale Middle School, CT

My Old Home

I miss the couch
I miss the chair
I miss the fighting over there.

I miss the kitchen
I miss the walls
I miss the bathroom duty calls.

Upstairs has its memories too
My room begins with a few.

I remember sliding down the railing
What I'd do when I'd go sailing.

With all the fun and games
I thought things would never change.

But it's all come and gone
The time we spent in My Old Home.

Nella Rouse, Grade 5
St Thomas More Catholic School, NC

Book

I am a book
Just take a look
Inside me and you'll see
One hundred pages
Filled with words
Just waiting for you to read

I was bought today
At Barnes and Noble
And well let me just say
There will come a time or two
When he will read me
Yeah someday

But until that day
I sit on a shelf
So lonely and afraid
I can't help but wonder
How long these other books have laid

Megan Raab, Grade 4
West Frankfort Elementary School, NY

The Out Doors

The out doors are full of things to do, but some people just don't realize it. Instead they sit inside and watch TV. When they could be outside playing with other kids. They could just go on a walk by their self. In summer, you could go swimming. In fall, you can jump in leaves. In winter, you could play in the snow, but make sure you're dressed warm. In spring, you could jump on a trampoline. In every season, you can do something by yourself or with someone. Either way get outside and have "FUN."

Cheyanne Albertson, Grade 5
L Ray Appleman Elementary School, PA

My Room

My room is a small jungle with tall grass that is toys.
The sunlight ignores the light blue walls, making my room shade, quiet, and serene.
The tiny sports carpet lies still near the door, greeting everyone who walks on it.
The legos, large and small, standing as still as statues.
My mirror, taking a glimpse around the room and showing a person's face whenever that person looks into it.
In my closet, lay undersized shirts that I last wore when I was 3.
The old book shelf holds dusty books that I have not looked at in quite a while.
My pillow, which holds infinite emotions, lets me sleep peacefully on it every night.

Brendan Canary, Grade 5
Abraham Pierson School, CT

24 Hours

Summer breezes blow into my window, as I wake, dancing like leaves blowing in the wind. School days are behind me and I'm free like a bird. Splashing, jumping into the blue pool makes me smile. Bike pedals turn as I fly down my hill. My bike is like a plane taking off. The sweet smell of rose bushes tickle my nose, and smoke filled barbecues burn my eyes. The sky is turning from blue to an orangey yellow as night turns the corner.

Elise Giannattasio, Grade 5
Hindley Elementary School, CT

The Bluest Blue

The bluest blue is paint in the art room, surrounded by greens, reds, and yellows, the blue paint mixes and dabs on your paper, stretching across to create something wonderful.
The bluest blue, is the sky surrounded by the white fluffy clouds which remind you of different shapes, the golden sun sets on a cloud peering down, sometimes reminds you of JOY!
The bluest blue, is a cheerleading uniform on a cheerleader surrounded by a screaming crowd, yelling parents, and demanding coaches, your teams wins and the air is filled with victory!
The bluest blue, is the ocean, surrounded by playing children, and tanning parents, you can taste the salty sea, the sand squishes between your toes, and the golden sunset looks great next to the bluest blue!

Camden Muddiman, Grade 6
Morton Middle School, KY

The Place I Call My Room

When the sun sinks slowly into the darkening sky, the newly risen moon shines through my window, gently illuminating the light colored walls, of the place I call my room.

Tucked away in one small corner, hides shelf after shelf of dolls and boxes that play beautiful music as the dancers inside twirl to an everlasting song.

Lying peacefully on the quilt that keeps me warm at night, sits a ragged old bear, that has witnessed all my life, and is one I held close to my chest, to dampen a frightened child's heartbeat, during a thunder storm.

Hanging on the wall sits a golden frame, and within the four corners lies an image. Each time my eyes fall on this image, I wonder how many eyes have viewed the same view. Brown, blue, green eyes, all gazing as if shooting at a forgotten bulls eye.

As I bury my face into my pillow as I have done every previous night, I know that sweet dreams will always be there, waiting for me, in the place I call my room.

Julia Horan, Grade 4
Abraham Pierson School, CT

Viking Fire

It is alas
A day of bright
Of stones of grey
And heart of light
Of soft milled corn
And deer of hunt
Until a cry of wretched delight
A cry of war of pain and strife
The Viking fire of no delight
As people run
The town 'tis alight
The Viking fire of no delight
The hill is filled with caves for hide
That the townsfolk know but to no abide
The smoke from fire can fill inside
The town a ruin and people in fright
The Viking Hordes now bask in delight
The mill in ashes and huts inflame
The Vikings will return again.

Cameron Berger, Grade 6
Norton School, CT

Beach

you walk,
   you run,
you skip,
   on the sand.

you jump,
   you play,
you sit,
   on the sand.

you feel the breeze,
   upon your knees,
and then go play,
   in the ocean.

how does it feel,
   to be really real,
and play,
   on the BEACH?

Calliope George, Grade 6
New Garden Friends School, NC

Goodbye Old Me

Goodbye old me,
I welcome a new,
As I show my vibrant hue.
Now I'm not in a box,
I am more open.
Goodbye old me,
I bid you adieu,
Because I'm not at all like you.

Daniel Cross, Grade 6
Lake Noxen Elementary School, PA

The Wind

The wind has its own personality.
Continually moving about, as if it has something to do.
Place to place tending its business, always secretive.
The wind brings storms of worry, doubt, and fear, always changing.
The wind brings breezes of happiness, joy, and love, always optimistic.
Hiding in the bushes, lurking in the trees, the wind is quiet.
Harsh, brittle and cold, the wind whips across my face, angry.
Sweet, damp, and lazy the wind blows across my face, content.
Coming in my open window, the wind is my visitor.
Quick, rushed, and hurrying, the wind scuttles along the treetops.
The wind is its own person. Forever shifting.
Calm,
Serene,
Beautiful,
The wind never dies.

Ann Fitts, Grade 6
J E Holmes Middle School, NC

The Best Place I Know

We packed our bags and got ready to go,
We left for the airport, moving fast, not slow,
We were going to a place where the orange trees grow;
Florida, the best place I know.

We were in the plane going 600 miles per hour,
Looking below us we saw the small towers.
It seemed like we were flying oh, so very slow,
It seemed like it would take forever to get to the best place I know.

We arrived there very late in the night,
Everyone tired from the three hour flight.
David and I peered from our hotel porch with a light,
To look at Florida's beautiful sight.

After two days we went to the next hotel,
John and I got so happy we started to yell
"I love Florida!" and I never wanted to go
Away from Florida; the best place I know.

Two days later, we left on the plane.
I'll remember this place, in my memory it will be framed.
David and I walking slow, because we know it's time to go
Away from Florida; the best place I know.

Nunzio Rosselli, Grade 4
Nelson Place Elementary School, MA

Where I'm From...

I am from delicious frosted sugar cookies, from hard candy, and corn bread.
I am from drawing.
I am from my favorite video games *Mario Kart* and *Banjo and Kazooie*.
I am from my strange brother, my Mom and Dad, and my cool friends.
I'm from both mild-weathered New York, and beautiful Ocean City
From endless Lego robotics building to going to my friend's house.
That's where I am from!

Maxwell Kammermeier, Grade 4
Honeoye Falls-Lima Manor School, NY

Eagle Friends

Soaring, through the freedom sky.
My feathers, flapping with the wind.
So glorious,
Suddenly, you look up towards me, a sad look in your eyes.
You needing a friend.
Me, dreaming, gliding, feeling, reaching.
Out to you.
Loving you, feeling you.
You needed a friend.
I felt you.
Soon, together, I was living quietly, in my nest above you.
Sleeping, eating, living.
Feeling, hoping you will catch me if I fall.
Looking, towards you.
Feeling you, dropping you eggs in the morning.
Loving you as my friend.

Molly Teece, Grade 4
Marsh Grammar School, MA

Fireworks on the Boat

BANG
Fireworks rise into the night sky
Brightening the darkness
Lighting the way
Smoky air fills the night sky
The moon shines down on the ocean
BANG
As the next colorful firework shoots into the sky
I whisper
"How do you feel right now?"
More smoke joins with the air
As the sparks float down
They whisper
"Great"
BANG

Perry Barth, Grade 4
Riverside School, CT

The Beach

The beach is a vacationing spot
Where there is sand,
And is very hot
The water is cool
Just as the hotel pool
The boardwalk, the games, the rides,
And the high tides
The beach is a great place to go
When you're there,
You can just 'go with the flow'
Laying in the hot sand when the sun is shining
Especially when the sun is oh so blinding
But time flies when you're having fun,
Fun in the sun
Have fun while it lasts.

Hailey Daniels, Grade 6
Christ the Divine Teacher Catholic Academy, PA

Graduating

My whole life I wanted school to just end
Now that I'm in fifth grade I wish it would extend
I will graduate with a sad look on my face
And all the sudden no longer am I in a race
I look down, tears rolling down my cheeks
Hoping that my best friend will not seek
I have had the best time here at school
But now there is no more being cool or being in a carpool
Everyone says goodbye
While everyone else starts to cry
My years at PJDS have been great
But now another school awaits

Mia Stein, Grade 5
Jack M. Barrack Hebrew Academy, PA

The Gecko vs the Snake

Today, I cannot climb any tree.
I don't even think I can catch a flea.
My spots have vanished; my tongue is dry.
My ears are making a scratchy sound.
I think my claws are stuck into the ground.
A snake is watching me from that tree.
It looks as violent as a killer bee.
If the snake decides, he will attack;
I know my friend, the tree frog, has my back.
Now, I am ready to go to sleep.
Then, the tree frog makes a loud, "Help me," peep.
So, I walk over to the frog's tree,
And see the snake doing a dirty deed.
The snake is harassing my best friend.
But, now it is my turn, and I'll defend.
I point my tail at the violent snake,
Then, I really give my body a shake.
My tail shoots off, as fast as a blink.
The scared snake runs off as fast as a mink.
"Ha," I say and give the frog a wink.

Reinaldo Jackson, Grade 6
East Shore Middle School, CT

Magic

There must be magic
In ourselves
That sprouts from roots and branches out
There must be magic
On the shores
Where baby turtles grovel to briny blues
There must be magic
Through the streets
When exchanges feed on shifting greens
And there must be magic
In the world
Where change and love live in every soul

Wilson Zhu, Grade 6
South Middle School, NY

Plant

Popularity is a plant,
Growing slowly,
To be the tallest,
Of them all,
To be the biggest.

But some never get up there,
They get strangled by the others,
Never get the sunlight,
Never get the chance.

Most get knocked down,
Back to the bottom.

While the strongest stems,
Remain at the top,
They will soon die out of position,
And new will,
Take the spot.

Nicole Amoroso, Grade 6
Hillcrest Elementary School, PA

Snow

Snow is like a soft,
white, glowing sheet
that is on your bed.
No two flakes are the same.
Each one is unique
because that is the way
the Lord made each of them.

McKenzie Lee, Grade 4
Bethesda Christian Academy, NC

The Internet

The internet is cool,
The internet is fun,
The internet is awesome,
The web is number one.
I travel all around,
On the internet,
YouTube's pretty fun,
And lol cats too I guess.
The internet is a tool,
The internet is not a toy,
These spammers are uncool,
A new iPod oh joy!
Don't click the little cookies,
Where exiting things you get
Computer's always freezing, viruses I bet.
Now you've heard my words,
Don't try to win for stuff,
You only always lose,
And your computer'll go puff!

Merrick Williams, Grade 6
Warrenton Middle School, VA

Horses/Stallions

Horses
Passionate, graceful
Cantering, trotting, galloping
An intelligent faithful friend
Stallions

Caroline Cline, Grade 5
The Cathedral School, AR

Cat

Cat
Fun, sweet
Annoying, sleeping, crawling
Cute ball of trouble
American Short Hair

Vanessa Mos, Grade 5
St Agatha School, NY

Shoes

Shoes are great
You can wear them on a date
You can pick your style
Pick the one that will make you smile
What color will you pick
Just make sure they are slick
Pink
Red
Orange
Yellow
White
Blue
Brown
Black
Some may even be green
Shoes.

Jenna Bruno, Grade 6
St Stephen's School, NY

Summer Fun!!!

Everyone!! come out and feel
The summer air,
Hot air but not so cold
Like the winter air.
The golden sun is shining
In the sky,
With a happy face.
Flowers are getting tired and thirsty
By eating the sun's rays.
Waiting for the rain to come
And take their thirst away.
So, water them every single day.
Go to beaches and have fun
But don't forget to put sunscreen on,
Enjoy the summer fun!!!

Subha Mojumder, Grade 6
West Frederick Middle School, MD

Stars

Billions of stars shine
Celestial art on high
I am mesmerized

Stars are very cool
Different sizes and shapes
No two are alike

Some stay and some go
Different colors ignite
Stars are beautiful

Alec Mason, Grade 5
St John Catholic School, MD

A Dream

A dream
Through the simmering sand
If I held your hand
I could swim
The skin shivering sea…

Alexis Dailey, Grade 5
Southern Pines Elementary School, NC

Her Heart Unlocked

Upon the tree
There was a lock.
It wouldn't come free.
It was like a rock.
I tried every key,
But to no avail.
I couldn't let it be.
I was ready to wail.
As I gazed at the sea,
I got lost deep in thought.
Alas; it was just me.
My vision almost naught.
My sorrow turned to glee —
Something shone so brightly.
The elusive key
Danced very lightly.
I dropped to my knee
With such gratitude.
Now there's a we;
No solitude!

David Fox, Grade 6
Discovery School @ Reeves Rogers, TN

Untitled

Comets are firing
Jupiter and its big eye
Meteors coming
Hot sun shining down on Earth
Space with all of its planets

Michael Gray, Grade 4
Stackpole Elementary School, PA

Mr. Man in the Moon

Mr. Man in the moon, you give me smiles
From what I can see, from miles and miles
Your beautiful home in the sky
Always will pass me by
As I spy on your beautiful stars
It's our secret, just you and ours
But when day starts to appear
And sadly, you are nowhere near
I think of the night, all misty and bright
But when night turns to day
I just smile and say
"I'll see you very soon
Mr. Man in the moon"

Brynne Fritjofson, Grade 6
Kelly Lane Intermediate School, CT

Shakepearean Sonnet

Throughout my years I have been muddled,
By Shakespeare's outdated works.
Even by the last line I am befuddled!
Each one must be full of quirks.

What was wrong with his brain?
Did he think he was cool?
Was his brain full of grain?
When I read his works, I drool.

He wrote about a lot of love.
He wrote about a lot of drama.
He probably wrote about a dove,
And guess who loves his works? My mama.

Why does everyone think he was really smart?
I think he should have made his hobby art.

Ally Murphy, Grade 5
Hilltop Montessori School, AL

Halloween Night

Halloween is a dangerous night,
when monsters and aliens could give you a fright.
WATCH OUT!!! A vampire is trying to bite.
Howling, and screaming and trying to get you,
is a giant ghost that is saying, "BOO."
Duck!!! He threw a cow that said "Moo."
Halloween is the scariest night.
It's not the night you would fly a kite.
It's the night for scary things,
like when an old witch sings.
The ghouls are all fools,
when they play with power tools.
Halloween is in sight,
I know it will give you a fright.

Tyler Lufkin, Grade 4
Nelson Place Elementary School, MA

Life

Verse 1: Life just goes on
When it feels it wants to
But the Earth ain't livin'
Forever like you

Pre Chorus: When you got a mountain
In front of you…
Just go for it. Take a chance.
And things won't turn out blue

Chorus: Climb the mountain,
Get over it and look where you have gone
Take a chance and go for it
Life's just gotta go on. Life's just gotta go on.

Verse 2: You made it over
Don't think that's it
There are millions more to go
Life goes on give it all you got
There is something important to know

Bridge: You're dyin'. They're cryin'
Take you one last breath
There are mountains in heaven
Just after death

Matthew Greene, Grade 5
Lockhart Elementary School, NY

Toys…

Toys sometimes live long,
And sometimes short lives,
Sometimes there are different ways a toy could die;
Rust,
Rain,
Puddle,
Dirt,
Misuse,
Sun,
Heat,
And many other ways,
Toys with short lives,
Are the ones that are played with the most,
However toys who aren't played with a lot,
Are the ones which,
Live longer,
Although they would someday depart because of dust.

Nicholas Burkel, Grade 5
Sunrise Drive Elementary School, NY

Discrimination

Discrimination is wrong
It's not right.
Every time it makes people fight.
They had unfair laws.

Charles Ingram, Grade 6
The New York Institute for Special Education, NY

Hammock

As I move…
    back and forth like running side to side water trickles like small ducks swimming through the water
        As I move…
            back and forth like running side to side I move my head and see wood splinters
    As I move…
    back and forth like running side to side as I close my eyes and relax with alone time

Maggie Mahanes, Grade 5
New Garden Friends School, NC

The Sources of Life

Everyone knows we need water, light, and air, but did you know why we have trees everywhere?
We use trees sometimes and we don't know it, paper, pencils, they should show it.
We also need coal, that's how we get plastic, if we had more of it, that would be fantastic!
Natural resources aren't all we need, pigs give meat so parents can feed.
Sheep give us nice, cozy wool, so if it's snowing, it will keep you from the cool.
If we didn't have chickens, would we have eggs, of course, but with a turkey you'd have to beg.
What sense would it make to steal a bird's baby, you'd might get away from a hawk, maybe just maybe.
As I was saying, stop cutting down trees, they give you the oxygen that you breathe.
It's important to recycle, too, or the planet will burn up and whose fault would it be YOU YOU YOU!

Julius Mays, Grade 6
Allbritton Elementary School, AR

Crystal Flower

The time is midnight, and this flower shines bright, the faraway moon is what's making it light.
The wind is swaying the beautiful trees; I feel the softness of the breeze.
The air is thick with the smell of pollen; I hear the twinkling of the petals falling.
The birds are snuggled in their nest; the fox are in their den to rest.
The colors are bright blue and green; don't you think this is a wondrous scene?

Nick Gilmore, Grade 4
Honeoye Falls-Lima Manor School, NY

Swimming

We swam through the Pacific, the big scary waves pushed us. We swam on, the big scary waves pushed us. We were losing strength, like a tired bird flying for ten days straight, the big scary waves pushed us. Seeing a boat we shouted, the big scary waves pushed us. We shouted on and on but, the big scary waves just swallowed our voices, the big scary waves pushed us. We saw no more boat, the big scary waves pushed us down, and down to DAVY JONES' locker. Working hard on his boat, the big scary waves pushed us.

Ivan Semyanko, Grade 6
Kelly Lane Intermediate School, CT

The Love of Music

Music has been around and around but the reason I like it is
Because it can turn your frown upside down
Music can also do the exact opposite.
Music is a way of communicating with the whole world.
People use all types of instruments and styles from the piano to the banjo
From the banjo to Mexico and Colorado.
From America to Russia, all over the world they use different types of music.
I wish I could tell you all the types but then none of us would go home if I did.
But don't forget about the people who invented it all.
Like Chuck Berry, Bob Marley, Elvis Presley, Willie Dixon, Charlie Patton, Sonny Boy Williams,
Louis Armstrong, and Michael Jackson.
I wish I could tell you them all but if I did none of us would go home at all
But I'm sure you get the picture.

John Clark, Grade 6
Morgan Math and Science Academy, MD

My Deepest Fear

My deepest fear is not of death or seclusion
But of myself and imperfection
I shutter when I hear the word failure
Or knowing I'm not good enough

Just one B can make me crack
Or the sight of a detention that I must serve
The only person who is pressuring me
Is me, myself, and I

We all know we're not perfect
but can't we try to be?
And if were not, am I the only one who cares?

Now as I write this little poem
I'm wondering to myself is this good enough?

Amanda Ryan, Grade 6
City of Pembroke Pines Charter Central Middle School, FL

Hope

Hope is to believe
It's thinking that you can do something
Hope gets you through the day
No matter what you should hope
With hope you can believe in yourself
And if you believe in yourself you can do anything
Hope is great
So Hope

Ashley Anderson, Grade 5
Jamestown Elementary School, PA

Dirtbike Crash*

The wind whipping through my hair
The danger of crashing
My adrenaline rushing
I'm stuck in a rut
I can't get out of it
I try to
But the rut throws me through the air
I land hard with a thump
I look over and my bike is lying on the ground
It's in gear still idling
Then everything goes black

Kyle Bair, Grade 6
Avon Grove Intermediate School, PA
*Dedicated to Mr. Yohannan

Dream

Slowly eyes close
Slowly you drift to dream-world
A pleasant doze,
You awake with a start.
    A crack of thunder.
You sink back to dream-land and continue.

Mairead Heiger, Grade 5
Avon Grove Intermediate School, PA

Fishing with Friends

I like to go fishing with my friends,
Sometimes we don't get home until 10 PM.
We fish everywhere,
    on the pier,
        in a canal,
            out in the Gulf.
We catch fish, big and small.
We always have fun fishing,
    even just sitting there listening.

Sage Nocera, Grade 6
Gulfview Middle School, FL

Apple

On the outside you look like the night sky filled with stars.
You feel like a bumpy old rock.
When I peel you, you sound like a noisy candy wrapper.
When I slice you, you sound like a busy saw.
Inside you look like a shiny moon.
You feel like a slimy wet toad.
You smell like sweet candy.
You taste like a delicious gummy bear.
Tell me, apple, how did you become so perfect?

Emmersyn Miranda, Grade 4
Glenwood Elementary School, MA

Lexi's Dreams

Dreams are what you think of life —
Your expectations to have a great time.
Dreams are your talents that you have yet to use.
Dreams are a butterfly waiting in its cocoon.

Dreams are a leaf falling from a tree.
Dreams are geese flying to the south.
Dreams are a chick in an alligator's mouth.

Dreams are a bird waiting to recover.
Dreams are the great things in life that you have yet to discover.

Lexi Hackerman, Grade 6
Garrison Forest School, MD

Green Forever

Green is the grassy fields of wonder
Green is the rainbow
Green is the sea that waves good-bye
Green is the trees that give us air
Green smells like clean spring air
Green tastes like the greatest apple of them all
Green sounds like the melody of a grass whistle
Green looks like the fresh flowing leaves
Green feels like the smoothest blanket
Green makes me feel like the wind
Green is my most favorite color

Zachary Sentz, Grade 4
Lincoln Elementary School, PA

Baby to Adult

Baby
Little, noisy
Growing, whining, maturing
Cute, cheerful, living, kind
Working, praising, driving
Smart, mature
Adult
Alex Whittington, Grade 4
Pike Creek Christian School, DE

Sandy Ocean

High tide
Gently flows in
Fish are swimming in
You can see their fins

A big wave
Breaks the calm
Surfers are on it
Having a bomb

The seagulls
And sailboats
Sandcastles
Plus floats

Oh, that sandy ocean
It brings us fun
Oh, that sandy ocean
Always basks in the sun
Kaleigh Swainamer, Grade 6
Freetown-Lakeville Middle School, MA

The Exercising Race

Run, run, run
it's a good thing to do.
Just make sure
that you tie your shoe.

Jump, jump, jump
as high as you can.
You should do it now
since you already ran.

Walk, walk, walk
for quite a while
now that you have jumped
and ran a whole mile.

Pace, pace, pace
they're not far behind.
Remember to take deep, deep breaths
while you make it to the finish line.
Kierstin Parricelli, Grade 6
North Pocono Middle School, PA

World

Land and water
Languages different
Killing wars
Angry people
Peaceful people
Polluting cars
Supporting life
Animals roaming
Technology blooming
— Reflection —
Blooming technology
Roaming animals
Life supporting
Cars polluting
People peaceful
People angry
Wars killing
Different languages
Water and land
World
Raeanna Crowe, Grade 5
Princeton Elementary School, ME

Hot Beautiful Days

The hot beautiful days
The crowded restaurants
Look at the beach
On hot beautiful days
Look at its colorful sunset
And look at the sunny places
On hot beautiful days
It sounds like
A peaceful state
People whispering softly
On hot beautiful days
The crowded beaches
And the crowded pools
Plain old Florida
On hot beautiful days.
Patrick McTiernan, Grade 4
Riverside School, CT

Flight

Above the world, floating gracefully
On top of a flower, taking a break
Inside a cage, please let me go!
Above the world, there are no limits
Away from its family, it travels alone
On the beach, landing on sand
Into the sky it soars
Above the clouds, floating away
Next to my arm, I stand perfectly still
On top of the world!
Haley West, Grade 6
Berry Middle School, AL

My Little Sisters

My little sisters are an image of me.

Katie, who I love.
She comes to me when she needs me.
I see light shining through her.

Annie, the youngest of all,
she holds on tight when she might fall.
I see a glow in her eyes.

Being seven and eleven doesn't matter;
they are BIG in my book.
They can come to me no matter what.
Every day they show me their light.
Emily Lucas, Grade 6
Gulfview Middle School, FL

Tigerstar and Firestar

Tigerstar
cruel, heartless
killing, fighting, scheming
Hitler, Shadowclan, Thunderclan, hero
saving, helping, caring
generous, pleasant
Firestar
Emily Walla, Grade 5
Tucker School, AR

The Wind

The wind is a horse
Which runs faster than the river
Flowing mane, waving tail
How fast do you have to go
To beat the wind?
Mikayla Taylor, Grade 6
Newport Middle School, NC

Midnight

I saw a beautiful doe,
walking across the snow.
She went for a bit to eat,
just a little nighttime treat.
As the apple glistened
and the moon was aglow.
Sarah Hamill, Grade 6
Bloomsburg Area Middle School, PA

Roses

Roses
Red, thorny
A wonderful scent
Delicate, pleasant, beautiful, delightful
Flowers
Heather Verdin, Grade 4
Ridgeway Elementary School, MD

I Love You

Mom I love you…
Without you, I get really sad.
On top of all the moms in the world, you're the best.
With you, love is never ending.
Beside you, nothing is impossible.
With you, my heart is HAPPY.
At all times, I LOVE YOU.

Tyler Bryson, Grade 4
St Joseph School, KY

It Was a Dark and Thrilling Night

It was a dark and dreary night
I was so thrilled and excited
And I didn't have a single fright
I was full of joy and so delighted
So hungry but couldn't a single bite

Waiting to pick her up so eager
To see her pointy ears
Her body so meager
Knowing I will love her over the years
Now she will be my cat forever

So sweet with that look on her face
She's so curious; you don't know what she will do
It's so different she keeps her walk at a steady pace
I had just one cat but now I have two!
Now all we have to do is name her Ace!

Megan Layne Gilman, Grade 6
Chickahominy Middle School, VA

Please Do Not Read This Poem

Please do not read this poem.
This poem is written for me only!
Stop reading me gosh!
There is nothing to see except words.
Anyway wouldn't you rather
play outside and make snowmen?
So put me down slowly
and get away from me!
Hey, mi amigo, why are you still reading me?
That isn't very nice.
I'm telling you to stop reading me.
You're breaking my heart!
You are not allowed to read this poem.
Put me down this instant dude!
Get away or I'll call the cops, the FBI, and the SWAT!
They shall drag you off in handcuffs.
They shall put you in jail
for people that don't stop reading this poem —
forever!
There's only one solution: stop reading me!

Danneurys Marte, Grade 6
Middle School 101, NY

One Last Shot

Ten seconds left on the clock.
Up by two and it's their ball.
"Swoosh," they score as the ball floats through the net.
"Timeout!" Screams the coach.
There's only five seconds left.
Little time to score.
James you take the shot.
Johnson, Jackson you two set the pick.
Tie game, no room for error.
As we jump back on the floor.
There's only a few seconds left, we have to score.
We get the ball halfway up the court.
This shot better not come short.
As I catch the pass on the inbound, I am surrounded by players.
I look very hard and I finally find an opening to the point guard.
I spin right and now the ball is in flight.
As he hauls it in with all his might.
He passes back as I dash down the floor.
I heave it up, it all comes down to this.
As it sinks through the net.
This is a game that I'll never miss.

Max Michalski, Grade 6
Neil Armstrong Middle School, PA

Angels

They watch over me when I am sad,
Steer me to one path make me glad.
All alone in the open,
They come unsudden and unspoken.
Don't know where I am nowhere to go,
Here they come with a bright glow,
Here we go up to the sky,
They make me feel like I can fly.
Helping others and me too,
It's like they choose what I should do.
Figuring out wrong from right,
Looks like I can see into the night.
Come down from the heavens,
Blinded by your light.
So scared sometimes they give me a fright.
I realize only my feet hit the ground,
With no sudden sound,
And they say,
We will watch over you
Forever.

Zac Knapp, Grade 6
Avon Grove Intermediate School, PA

The Thrill Guy

There once was a kid named Phil,
he always liked to thrill.
He'd jump up and twist,
but one day hurt his wrist,
now he knows he doesn't have skill.

Nicholas Ciarlante, Grade 4
Stackpole Elementary School, PA

Love/Hate
Love
Warm, flexible,
Loving, caring, convincing,
Hopeful, happiness, painful, conflicts,
Depressing, disliking, fighting,
Cold, evil,
Hate
Bobby Jo Engle, Grade 6
Lake Noxen Elementary School, PA

Pencil
A long yellow stick sits at my desk,
with a pointy tip,
as sharp as a knife,
goes down on my paper,
to write and write.
Brendan Smith, Grade 4
Abraham Pierson School, CT

Fish!!
Fresh fish is so delicious,
It's also nutritious.
I like you when you're hot,
But sometimes you're not.
You make me so hungry,
Especially when it's sunny.
I cook it on the grill,
And there goes the chill.
I could eat it every meal,
Even if it tastes like seal.
Matthew Gummo, Grade 4
Watsontown Elementary School, PA

Light Blue
Blue is sad
He hates basketball
He is very slow
Blue is ugly
Blue is a good friend
Blue loves to play baseball
He likes to eat fruit
He loves to read
Blue is under my bed
Blue hates the color red
Blue is in the sky
His favorite food is pizza
Blue is not scared of anything
Blue is my best friend
Blue likes to jump
He likes to get in the pool
His favorite subject is math
Blue is very smart
He hates to be wrong
Blue likes to fish
David Ball, Grade 4
Youngsville Elementary School, NC

Haley Kane
Haley
Fun, friendly, shy, artistic
Daughter of Joe and Christin
Lover of golf, summer, and roller coasters
Who feels excited when trying something new, relieved at the end of the day,
and believes peace is what matters most in the world
Who fears time might pass her by, death, and disease
Who would like to travel the world, take lots of pictures,
and have the time of her life
Resident of Lexington, Kentucky
Kane
Haley Kane, Grade 6
Morton Middle School, KY

Seasons
Spring is green
Like the grass covered in dew,
And the unblemished frogs leaping into the pond filled with lily pads,
And ripe grapes ready to be eaten.

Summer is yellow
Like the fragile and beautiful sunflowers ready to bloom,
And the ripe delicious bananas,
And the scorching sun reaching out to us.

Autumn is brown
Like the branches of a tree waiting to be climbed by little children,
And a scrumptious brownie teasing me,
And a hawk hovering over our heads

Winter is white
Like snowballs waiting to take a ride in the air,
And a blank sheet of paper laying down on a desk,
And a paint cover on a nice smooth wall.
Nalin Suri, Grade 5
Oliver Hoover Elementary School, FL

Fall
Red, yellow, orange all over the ground,
The trees are sad, they have grown a great frown.

Their leaves are gone — all over the ground,
another winter is coming, that is not a good sound.

The cold snow, the awful blizzards, the kids' mothers say,
"C'mon, it's time for dinner."

At last spring has come, everyone is on the go,
and look at those leaves, I mean just look at them grow.
They're not red, yellow, or orange, they're normal, just plain green.

All is fine till next fall,
when the trees' leaves turn red, yellow, and orange
and fall to the ground.
Tyler Douglass, Grade 6
Gulfview Middle School, FL

Snowy Weather

S now is pretty but tastes very icky.
N ice and white but not bright.
O utside it snows and lands on your nose.
W hite and fluffy it falls from the sky.

Mia Gowdy, Grade 4
Bethesda Christian Academy, NC

Rain

Its raining,
it is all black and white, with the thunder roaring.
Giving a goosebump through the body.
It is a blessing from God,
making the earth moist and fertile.
I shiver into my blanket, hearing a soft lullaby.
Falling asleep with the soft whisper going through my ear.
Going to sleep with hopes of a sunny tomorrow.

Raima Shafiq, Grade 6
Muslim Center Elementary School, NY

Opposites

What's the opposite of hunting?
Maybe it's a deer that's grunting.
Hunting deer is so fun.
And you might not even get one.
What's the opposite of football?
You might not get anywhere at all.
What's the sense of running around?
When all you get is smashed into the ground.

Trystyn Summerville, Grade 6
Freedom Area Middle School, PA

Protect Her

We're polluting the Earth now can't you see.
We're turning our home into tragedy.
Mother Nature needs help these days.
For this is not just a short phase.
She needs help to live beyond.
Now it's time that we respond.
Now let's clean up Earth's wonderful face,
For this could become a beautiful place.
The time we have is wasting away.
Now it's time we make it ok.
It's time we reduce, reuse, recycle.
Instead of a car, take a bicycle.
Recycle bottles and cans,
So we will have some beautiful lands.
In the future, I can see it now,
Our Earth is so clean, I can only say wow.
Let's have our Earth looking like this.
Let's keep it clean so we won't miss!
We can remove this entire blur,
All we have to do is protect her…

Just protect her!

Jordan Butler, Grade 6
Captain Nathan Hale Middle School, CT

Lost (I Am)

I am lost
I wonder what is becoming of me
I hear the howling sand rush over me
I see this black figure coming towards me
I want to get out of this horrible place
I am dying under the desert sand burning me underneath

I pretend that I'm going to be all right
I feel my heart pounding I feel my body burning
I touch the hot dry sand
I worry that I'm going to die I'm only 9
I am dying!

I understand that I must die but I'm only 9!
I say to God please don't let me die
I dream that someone or something is going to save me
I try to move but the sand is sucking me in
I hope I'm not dying
I am dying.

Cassidy Tucci, Grade 6
Kelly Lane Intermediate School, CT

Assignments

My teacher assigns our class an essay,
so I click my pen and begin to write.
My pen zooms across my paper,
as if it were a launching space ship!

My mom assigns me to clean my room,
so I grab a trash bag and a broom.
I find many piles of dirty clothes,
along with some dust bunnies too.

I assign myself to take a look at our beautiful world,
so I walk outside to observe the wonders I've not seen before.
All the way from beaches and shores,
to mountains with snowcaps and waterfalls!

I ask you, what is your assignment for me?

Summer Weaver, Grade 6
Gulfview Middle School, FL

Watching

Spring is almost here
But it feels like she left me just yesterday.
I thought I saw her walking towards me,
But then I blinked
And she was gone.

When I see her picture on the wall
I know she'll always be watching,
Watching over me.

Shelby Cox, Grade 6
Discovery School @ Reeves Rogers, TN

Father Daughter Dance

All the girls get ready for the dance,
The dads wear their special tie and tux,
I take his hand,
It's like we're in our own land,
I say, "I love you,"
He says, "I love you more,"
After awhile our feet feel sore,
But we still dance until the end,
They send you away with a crown,
Made especially to match your gown,
We ride home as quiet as can be,
I'm glad you came to the dance with me!

Cristin Hickey, Grade 4
H Austin Snyder Elementary School, PA

When I Mowed

When I went to mow
I ran over a hoe
I cut my toe
I cut my grass too low
Oh no!
I forgot it was for show

Nick Huggins, Grade 4
Fishing Creek Elementary School, PA

Nice

Hannah Schneider
Who is
Funny, nice, smart
Daughter of
Matt and Tammy
Lover of
Soccer, candy, siblings
Who feels
Happy, love, forgiveness
Who needs
Friends, family, hope
Who gives
Love, fun, understanding
Who fears
Outside in the dark
Who would like to see
Joe Jonas, Heaven, Chicago

Hannah Schneider, Grade 4
St Alexis School, PA

Sadness

Sadness is blue.
It sounds like a scratch on a chalkboard,
It smells like the salt water at the beach,
It tastes like leftover broccoli,
It looks like a baby crying,
It feels like a really bad sunburn.

Katie Collins, Grade 4
Sacred Heart School, PA

Church

Happiness flows
Everyone is welcome
Peace in hearts
Body of Christ
Singing of love
Prayer of God
Sacred building
Heavenly host
Beautiful sculptures
Stain glass windows
Rows of people
Angels singing
Holy Spirit blessing
Word of God

Nathan Ciffa, Grade 6
St Stephen's School, NY

Summer Break

I am so excited in 2 days
Because it will be summer break
I am going to the beach
Hopefully there will be some heat
I will swim with the waves
And go with the flow
And feel the wind blow
I will feel the breeze in my hair
While I am eating a pear
I would like to see a dolphin
Because they are lovely
Please let summer break be here

Emily Payne, Grade 6
Warrenton Middle School, VA

Life with Courage!

Life has many tasks
Many mountains we need to climb
So many problems to figure out
But courage makes us strong
So we know right from wrong

When the day breaks
And night falls it gets scary
But courage makes you stand tall

Life may push you around
Be sure to make your sound

The world keeps spinning
And courage keeps winning

Courage comes with life,
Keep yours glowing
And always showing!

Sydney Fournier, Grade 6
Normandin Middle School, MA

Oceans

I can hear the waves,
Crashing into each other,
Can you hear the waves?

Janet Lara, Grade 5
Avon Grove Intermediate School, PA

Spring

I like spring it is finally here.
Flowers are blooming let's all cheer.
Bunnies are running in my backyard.
Birds are chirping in my yard.
Grass is green, trees are flowering.
In April it is always showering.
Hip hip hooray for spring.
My favorite time to sing.
People are happy to be outside.
Grilling and playing all the time.
Winter cold is finally over.
Spring is here put away the cover.

Austin Raines, Grade 5
St John Catholic School, MD

Rain

Water dripping,
Gutter filling
Harsh,
Gentle.

Humid, cold,
Puddles.

Soak my
Clothes through
My jacket.

Baseball game
Rain-out
Soccer game
Mud-bath.

Terrible — flooding,
Miracle — drought ending,
Relief from the hot summer,
Glorious rain.

Marcus Barbu, Grade 5
Public School 128 Juniper Valley, NY

Autumn

When fall
Comes, cool winds blow
Then the short days go to
Night and the harvest moon shows its
Bright light.

Shania Braman, Grade 6
Bedford Middle School, PA

Love*

Love is Mom baking cookies in the oven
It is like a puppy welcoming you home
It's the warm feeling of a hug

When I wash Mom's car I'm showing love
Love is helping a friend
It's a place to stay when all's lost

Love's a wondrous thing
Love is what it is
That's the way I like it

Abbie Thompson, Grade 4
Youngsville Elementary School, NC
*Inspired by John Denver's, "Perhaps Love…"

Frozen Mountain Peaks

White is snow
White is clouds
White is paper
White is a pillow
White smells like vanilla
White tastes like cold ice
White sounds like cooing doves
White looks like a cat
White feels like a feather
White makes my breath frosty
White is a mountain peak waiting to be climbed

Amna Zigic, Grade 4
Lincoln Elementary School, PA

Our Lovely World Our Lovely World

Cotton candy swirls in the morning sky,
Grasses drying off after a midnight shower,
The birds are peeping all around,
The world is waking, the sun is smiling,
And life is good.
So I will take a moment and
Rejoice.
For the Earth is at peace once again.

Anna Kilpatric, Grade 6
West Frederick Middle School, MD

Holocaust

H atred for Jews
O ccupation
L ots of ghettos
O ur lives were not our own
C oncentration camps
A dolf Hitler
U nderstanding differences
S wastika
T reating others the way they should be treated

Adam Person, Grade 5
Shafer Elementary School, PA

Fairfield's Beauty

So many things to see in the marsh,
Quite a few of those smelled very harsh.
I liked the scent of the nice fresh air,
But the skunk cabbage — that was a scare.

Birds were flying from tree to tree.
Boy, I wish that it could be me.
The sounds the frogs made were like little burps,
While the birdies up high made lots of chirps.

The pond was very murky,
It was pea green and quirky.
I wanted only to catch a big fish,
And that was by far my one greatest wish.

As I walked along a very small path,
A frog was taking his daily mud bath.
I could taste the pure and sea-salt air,
And feel the wind blowing my hair.

Now I get ready to leave this cool place,
I feel like I just lost a big race.
I will not forget the day I spent,
All that I saw and how much it meant.

Edward Cybulski, Grade 6
East Shore Middle School, CT

I Am a Good Student

I am a good student,
I wonder if I'll see my friends,
I hear what the teacher is saying,
I see my graded papers,
I want to be intelligent in class,
I pretend I am not a bad student,
I am a good student.

I touch the books in the library,
I worry if I get a terrible grade,
I cry if I don't do things right,
I am a good student.

I understand the cursive I do,
I say to my teacher I'm doing my homework,
I dream to have more teachers like my reading teacher,
I try my best in school,
I hope I am never absent,
I am a good student.

Doris Diaz, Grade 4
Meadow Park Elementary School, FL

Untitled

The sun and the moon
"My winds are cold," says the moon
The sun says nothing

Jacqueline Rose, Grade 4
Stackpole Elementary School, PA

Change
Change
Don't sit on your butts
Get up and change
The world

Change
We shouldn't wait
Bring our soldiers home
For Christmas

Change
If you have
The power to
We all do
I know I do
Meghan Bailer, Grade 6
E T Richardson Middle School, PA

The Butt in Tibet
There once was an old cigarette
Who loved driving his big Corvette
But then he got smoked
And alas he croaked
Thrown out as a butt in Tibet
Griffin Sernoffsky, Grade 6
Captain Nathan Hale Middle School, CT

Mat Ball
Mat Ball
Have some fun,
kick a ball.
Run the bases,
be an ace.
Just have good time.
But don't overdo it,
you will get hurt bad.
Then you will be tired, sad, and mad.
Then first part sounds fun,
but the rest sounds bad.
Dean Jackson, Grade 5
Southern Pines Elementary School, NC

The Sky
In the sky
you can imagine many things,
pirates, dragons, cupcakes, rings.
When you're sad
just look up there,
it's just like going
to the fair.
As you get older,
they fade away,
you're not longer a kid,
they cannot stay.
Liam Chen, Grade 5
Melville School, RI

My Elmo
The day Elmo was going to leave me.
I cried I knew I would never seem him again.
My dog Elmo would never sleep with me when I needed him.
Never to see his brown, black, and white fur.
Never to see him jump on my bed to greet me in the morning.

I watch as my dad put the limp dog's body in the car.
His bushy tail did not wag like it always did.
When dad came home and the door opened he would not be there.
Just an empty box where he laid before he left me.
Never to comfort me.

I would never feel his warm wet tongue lick my face.
He wouldn't wipe the tears away that I have now never to fill the hole in my heart.
I would never see him again my dog was gone.
Along with the part of my heart that held him close and would never let go.

I cried for days, weeks so many tears.
No dog would replace him.
Nothing would replace...
    My Elmo.

Emily Cummins, Grade 6
E T Richardson Middle School, PA

Happiness
Happiness is something that draws a smile on a person's face.

Happiness is the rising sun.
Its whitey glow and beams of light brighten the sky.
A feeling of joy springs in every child's soul.

Happiness is a basketball.
Children dribble, shoot, and dunk.
And the fun never ends.

Happiness is a pile of brown, crisp leaves.
Children dash and jump into it for lots of fun.

Happiness is cottony snow.
It covers the ground like a thick white blanket for children to play in.

Happiness is a yummy cup of hot chocolate served on a freezing winter day.
It warms and revives a child's spirit.

Happiness makes the world bright.
Go out and spread it!
Harry DeKay, Grade 6
Haynes Academy for Advanced Studies, LA

The Wall
There's a wall holding me back to all my...dreams
That walls a passage to my life, but why is it me...
I need to let loose not care anymore take a sip of my drink
Look galore in the sky and picture the clouds as my dreams flying by...
Dominique Scarabaggio, Grade 5
Public School 3, NY

I Am

I am a strong believer
I wonder when the world will end
I hear the wind whistle in the sky
I see sparkles in the night sky
I want to know the things that can't be answered in life
I am a strong believer

I pretend that I am the richest person in the world
I feel happy every day
I touch the hot sand across the beach
I worry the sun will eventually crash down on Earth
I am a strong believer

I understand the hard things in life
I say it may come to an end
I dream that it never happens
I try to believe
I hope terrorism will not take over
I am a strong believer

Emily Jackson, Grade 6
Kelly Lane Intermediate School, CT

Time

Pens and pencils work to dawn.
Files from files, yawn after yawn.
The clock is ticking, time to catch the train.
You finally come home again.

Caroline Murphy Racette, Grade 4
St John the Evangelist School, MA

Violet

Roses are red, violets are blue
Little Miss Violet I love you

Bright red hair, lavender colored eyes
You sure are a cute surprise

You are a miracle, I never stop thinking about you
Even in school, I always think about you

Those little toes, those little hands
You can crawl, oh yes you can

You kiss your baby doll, you pull yourself up in your crib
You even let us put on your bib

I make you laugh, I make you cry
Even though I don't try

Oh little Vi, as sweet as can be
You remember you'll always have me

Roses are red, violets are blue
Little Miss Violet I'll always love you.

Madison Packard, Grade 5
Geiger Elementary School, ME

I'm a Pencil

I'm a pencil with lots of talent
"Talent" I have for you.
I work for you every day
With broken point you rush to sharpen me.
"Bold" and bright I shine for you
Your grades are due
You counting on me, to work for you
If you make a mistake or two don't forget
To look on my head.
I will erase for you
Clean work I promise you.
"Bright" and bold I shine for you.
I work for you
A pencil I am!

Renna Taylor, Grade 5
Sea Castle Elementary School, FL

Herb Magee

Coach with most wins in Division II ball,
Inducted into Philly Sports Famed Hall.
He is honest when he speaks, and yes, that is clear,
Goes to Season's Tip-Off Tournament every other year.

Coach is confident, friendly, and never mean,
He has two daughters named Kay and Eileen.
Eileen's two daughters are Katie Stec and me,
I am proud to be the granddaughter of Herb Magee!

Karly Stec, Grade 5
Villa Maria Academy Lower School, PA

Black Is My Friend

Black is a crow,
Black is night,
Black is my best friend,
I love the dark,
Black is with me for the night,
I hate when he has to go.
He is my shadow that follows me around.
He likes to bully people,
He loves me so,
I can't let him go,
He has no friends except me,
He is a sour piece of candy,
He is the wolf howl at night,
He is my dog,
Black is a skunk,
A Yak,
A ring on a raccoon's tail,
The masks that people wear,
He fails grades, but not in my book,
He is the black horse that is not tamed
That roams around at night.

Camryn Hill, Grade 4
Youngsville Elementary School, NC

Somewhere

Somewhere there is suffering.
Somewhere there is hate.
Somewhere there's a woman,
without food on her plate.

Somewhere there is dying.
Somewhere there's arrest.
Somewhere there's a teenager,
who is badly depressed.

Somewhere there is sobbing.
Somewhere there are poor…
Somewhere there's a boy waiting,
for his dad to come from war.

Somewhere there are racists.
Somewhere someone feels hoarse.
Somewhere someone's parents,
are ready to divorce.

But…
Somewhere there is laughter.
Somewhere there is love.
Somewhere people are happy,
and thanking that spirit above.

Diana Sinanian, Grade 5
Cool Spring Elementary School, VA

Boar's Head

Boar's head on the wall
Staring a hole through my head
Please burn that thing now!

Ben Palmer, Grade 6
Discovery School @ Reeves Rogers, TN

Planes

Planes,
Hear the rumble of the engines,
The whistle of the wind,
When it whistles over the wings,

Planes,
Through the endless wonders of the sky,
It flies,
Soaring through the puffy clouds,
As it flies,
To vast destinations,
Of far-off countries,
Of Africa,
Asia,
China,
North America,
And many more.

Mustafa Ghasia, Grade 5
Arthur S May Elementary School, NY

The Tree

The tree's
Green leaves
Are like
The ocean
At night
The wood is
Rough
Like the
Side of our desks,
But
When the tree
Gets too old
"SNAP"
The tree
Falls
Apart,
And is dead
Forever,
But waits
To come back
Someday.

Steven Magda, Grade 4
Riverside School, CT

Day/Night

Day
hot, sunny
blazing, steaming, warming
dawn, tea time, twilight, midnight
calming, relaxing, sleeping
cool, dark
night

Grace Ann Boudreaux, Grade 5
The Cathedral School, AR

I Am

I am proud and happy
I wonder about my baby brother
I hear my mother's voice
I see many people
I want lots of money
I am intelligent and a good child
I pretend that I am a teacher
I feel joyful
I touch Malone's cry
I worry about my family
I cry on Malone
I am a dancer and singer
I say the world is free
I dream of being a break dancer
I try my best
I hope that Mrs. Malone stays safe
I am a singer and dancer

Davion Bell, Grade 4
Black Fox Elementary School, TN

Moonlight Mustangs

I see mustangs in the moonlight
They call to me at night
I see all the dapples and grays
The mustangs call to me
Then the mighty stallion rears
His white coat gleaming
Then away they run
Out over the fields
I watch them until the last of them,
Vanish into the moonlight
Atop the hill the mighty stallion,
Rears one last time.

Caitlin Woodson, Grade 6
Bishop Walsh Middle High School, MD

What Is Writing?

An expressive language,
A way to get attention,
Squeaky erasers,
Poems,
Information,
Lead pencils,
Narratives,
Hooks,
Punctuation,
Caps,

That is writing.

Hunter Santana, Grade 4
Meadow Park Elementary School, FL

Someone

Someone living in Kalamazoo
wrote a clerihew.
It was so bad
and made him mad
so he started something new.

Madison Thrasher, Grade 6
Bedford Middle School, PA

The Hopeful Soul

There is a dark heavy cloud,
over my dry cracking land,
I am the sun,
I am the hope,
I break through the clouds of despair,
and bring love into the land,
I am the rain in a drought,
I am the crops in a famine,
I am the life in her soul,
the Depression is among us,
and to stay strong,
we must find hope.

Carolina Fowler, Grade 6
Chapin Middle School, SC

Pen and Pencil
Pen
Permanent, ink
Interesting, exciting, writing
Communicate information, illustrate pictures
Drawing, sketching, erasing
Mechanical, wooden
Pencil

Karen Le, Grade 6
St Agatha School, NY

A Whole New Day
A brand new day with its morning sun,
A whole new cycle has just begun.
And here one person in solitude I stand,
But how the silence is piercing my mind.
I long for sound, just one little cry.
The serenity is disturbing more than I found,
The clouds are not moving, nor is the ground.
Where will I get? From where do I come?
I stand here in mystery, just me, I, the only one.
As I start to ease forward with care,
I suddenly leap out of the silence and break into a run.
The sun feels heavy, a new day has just begun.
With the wind, I fly towards my goal,
Where am I going? Is it no place at all?
Yet I charge for the pleasure, run for the glory.
Sprint toward the end, what is controlling me?
Then, as I start to slow down with a skid,
I realize, and think, of what I just did.
I have gone far, from where I have been.
This brand new day just came to an end.

Ciaran Hedderman, Grade 5
Hamagrael Elementary School, NY

Happiness Is a Light
Happiness is a light
Brightening up a room and,
Shining all around.
Glowing in the darkest places.
Making the dark places
Light again.
The light shows you
Where everything is
in a dark room.
Someone's eyes, coming from a dark room
To a light room,
Need to adjust.
But Beware!
When a bulb burns out or someone flips the switch
The light goes out!
Replace the bulb
Quick!

Ryan Harvey, Grade 6
Hillcrest Elementary School, PA

Snow Day
I was sick
On a snow day
I would have had first pick
Only if I wasn't sick

I can't believe I'll miss playing today
And am going to be all lonely
While my friends go out and play
Then they knocked on the door and said
"Hey, can you come out and play?"

I responded, "I'm sick in bed."
"Good luck, Buck!"
They said while shaking their heads
I walked to the window and saw a bunch of kids

Awww, shucks!
I hate being sick
It really sucks
They're having fun while I'm down in the dumps

Finally my brother came in
All he did was pick
But next time
I bet he'll be the one who's sick!

Hananiah Brogdon, Grade 6
Linkhorne Middle School, VA

Opposites
I see roses that are blue,
I see violets that are red.
Mixed up…in an opposite world.
The sky is green and the ground is blue.
The colors of the rainbow are opposite too.
I'm stuck in this crazy world.
Where the sun is white and the moon is yellow,
Where night is day and day is night,
Where you wear hats on your feet and shoes on your head.
What a crazy world this is where everything is opposite,
Wait a minute…I am upside down.

Katelyn Walls, Grade 6
Discovery School @ Reeves Rogers, TN

The Boomerang
I'll
let you go
because I know,
you'll come back to
me. A brilliant angle, not
so deep,   in my backpack
I shall keep   until I find
a perfect place   to set you
free, so whirling   quickly back
to   me.

Max Tajmir, Grade 6
Berry Middle School, AL

What's Wrong with Boys and Girls?

Boy
Immature, fun
Sweating, running, fighting
Fists, swears, dance, books
Yelling, bossy, whining
Weird, pushy
Girl

Jake Elton, Grade 5
Avon Grove Intermediate School, PA

Yesterday

The land of yesterday
Lived a day, yet passed
Its people aged with wisdom and solace
You can recall what they've told you

Future does not exist,
Only past
They do not move forward
But deeper into what they can recall

Natasha Radtke, Grade 4
PS 10, NY

Irish Step

I love it
R ewarding
I deal for free time
S o much fun
H ard work

S ilver and gold medals
T wo times a week
E nergizing
P ractice 20 minutes a night

Jackie Aylward, Grade 6
Albert D Griswold Middle School, CT

Karma

Good and evil
sometimes you get the good side
sometimes you get the flip side
I'm the life coin
I make you happy
I make you sad
I'm the ying-yang
brightness
and darkness
good deeds done
bad deeds committed
there is no middle
just rewards
and punishments
who live through me
the whole time away

Justin Hoffman, Grade 6
Avon Grove Intermediate School, PA

A Leaf

A leaf leaping out off the tree that has been resting
All year long gliding down gracefully like a feather the leaf green as could be
Like light reflecting off the top of the green tree
Fall slowly turns the color of the leaf
Slowly
Slowly
Slowly
Turning crimson red
Burnt yellow
Pumpkin orange
It gruffly drifts down
Light as a feather
Falling
Falling
Falling
The leaf screaming as it falls
Down to its deadly fate
As the landing looks soft but
It plummets hard down to the ground

Max Miller, Grade 4
Goshen Elementary School at Hillcrest, KY

My Greatest Fear

My fear is released not when the darkness takes over
Not when I come to something unknown
Or when I am about to die for in death, there is a heaven
My greatest fear is the absence of love or when happiness is only a word
Or if I never understand true bliss and if I destroy the soul of another
My greatest joy is the anticipation to be holding my newborn baby
Or to find happiness where you least expect it
Or to see the real beauty that our Earth is capable of
For, unlike joy, fear is an object that you choose to use or see
And when the world is crumbling down
And when death is about to shake your hand
Or if you see love one more time before it dies in the battle
Then you'll let fear in because why wouldn't you be afraid
If everyone you know vanished if your time is up if love doesn't exist
But loved ones are holding my hand preparing me for my life
Which is yet to come and catching me when i trip over my own sorrow
And loving me when I forget that love is possible
The journey of life must always come
And there will be battles to be lost and battles to be won
But fear will always be on the opposing side wanting to pulverize me
But I shall fight and I shall win

Anastasia Hanson, Grade 6
City of Pembroke Pines Charter Central Middle School, FL

Where I'm From

I'm from a family that forces me to eat a disgusting vegetable called "broccoli"
I am from playing soccer 24/7 and never giving up
I'm from a mother that scowls like a starving tiger.
I am from a poor but happy country named Colombia
I'm from skating and getting a terrible concussion
Concussions hurt.

Sebastian Cano, Grade 5
Hamilton Avenue School, CT

Family

My family is nice.
They are as sweet as spice.
Laugh, talk, hooray!

We laugh and play.
We play all day.
Ha Ha Yay!

Mary C. Sgro, Grade 5
Our Lady of Grace Elementary School, PA

The Barn Owl Feast

There once was an owl with a heart shaped face.
He lived in a very dark and dingy place.
His home was as dark as the midnight sky.
The owl was never afraid to climb and fly.
The creepy, white barn was the owl's dark home.
He was not alone because the mice will roam.
The owl will feast when he hears the mice feet.

Their little hearts beat when he swoops down for meat.
He grabs their crown, and he won't let them down.
Especially when others are not around.
The owl could fly like a brown crazy hawk.
When people are sleeping, the owl shouldn't talk.
The barn owl's feathers were as white as snow.
When it is nighttime, the scary owl's eyes glow.
Last night the owl screamed loudly and woke up,
The town of Milford, Orange, and my fun pup.
The owl moved it's beautiful wings to shake.
The animals below are his to come take.

Kristen Sheridan, Grade 6
East Shore Middle School, CT

Friend

I need to know if you're my true friend,
will you be by my side until the end?
Can I tell you my secrets deep,
and trust them in your heart you'll keep?
We are neither of us without our flaws,
can you accept mine as I will yours?
I'll be a shoulder to cry on when you're blue,
will you be there for me when I need you?
No matter how busy I will make time for you,
if you are busy will you make time for me too?
I will take your hand and comfort your tears,
will you hold me and soothe my fears?
I will give you joy and many warm smiles,
can we share that even across many miles?
I will not forget what's important to you,
will you remember what's important to me too?
With you my most favorite things I'll share,
if only I know do you truly care?
If you can accept me as I do you,
then I will know you are a friend most true.

Abdulai Mohamed, Grade 5
PS/MS 004 Crotona Park West, NY

Summer!

When I think of summer
I never think of anything that is a bummer.

I always think of summer,
Because it will be funnier.
The warm winds make waves
That make the sand moist on summer days.

The flowers are in bloom
Like the colors of the rainbow.
They smell like heaven, sweets, and ocean waves.

The animals lose their winter fur,
Because winter is a blur.

Shania Stanton, Grade 6
Celina K-8 School, TN

Perfect Day

As I walked through the moist, green grass,
I saw something perfect, I could not pass.
A beautiful basking rock shimmering like a star at night,
Climb up that rock, I think I might.
Rest like a statue on this rock,
Basking in the warm sun around the clock.
After my long, warm day of sunbathing was finally done,
A new journey had begun.
I went and walked under the tree;
The limbs were shady arms protecting me.
I relaxed comfortably in the cool grass letting off heat.
Then I strolled to the pond to eat.
I dove in and sunk like a stone.
It won't be long until I am alone.
My wonderful day was done and so was my long, splendid year,
To wake up with the bright sunlight there.
Everything will be just right,
I tuck it in and I call it a night.
I had the most perfect last day before my hibernation,
Please remember my location!

Janae Owen, Grade 6
East Shore Middle School, CT

Dancing

Across the floor click, click, click
On the stage dancing to the beat
Around me, more dancers
Over the last two years, it's been my thing
Within me a passion
'Til my legs give in
Inside my heart is pounding
Outside my face is smiling
Beside me my arms flex
Instead of waving them all over the place

Katelyn Cole, Grade 6
Berry Middle School, AL

Chocolate Gummy Bears

The freshly brewed hot chocolate that has just been drowned in boiling water.
It's a mummy wrapped around with invisible colored bandages as it gets trapped in a chocolate sarcophagus.
It's covered with cinnamon colored pimples, as the sepia colored skin stains my fingers.
The nose is sticking up, trying to breathe.
It dances while it crashes down into the transparent jar.
The luminous skin makes my mouth water, urging me to have more,
As it sits silently waiting for their predator to eat him up.

Erica Fu, Grade 6
Nathaniel Hawthorne Middle School 74, NY

Last Chance

Words are unique, with minds of their own.
They have power to hurt, to make a man groan.
Also to cheer, to encourage someone,
Digging deep for a smile when the day is done.
Yes, words can draw a feeling or two.
Yes, they can mock, but also help, it's true!
They are weapons, sort of, in a way.
While they've battled for centuries, they cannot retreat to this day!
It's an honor to have words, and to have skills to think fast.
Only surging, only surging when the time comes at last.
He must be careful, though; must not mess up.
If he does something wrong, the words will furiously erupt.
You see, when a word is out, out in the air,
It's like a bullet that's been shot, for it SHALL always get there.
If it's not perfect, it could wound your best friend.
And as we all know, a wound takes a long time to mend.

Words are still beautiful. They still dance and enchant.
But whatever you say, wherever you are, remember: each word you form is your last chance.

Clare Miller, Grade 6
Visitation BVM School, PA

A Magical Land

Silent and
peaceful   the desert   lives until
the animals   wake then   the desert
is rich with   sounds and life.   Birds are
flying from   one saguaro to   the next; landing
silently on   the arms of the   gentle green
giant, calling   to each other in   voices of
beautiful song. Snakes slither   soundlessly on
the sun seared floor. All senses alert. Bright desert
flowers are in bloom. Spots of color contrasting
the green cacti. With insects and birds
collecting its sweet nectar. Dominating
the desert, saguaro cacti are beautiful
creatures. They
are vital to life in
the desert. Maje-
stically looming
in the background,
purple and gold mountains complete the glorious desert scenery. To the general population of America, the desert holds a
stereotypical image: dry, brown, lifeless, and dead. All who believe that are missing out on the true beauty of this magical land.

Krysta Przestrzelski, Grade 6
Charles D Owen Middle School, NC

Poems

Why are poems so hard to write?
I try with all my might.
And I still can't write a poem.
Poems are so hard to write.
To become a poet,
You really must have to know it.
Poems can be fun to write.
But for me it would take all night.
I really deeply love poetry.
For me poetry is like being free.
Some people make a living on writing poems.
But for me that is not to be.
Poems are so good to me.
I treat them just like a tree.
Even though I know 'em,
I still can't write a poem.

Andrew Schaich, Grade 6
Charles D Owen Middle School, NC

US Military

Everyone in it has hearts of glee
They fight for you and me
We stand in a land of free
Think of war, how terrible it's been
Seeing all the suffering men

They conquer their fear how rough it's been
Fighting through years
Through many objectives
Complete or failed, they never stop
They risk their lives day through night
Give them your soul
Give them your life
Remember what they've done
So keep them in your guiding light

Shane DiStefano, Grade 4
West Frankfort Elementary School, NY

If I Used an Attic

If I used an attic,
I would store not only junk, but memories.
It would be like walking into a wormhole
Without a tiny glimpse of the future.
If I used an attic,
I would try to savor every moment I spent in it.
I would feel cozy inside of it, just like I would
In front of a hot stove or sitting by an open fire.
If I used an attic,
I would show my grandparents my progress
While sitting on the couch in the attic.
I would not let it get junky in there because it would
Trash many precious memories.

Nikki Jackson, Grade 4
Spartanburg Jr Writing Project, SC

The Sky

I see the sky, the flowers blooming and the river singing.
I feel strong as I watch the sky, as it watches me.

I hear the wind coming in fear, and the sky crying in tears.
As the river flows I hear the silence of the sky.

I wish I could touch the moon and see its life as it can see mine
I imagine I could touch the sky and it could touch me.

I know the power of the night and the shine of the moon.

Tyrone Jackson, Grade 6
Suffern Middle School, NY

Army

They protect us,
They spare their lives for us,
They protect the U.S.A.,
You may cry when your mom,
Or dad doesn't come home alive,
But don't cry when they're protecting you,
And everyone around you,
So when they come home,
Don't jump all around them,
And pretend they never went,
To war,
Because they protected you,
And everyone around you,
Greet them home and care for them,
Respect them,
Don't forget to thank them,
They put their lives at risk,
For the U.S.A.,
They spared their lives for us,
They protected the U.S.A.,
Thank them.

Tyler daSilva, Grade 4
Naquag Elementary School, MA

Love*

Love is the moon shining brightly on a beautiful summer night.
Love is me and my mom baking cookies on Father's Day.
Love is good.

Love is like a rainbow after a storm.
Love gives people a home and clothes.
Love keeps you safe.

Love never hurt anybody because well, because it's love.
Love will keep you happy even when you're sad.

Love wants to help when there is no help left.
It keeps going and never stops.
Love is good.

Emma McManus, Grade 4
Youngsville Elementary School, NC
*Inspired by John Denver's, "Perhaps Love…"

Snow

I would very much like to go
Where I could play in the snow.
My snow sled would be plastic.
It would be fun also fantastic.
I would make angels out of snow.
You would see one wherever you go.
Yes, oh yes, it's very true.
This is what I want to do.
I would very much like to go,
Where there was lots of snow!

Hannah Mishler, Grade 4
Bethesda Christian Academy, NC

Seasons

How I love winter,
I'll never get a splinter,
I love it when it snows,
And the pink color of my nose.

How I love spring,
When doorbells ring,
The grass is always green,
And nobody is mean.

How I love summer,
When nothing is a bummer,
And I can get cool,
By jumping in the pool.

How I hate fall,
I have to go to the mall,
Get ready for school,
And follow every single rule!

Erin Umlauf, Grade 4
Stall Brook School, MA

Mom/Dad

Mom
Smart, pretty
Growing, adoring, caring
Woman, protector, man, father
Playing, loving, boring
Intelligent, bossy
Dad

Matthew Maldonado, Grade 4
Ridgeway Elementary School, MD

Snow Storm

Falling and falling
Everywhere you will see it
Whiteness is falling
Down and down it falls all day
It will never ever stop

Christopher Bielica, Grade 6
Normandin Middle School, MA

Love and Hate

Love
Romantic, passionate
Caring, sharing, hugging
Friends, friendship, hatred, enemy
Crying, stressing, upsetting
Mad, miserable
Hate

Janet Muñoz, Grade 6
St Agatha School, NY

Yellow

Yellow is a daffodil
Yellow is a stick of chalk
Yellow is a golden ring
Yellow is a vanilla cupcake
Yellow smells like a lemon sponge cake
Yellow tastes like a glass of lemonade
Yellow sounds like a shiny new bell
Yellow looks like a bunny
Yellow feels like a brand new pencil
Yellow makes me feel happy
Yellow is a dandelion

Alexis Reiter, Grade 4
Lincoln Elementary School, PA

Forgiveness

I must find a place where I
Can escape the troubles of
The modern world.

I need to find a place where
Relaxing is easy and the days
Slowly pass.

I need to find a place where
The possibilities are seemingly
Endless.

I need to find a place where people
Are all joyful and forgiving for
I
Am
Not
Perfect.

Nicholas Barr, Grade 6
E T Richardson Middle School, PA

Birds

Birds
Small, pretty
Singing, flying, nesting
Beautiful singer at work
Majestic

Courtney Conder, Grade 6
Jackson Christian School, TN

Really Red

Red is,
the gorgeous velvety rose
gracefully
bowing its head
in the soft summer breeze.

Red are,
my blushing plump cheeks
embarrassed
by the kiss
stale upon my cheek.

Red are,
my tired bulging bloodshot eyes
wandering
back and forth
around the smoky room.

Red is,
the furious flaming forest fire
devouring
every living thing
in its path.

Red is beautiful!

Rebecca Grimmer, Grade 4
Waynesburg Elementary School, KY

An Elephant's Prayer

In this hot desert
Of destruction and death
I must pray for protection
From mankind
And the desert's hot breath

David Eke, Grade 6
Kelly Lane Intermediate School, CT

Water Bottle

Water bottle
Open
Crack
Drink
Gulp
Gulp
Refreshed
Water bottle
Open
Crack
Drink
Gulp
Gul...

Empty!

Andy Tu, Grade 5
Public School 128 Juniper Valley, NY

Saluting America

Dear Soldiers,
In the summer afternoon, the sound of car horns and sirens
With a smell of oil and gun powder, the air hot and dry.
There was bright lava red and white lines.
There were white stars and a blue uniform.
You could see in the background a great big flag, as I salute it.
Thank you soldiers!

Bryan Fletcher, Grade 4
Honeoye Falls-Lima Manor School, NY

Holocaust

The Holocaust was a terrible time
When they arrived at the death camps
They were told to stand in certain lines
The hatred the people made
The consequences the Jews paid
They were liberated in 1945
Some died and some survived
When they were let out
Some couldn't find their homes
They were lost and all alone
Some couldn't live without their families
Now you know why the Holocaust is important to me!

Katherine Wallace, Grade 5
Shafer Elementary School, PA

I Am Your Conscience

I am your conscience.
I wonder why you don't listen to me.
I hear good and bad.
I see what you don't want Mom and Dad to see.
I want what is right and just.
I am your conscience.

I pretend sometimes that what's wrong is okay.
I feel guilt.
I touch others when I make you do right.
I worry that you've done more wrong than others.
I am your conscience.

I understand that you make mistakes.
I say that all have room for forgiveness.
I dream that you will always do what's right.
I try to decide what's best.
I hope you will always follow my guide.
I am your conscience.

Shannon Elizabeth Greene, Grade 6
Kelly Lane Intermediate School, CT

Basketball

I like to play basketball in the fall.
When I'm about to shoot sometimes I stall.
Foul shots are always my worst,
But when I miss I never curse.

Dylan Garcia, Grade 6
Warrenton Middle School, VA

The Snake in the Corn

I'm a corn snake that slithers, slides, and squirms,
Through the farmer's mice infested cornfield.
At certain times though I might have to yield,
To look around for the farmer and gun.
Because if he's near, I will have to run.
I hear a tapping and scatting noise near.
I think it's my lunch which isn't too clear.
I slide through the brush rushing like a deer,
As I watch him go with the ax of fear.
My stomach growls like a great lion's roar.
Suddenly I forgot what I came for.
Starving, like I am only made of bones,
My small empty stomach growls, groans, and moans.
The stalks are my guards as Farmer went by.
Glad I'm camouflaged so here I can lie.
I see my lunch just sitting there like me.
It looked very queer from what I could see.
I lunge right by, hoping I would not die.
Then he swung the ax, I'm thinking, "Good bye."
Smelled a lot like death, but I'm glad he missed.
I wondered why we could not coexist.

Trevor C. Osborne, Grade 6
East Shore Middle School, CT

God's Gifts in My Life

G od gives me a lot
O ne gift is love
D uring creation He gave me courage

G od gave me the Holy Spirit
I t is great to have peace
F irst, in creation, I also received a brain to learn about Jesus
T he best gift is prayer
S unday is when you thank God by going to church

Samantha Longobardo, Grade 5
St. Patrick's School, NY

The Beach

The sound of waves crashing ashore,
Something we wait to hear,
For when we hear those enchanting sounds,
We know the beach is near.

The sun beating down, on water so blue,
Something we wait to see,
For when we spy those sparkling waves,
We know that over, is the never-ending plea.

That salty air, that fishy tang,
Something we wait to smell,
For when we breathe that beachy scent,
We know that all is well.

Sarah Larson, Grade 6
Chickahominy Middle School, VA

I Feel Alive

I feel alive,
When the wind blows,
I feel alive,
When the sun rises,
I feel alive,
When the snow glitters,
I feel alive,
When there are sprinklers,
I feel alive,
When I tumble,
I feel alive,
When I stumble,
I feel alive,
Because this is me.

Rebecca Dupuis, Grade 4
Trinity Lutheran School, FL

Jonney Is a Rabbit

Jonney is a rabbit,
But he has a bad habit.
He likes to take some carrots,
But he is afraid of parrots.
So if you guard your yard with a parrot,
He won't take your carrots.

When he sees the parrot,
He'll run away without a carrot.
When he gets back home,
Which is under a garden gnome,
He'll sit down and say,
"Wow, what a day!"

Collin Machamer, Grade 4

The Man from Gent

There once was a man from Gent,
Who sang wherever he went.
   He went to the fair,
   He tried to sing there,
To make enough money for his rent.

JoAnne St. Clair, Grade 4
St Barnabas Elementary School, NY

The Soldier

I was on guard that night,
When the rocks began to shake.
I was frozen with fright,
When the Earth began to quake.
They said to say I was asleep,
When some soldiers passed away.
We fought and fought,
Until we were all dead.
Courage arose that glorious day.

Zachariah De Souza, Grade 4
PS 10, NY

Can You Imagine

A duck that doesn't quack
A fat guy that doesn't snack

A ball that can talk
A tree that can walk

A shoe with fire laces
A celebrity that doesn't go places

A dollar that's worth something
An elephant that weighs nothing

A country that's drug free
Hollywood without TV

A computer without education
A shopping spree across the nation

Samuel Sharpless, Grade 6
Freedom Area Middle School, PA

Oak Tree

As you sway
In the wind
I hear a rustling sound

I peer into your leaves
And see
Nothing

I climb your branches
And inch closer to the top
And I see
A nest

Aaron Subashiq, Grade 5
Public School 128 Juniper Valley, NY

Baseball/Soccer

Baseball
hard, dirty
hitting, running, sliding
dugout, field, red card, yellow card
kicking, running, blocking
arduous, grimy
Soccer

Carlos Jeffery, Grade 5
The Cathedral School, AR

My Favorite Sports

I like to watch football games,
even basketball with Lebron James,
though my favorite team is the Lakers,
I like Kobe Bryant's faders.

Daniel Joynes, Grade 6
Warrenton Middle School, VA

Candy

Snow is really just
Peppermints and sugar clumps
Clinging to the trees.

Michele Wang, Grade 5
Fairfax Collegiate School, VA

The Moon and the Stars

I stare with unblinking eyes
At the amazing sight above me
Thinking many things
But too captivated to wonder
Did time stop?
Never have I been so mesmerized
On feasting my eyes on a sight like this
The sight of the moon and stars.

Charlie Stein, Grade 4
Riverside School, CT

Night Fall

Green trees,
Dancing with glee.
Pretty flowers,
Posing with pink power.

Scurrying mice,
Happy the weather's nice.

Water flowing,
With the sunlight —
Practically glowing.

Steamy vines,
Hanging in straight lines.

Crunchy underbrush —
The noise makes animals rush.

Boulders the size of Everest,
Towering over the forest.

I think nature
Is peaceful and calm —
At least until
Nightfall.

Kaitlyn Ross, Grade 6
E T Richardson Middle School, PA

Green

Earthly, natural
Recycling, helping, preserving
More than a color
A lifestyle

Alexis Broadnax, Grade 5
The Cathedral School, AR

The Sweet Girl

Pink is shy but very sweet.
She loves the taste of candy and has trouble falling asleep.
She loves the color brown just like brownies.
She never gets mad but when she does she cries.
Pink loves to read everything 2 pages to 2000 it does not matter.
I have to say she is the best friend you could have.
She loves to go to the pool and New York.
Pink loves to go in the woods.
When she is big she wants to be a vet.
I love pink and pink loves me.
She is the best friend you could ever have.

Morgan Scott, Grade 4
Youngsville Elementary School, NC

The Puzzles of Life

The puzzles of life are beyond me
Changing and creating different beliefs
The love of life is filled with lots of things
Heart felt compassion pouring out of thee
The devastation of life occurs very often
Hurting and breaking destroying and making
The keys of life are three different keys
Love, Hope, and Joy
The tragedies of life are never fair
So do what you can do and leave the rest to God
The puzzles of life are beyond me
Changing and creating different beliefs

Keresa Richards, Grade 6
Imagine International Academy, GA

Oh Old Dog of Mine

Oh old dog of mine
I can still see your face shine
After school every day
Yet my last memories of you aren't pleasant
I remember looking into those watery eyes
You were waiting for the pain to stop
You wanted to go fast but we wouldn't let you
Instead we made you live those last painful days
Maybe if it was a little sooner you'd be here now
But we were late, too late
But we wouldn't let go of you
Oh old dog of mine
I can still see your face shine
But now it's just in my mind
Rocky you had to go but now? So young?
I remember the last time I saw you lay your head down
'Cause the next day after soccer
My mom told me she took you to the vet again
But not to help you live but to stop the pain
Oh old dog of mine
I can still see your face shine

C.J. DeAngelis, Grade 6
Norton School, CT

Rush and Hurry

Rush and hurry, rush and hurry,
why am I always in a scurry?
I am always in a rush
and never can slow down.

Time to go, time to go,
everyone thinks I'm too slow.
I like to enjoy the things I do,
but never get a chance.

I am running late, I am running late,
this issue causes big debates.
I wish I could enjoy things
instead of rushing through.

I finally slowed down, I finally slowed down,
but believe it or not, it caused a big frown.
My list of undone tasks
was as long as the Mississippi River.

Time to rush and hurry.

Sierra Jones, Grade 6
J E Holmes Middle School, NC

Sadness

Sadness is like the color gray,
It sounds like crying,
It smells like rain,
It tastes like seaweed,
It looks like a puddle of water,
Sadness feels like you just lost your best friend.

Miranda Marchiani, Grade 4
Sacred Heart School, PA

Highway

I see the world,
I look out and see,
All the people in front of me.
They have lives, thoughts too.
I sometimes wonder what they do.
But I have places to go,
See people I know.
So I move on.

Grace Kennedy, Grade 6
Stratford Landing Elementary School, VA

A Chipmunk

I see a chipmunk fast and quick.
He scurries up a little stick.
He finds himself, a plunder of nuts,
The chipmunk eats, and makes little cuts.
He stuffs them in his cheeks,
The critter runs, and some nuts, out they leak,
Out of the chipmunk's little cheeks.

Ingrid Henriques, Grade 6
Mount Zion Christian Schools, NH

Orange Is Cool

Pumpkin is orange
It tastes like pie.
It sounds like boo.
It smells like seeds in the oven.
It looks like a cat.
It makes me feel scary.
Patrick Shank, Grade 4
Lincoln Elementary School, PA

Sad

I miss him
The light was reflecting
Off the glass in the room
Him laying there in bed
With people all around
Everybody talking
People talking
I miss him
Rhaya Winsky, Grade 6
Charlton Middle School, MA

Autumn

Leaves falling from trees
As I walk outside it's cold
As I remembered
The chilly air means autumn
Autumn is finally here!
Jamie Paiva, Grade 6
Normandin Middle School, MA

Summer

I'm waiting for summer to come,
For kids to have no school,
For ice cream to melt,
For pools to open,
For friends to come over,
For no work to be done,
For horse shows to win,
For places to go,
For time to relax,
And then I'll know it's summer.
Hayley Miller, Grade 6
Discovery School @ Reeves Rogers, TN

Dragons

Dragons in the clouds flying there
Blazing breaths of fire air
Always battling black strong knights
When he sees a dragon
He goes and fights
The fight was furious
Then he comes home victorious
But his eye jerked a tear
And his mom kissed him on the ear.
Lance Buhler, Grade 4
Athenian Academy, FL

Gone to Florida

Under my bed,
I found a picture,
Ripped but not destroyed.

I had been thinking of them,
I crawled out from under my bed and plopped myself on the couch.

I saw it: a picture before they left,
A piece of my soul,
Something I would remember.

I started to think,
They have always been there for me and helped me through tough times.

It wasn't true,
They left,
They could come back from Florida.

I sat there,
Thinking of all the great times I had with them,
Sad times, happy times.

They were always there for me,
Even when they were in Florida.

Amy Drake, Grade 5
Melville School, RI

Tempted

If they can do it why can't I?
I know some of the damage it can do but not all
It would make me feel so good for the moment
Horrible the next
So much fun until you get caught
I could just walk away but they would all laugh
If I stay I would fit in but I would lose my place with my other friends
Is this normal to be thinking about doing something like this?
What would my parents think? Would I still be able to play sports?
Then comes the most important question, are these people really my friends?
Would my real friends do this?
No.
I just walk away from it let them be stupid and do that, but I won't I won't stay.
Ally Samick, Grade 6
West Frederick Middle School, MD

Jacob Hiller

Jacob
Shy, caring, smart, creative
Brother of Camille Hiller
Lover of ice-cream, games, and God
Who feels happy, excited during holidays, and nervous before tests
Who fears spiders, scorpions, and tests
Who'd like to see global peace, the Olympics, and Australia
Resident of Dundee Drive
Hiller

Jacob Hiller, Grade 6
Morton Middle School, KY

Deepest Fear

Our deepest fear is not of death but after, where we shall go.
We live our lives full of choices but which is right, who knows.
There are different religions and different lifestyles
and when you are an adult you choose.
But people still have the question in the back of their mind saying, Whose?
Whose? Whose?

My deepest fear is not where I will go because I am confident of my belief here on earth.
What I am most afraid of is not helping others and finding our worth.
I feel like this world is becoming a sick place.
It is really scaring people because it is changing at such a fast pace.
Sometimes I want to go around and be a little helper bee.
I would love to help others with their fears so they can be set free.

Danny Meltzer, Grade 6
City of Pembroke Pines Charter Central Middle School, FL

130 Degrees

I'm in Arizona.
Summer hit me like a cobra ready for the kill.

The sun feels like a slap in the face and the swimming pool is no remedy for my burning hot skin.
The sun's rays are shining across the water and the grass is dried out and *light green*.

I'm glad the weather is hot and will stay hot.
For this is where I have lived for my whole life and will stay for my whole life.

Sarah Fournier, Grade 5
Melville School, RI

My Fifth Grade Year

August — the new school building is here, and 5th grade is so very near.
September — school has started with a "POW!" I'm having fun and I don't know how.
October — Halloween and my birthday are so very near, it will be a celebration when they are finally here!
November — my head is full I've learned a lot, hope I do good at the turkey trout.
December — Christmas is here, and so is our break, I need it to last long for heaven's sake.
January — the New Year is here, and our first school dance is near.
February — it's Valentine's Day, red and pink everyone say hooray.
March — ready for Saint Patrick's Day, and the sleep over, it's time to play.
April — time for spring and time for the big bunny. I hear he is really funny.
May — it's time for Pass testing, some birds on our porch are nesting.
June — school is out, and I love it without a doubt.

Rachel Bailey, Grade 5
Waccamaw Intermediate School, SC

My Deepest Fear

My deepest fear has nothing to do with goblins or ghouls.
It also does not have to do with fearing being either too perfect or not perfect enough. No, my deepest fear is the feeling of being embarrassed.

Embarrassment, that is the reason for my constant silence during classes. It is also the reason for many other things, such as being called on by teachers to give an answer, when the answer winds up being wrong.

Or, being able to express myself and my own individual opinions without worrying of the bad or hurtful opinions or remarks of others. The feeling of being constantly made fun of for the enjoyment of others is my deepest fear. Some may say it is best not to listen to others' opinions. But it is hard at my age of 12 not to listen and maybe even agree.

Jason Forbes, Grade 6
City of Pembroke Pines Charter Central Middle School, FL

Journey

Trapped in a world of imagination
But trying to get away from reality
A journey will free you
From the chains of reality

And take you into a different world
A world you can make your own
And cherish what is ahead
When you stop to think

You get pulled back
By your mind
Your heart
Your soul

Your will to be there
You go a long way
On a journey
Alex Grajek, Grade 6
E T Richardson Middle School, PA

I Am Deaf

What is that teacher saying up there?
The words never enter my ears.
See the mouth moving no words
Seeing but no hearing
Are the birds chirping?
I cannot hear
What they say
I am,
Deaf.

Shelby Kellner, Grade 6
L Ray Appleman Elementary School, PA

Tarpon Springs

A tarpon
jumping out
of the water
splashing
splashing
splashing
the sun was setting
the wind was blowing
there wasn't
a cloud
in sight
my arms
were breaking
I thought
I'm too excited
will the
tarpon break free?
Gavin McLay, Grade 4
Grace Lutheran School, FL

Gone

Monday, Tuesday, Wednesday
all the way to Friday
My heart beats.
Faster
Faster
My tears wander down my face
Harder
Harder
I am a waterfall

Then Friday at noon
My dad shows up at the house
I dart toward him
and hug him as tight as can be

Why does he have to go?
I love him
and always will

Then it repeats.

Monday, Tuesday, Wednesday
all the way to Friday.
Rachel Morrison, Grade 4
Garrison Jones Elementary School, FL

What Is Autism?

My brother
A terrible disease
A war
A connection
A family
Life!
Autism, the battle that never ends.
Allison Sherman, Grade 6
Arthur I Meyer Jewish Academy, FL

Death

Nobody wants to hear it
And it is very sad
Sometimes you can predict it
But sometimes it just happens.

It can be violent,
But can also be peaceful
It can break a family apart
In just one second.

It is the worst thing in life
But it happens to everyone in their time
A heart is always broken
When this dreadful thing happens.
Corey Doughten, Grade 6
Avon Grove Intermediate School, PA

Life's End

My life is at end
It sit here in curled crocus flowers
All drowned by the weeping of tears
It is black that surround
On the inside and out
I shall go to the stars
Where a golden gate stands
In the sky's hands.
Kodie Chontos, Grade 4
PS 10, NY

The Race Horse

Rush of the thundering hooves
Pounding the sandy track
The run to get to the winner's circle.
Who will it be?
The bay?
The black?
Or the one beyond them?
The gray?
The chestnut?
We may never know.
Swift as an eagle
Running with the wind
Horse and jockey work as one.
They run
rain or shine,
mud or dust.
They are
speedy as a bullet
THE RACE HORSE.
Emma McDonald, Grade 6
New Garden Friends School, NC

My Cats Licorice and Morgan

Happy kitty, he's a treat
Happy kitty loves to eat
Licking pretty fur so neat,
Happy kitty! He's a treat!
Pouncing on foreign objects so high,
Licorice is nocturnal and never shy!

Now comes Morgan
Who's a bit shorter.
She walks down low
And her tail is like a flag
Pointing where she wants to go.

Together they are a tribe of two
Always happy and never blue.
They give me a friendly greeting,
And then we have a furry meeting.
Alistair Liptak, Grade 5
Melville School, RI

The Great Game

It is an incredible basketball game
The Cavaliers against the Lakers
The game starts the Cavaliers
Are under control the 1st ends
The second quarter is now underway
The Cavaliers are winning 31 to 11
The Cavaliers are playing incredible
James with lay-up after lay-up
The second quarter ends 61 to 21
The third quarter has now begun
The Cavaliers are not playing well
The Lakers are playing amazing
They want to get back from the
Huge deficit that they're in
The fourth has begun the Lakers still fighting
Kobe Bryant with three after three
Two minutes left 94 to 103
Kobe Bryant knocks down the three 97 to 103
The Cavs don't score Kobe hits another three
Kolbe with the last shot full court swish!!!

Tom Gagola, Grade 6
St Stephen's School, NY

Summer

Everyone likes to be outside.
They like the ocean with a tide.
Swish, swoosh, SPLASH.

Everyone likes to be cool.
So they jump into a pool.
Ooh, ah, KAPLOOSH.

Katrina Lundquist, Grade 5
Our Lady of Grace Elementary School, PA

Ermines

White in the winter,
Brown in the summer.
Where they live,
I sure do wonder.
Norway, Sweden, the Soviet Union;
There you will find them; the sweet fine ermine
They weasel, they walk.
They don't really talk.
I keep watching the clock 'til my mommy comes back,
With my sweet, fine ermine.

Rachael Champion, Grade 4
Pike Creek Christian School, DE

Comparing Things

A book is like an adventure in between covers;
A cloud is like a poodle;
A bird is like a happy little sunbeam;
A baby is like the sun coming out after a heavy rain;
A kitten is like a small creature inside a bundle of fluff.

Tamara Lehew, Grade 5
Claysville Elementary School, PA

Summer

The trees are green, so is the grass.
Winter and spring have come to pass.
Fishing for cod, some trout, and bass.

Hot dogs, and burgers on the grill.
Rolling down a grassy hill,
I love summer, it's such a thrill.

Swimming in the sea, playing on the sand.
Walking around, everyone is so tanned.
Spending more time in water than on land.

Corinne Lumadue, Grade 5
Our Lady of Grace Elementary School, PA

roller coasters

over the electric steel rails
through the dark man made tunnels
into the breeze rushing through my hair
in front of a man yelling wildly like a little girl
past the tiny people on the ground
between the seat and the bar holding you tight
beside my sister as white as the clouds
underneath the blue ceiling
above the thin air
toward the people waiting to feel my feelings

Ashley Malloy, Grade 6
Berry Middle School, AL

I Will Not Forgot Him

Looking into his eyes from my heart
Feeling a cold shiny tear running down my face
Looking at me so proud, brightening my day
Smiling goodbye and putting his head down

Looking up
Calling for him
He answers weakly
Blowing him a kiss
Falling into a puddle of sadness
Another cold shiny tear running
So sadly down my face
Hearing his voice for the last time
Slowly fading away
Wanting him to be with me forever

One last sad shiny tear running down my face
Tasting all the happy memories
All the laughs
Remembering him from my heart
So fragile, so old
My uncle
Will he come back to me?

Haylee Kantor, Grade 4
Goshen Elementary School at Hillcrest, KY

Black

What does the color black mean?
At night it is always seen.
If your world is empty,
You are looking at that lifeless screen.
Breana Avila, Grade 4
Princeton Elementary School, ME

An Ode to Flowers

An ode to flowers
They grow in tall towers
They spring up in France

The winds make them sway
They bloom every day
But they get a lot of ants

They all have pollen grains
That wash away when it rains
And across them all butterflies dance
Jamie Moulton, Grade 6
Captain Nathan Hale Middle School, CT

Monkey

In the rain forest,
A monkey swings in a tree,
On a summer night.
Hunter Battista, Grade 4
Public School 207 Rockwood Park, NY

Sunrise Sunset

From sunrise to sunset
I wait in my boat
For the fish
To come afloat

From sunrise to sunset
I read my book
Waiting for a fish
To catch my hook

From sunrise to sunset
I eat my lunch
Waiting for the fish
To take a munch

From sunrise to sunset
I wait with my fishing gear
For the fish
To come near

From sunrise to sunset
I will wait all day
For the fish
In this little blue bay
Liora Bernstein, Grade 6
Arthur I Meyer Jewish Academy, FL

Too Sick for Words

My legs are aching they feel uneasy,
My stomach hurts and I feel wheezy.
My eyes are so worked out they just might pop,
I'm so tired I just might drop.

I'm so tired, but I can't go to sleep,
Not even if my baby brother doesn't make a peep.
I can hear the TV, it's up way too loud,
But all my ears hear is an annoying pound.

The pillow that my head is on is just not enough,
And a trip to the couch would knock the air out of me with a "puff."

I know you're tired, and so am I,
But in my room I just might fry.
So before I wrinkle and dry away,
Will you take me to the doctor today?

Amy Daniels, Grade 6
Winfield Middle School, WV

What the Third Eye Sees

The Third eye sees me biting my nails when my mom isn't looking.
The Third eye sees me reading past lights out.
The Third eye sees me eating candy when I'm not supposed to.
The Third eye sees Dad eating all my chocolate at night.
The Third eye sees my classmate talking to her pencils.
The Third eye sees me sticking up for my friend.
The Third eye sees all.

Roman Latulippe, Grade 6
Hudson Memorial School, NH

Softball

The nervous yet anxious feeling in your stomach.
You're up to bat.
Holding your green cyclone metal bat.
Waiting for the ball.
The pitcher throws.
One strike, says the umpire.
The next ball comes to me, and I hit a grounder to third base.
I run with all my might and power.
I was safe.
The next batter hits.
I am on second.
The next batter is up.
I steal a base. I am at third.
The batter hits. I run fast.
I went home!
My team was ecstatic; they were screaming and had joyful faces.
I was excited and couldn't believe it.
It was the last inning for the other team.
Another teammate and I got two girls out. Two balls to two strikes.
Our pitcher threw, and the batter was out.
We won the game!
Gabriella Congi, Grade 6
St Stephen's School, NY

Wrestling vs Soccer

There are kids wrestling other kids
And getting pinned
And in soccer kids are kicking
The ball into a goal like a bin

There is a sweet smell in the air
Along with the smell of the mat
In soccer you smell the spring air
Moving fastly past you like a gnat
You can taste the rubbery mouth guards
Sitting in your mouth like a sleeping bat
While in soccer you can taste
The concession stand hot dogs
That are as tasty as a fasnaught

You hear people getting smacked into mats
While in soccer you can hear
The loud kick of the ball
You feel the cushiony mat that is also hard
In soccer there is soft grass

Kraig Freeman, Grade 6
Bendersville Elementary School, PA

I Am

I am
Nice, Funny, Caring
I care a lot about happiness.
Friendship is important to me.
Enjoyment is important to me.
To me life is very important.
Being yourself is the best thing you can be.
You shouldn't be rude because you won't have friends
And you should be nice and kind.
I stand up for myself and others, too.
I like to enjoy life and make the most of it.
I wish some people would be more caring.
I am

Kyli Hermick, Grade 6
Freedom Area Middle School, PA

The Game

Football is like sunshine on a rainy day.
I love to watch it, even when I have to pay.

If it's on TV it doesn't cost money
THAT really makes my day sunny!

Runners move as fast as lightning.
A really bad hit can be frightening.

Football is leather and lace dreams.
I love to hear the crowd when it screams!

Mac Anderson, Grade 4
Edwards Elementary School, SC

Race

It was the day of the race,
I was slow and felt like a disgrace.
There was my sister to cheer,
But my heart was beating so fast I could not hear.
I was standing in line waiting for my turn.
Being so nervous my stomach started to churn.
Then it was my time to run,
The guy I had to beat I lost to before this wouldn't be fun.
But my gym teacher raised his hand and put it down.
I could hear my feet pounding the ground.
I saw my sister cheering with her friends all around.
But it wasn't quite a race but a 100 yard dash,
When I ran it last year I got a big rash.
I tried to pace myself but could not,
Now I was sweaty and hot.
Then we came close to the finish line,
If I really ran the results would be fine.
But I started to lag,
It was really a drag.
Then we crossed the finish line we were done.
Even though I lost I guess the race had been a little fun.

Kenison Garratt, Grade 6
Salem Middle School, NC

A Mystery

Nature is a mystery
I'll never know what's next
Rain, snow, wind, and sun
Anything can happen

Nature can be a good thing
Can even bring something bad
Either way I can't control
The mystery of nature

Hurricanes, tornadoes
Are things nature will bring
Good or bad
I can't control

The mystery of nature

Angie Giang, Grade 6
E T Richardson Middle School, PA

Sammy, Sammy, You Were a Great Dog

Sammy you were a great dog,
And I loved you.
You were very obedient,
And you had good manners, for a dog.

I remember that day,
When you were very tired,
You would lie on top of your coop,
Like king of the world.

Matt Miller, Grade 6
Lake Noxen Elementary School, PA

Soccer

It is green
grass all over it
and it has a goal
with a center field.
There is a goal box.
There is a right
and left wing
and center field.
There were lots
of fans
cheering for the player.
The cars on the road
they were beeping
their horns
at the people to move
if the light was
green
green
green.

Calie Allwardt, Grade 4
Grace Lutheran School, FL

Taysha

Taysha is a girl
Likes to listen to Linkin' Park
She likes the sound of music
Likes to stay in the dark

Taysha Perez, Grade 6
Normandin Middle School, MA

My Backpack

Have you looked in my backpack,
It's as big as Santa's sack!

There's notebooks,
Footballs,
Letters,
And more.

My bag is so heavy,
I dropped to the floor!

I can't get up,
I need some help…
There's that lotion for my scalp!

There's pencils,
Flies,
And homework passes.

But, don't forget,
My backpack's all mine!

Sarah Meleski, Grade 6
Freetown-Lakeville Middle School, MA

Revenge

Revenge is a mean girl
Who yells all day,
She has been hurt
Her memories won't fade away

She won't stop screaming
She won't be ignored
She doesn't have a button
There is no cord

She will get you in trouble
She will make you regret
You want her to go away
But she's not done yet

Now you're in the deal
They say you are wrong
She's the one to blame
But she's already gone…

Tyana Morris, Grade 6
Newport Middle School, NC

Fly

I wish I could fly
High in the sky
Above the trees
Farther than the bees
Farther, farther, farther
Faster I fly into the blue
Waiting for my wish to come true.

Courtney Brown, Grade 4
H Austin Snyder Elementary School, PA

Bloom

Drip, drip, drip
Black as night
how does it bloom
full and un-grown.
the dew slips and slides
and makes the flower
shimmer in the rain
then the sun comes out
and the flower blooms.

Cassidy Hall, Grade 6
Canterbury School, FL

A Cat

I had a cat that was crazy
His favorite toy was a daisy
He got so fat
He stayed on a mat
And that's how he became so lazy

Justin Zulueta, Grade 6
Normandin Middle School, MA

What Is Love?*

Love is like a rainbow
It's everywhere we go
The smell of fresh cookies
Coming straight out of the oven
The peaceful sound
Of a waterfall
The tenderness in my heart
A warm fire
A nice big hug
From your parents
It's a nice hot
Cup of hot chocolate
What is love to you?

Talaysia Pettiford, Grade 4
Youngsville Elementary School, NC
*Inspired by John Denver's,
"Perhaps Love…"

Dog and Cat

Dog
Hairy, clever
Helping, playing, barking
Bone, squeaky toy, mouse, claws
Resting, jumping, chasing
Lazy, scary
Cat

William Hoo, Grade 6
St Agatha School, NY

Landing

Click!

Snapping my helmet on tight.
I grip the handle bars.
Getting ready for the action
That is about to happen.

First, I go down, then up
Then down, up, down, up
Then I quickly jump off.

Next, pedaling as fast as lightning,
I ride to the big ramp.
Getting ready to fly.

I jump off the ramp.
Feeling the cool wind
Try to push me back.

Spinning the handlebars…1, 2, 3
Caught the handlebars.
Sticks the landing.

Daniel Hua, Grade 5
Abraham Pierson School, CT

John Deere Green

The city folk called it a redneck machine,
But I just called it John Deere Green.

It was a 4455
Bad to the bone;
And man that paint job,
How it shone!

I painted that hood as green as I could;
And boy did it ever look good!

I shined it up and took it to a show,
Just to see how much it'd tow.
40,000 pounds is what they said,
When they took it back to the shed.

I've plowed so many fields;
And measured lots and lots of yields,
But I only could've done it,
With John Deere Green.

My old tractor's gone now;
It'll never again hook to a plow.
I sure do miss that green hot rod,
It ran so well through them dang mud clods.

Hadley Hutchison, Grade 6
Jackson Christian School, TN

Beach

For its only sunshine lie down on you
Its gentle winds quickly passing through
What was gentle is now waves crashing
Then you quickly go dashing
The sand gushing up between your toes
The smell of fresh cooked food wafts up your nose
But there's terrible danger near
No one knows but they will soon be in fear
The sand stings your face
Still moving at a fast pace
There is a spiraling storm close behind me
For that is the only thing I can see
It's now or never
I pull a lever
A door shoots open
Just keep on hoping

Regan Cook, Grade 5
Avon Grove Intermediate School, PA

Spring

Flowers showing buds colorful and bright
Animals awaking from a long sleep
Green grass reaching up out of the melting snow
Plants growing new leaves
Spring has come

Peter Marzo, Grade 6
Kelly Lane Intermediate School, CT

What Is Summer?

Children drawing on sidewalks,
Baseball fans cheering on their teams,
Vacations and trips to new places,
Little girls playing double-dutch in the streets,
Hotter and hotter weekends,
Sleepover after sleepover,
New friends and new memories,
Blue birds singing new songs,
Daisies sprouting everywhere,
Beaches overflowing,

That is summer.

Emily Smothers, Grade 4
Meadow Park Elementary School, FL

The Thunder Dance

The thunder and lightning love to dance
A walk and a strut and a leap and prance
The lightning flashes as the thunder sings
I go outside and dance along
Then I start to sing a song
When it is raining the harmony starts
The lightning flashes across the sky
As a shooting star starts to fly
The thunder claps and it is done
Although it is just fine
I had wished upon a star
For another thunder dance of mine

Camerin Zell, Grade 5
Sippican School, MA

Flying Through Space and Time

I'm flying through space and time.
Seeing everything that happened and is still to come.
The Mesozoic era, and 3265!
I know if dragons are real.
I know if we colonize other planets.
I know if global warming takes over,
If we even survive!
But I'm not telling.
There's no way I'm telling.
I saw King Arthur's death.
I saw when the planet was created.
It was amazing.
Imagine the 4th of July times 1,000.
Millions of multicolored stars,
Shooting all over the place.
I know who planned the murder of Lincoln,
But I'm not telling.
The future would be unraveled.
Bad things would happen if I did that.
I'm flying through space and time.

Augie Bottorf, Grade 4
The Lee Academy, MA

The Unforgotten

So little time, life to thrive for, say goodbye to the condemned
Unfulfilled destiny to be here in the perpetual future,
To find life they lived for death they die for and people they fight for.

Still here in our lives, in our hearts, still waiting, longing for us,
Us longing for them, to find the benefit, of life and death.
We knew them well, loved them as far as love can bring us,
They help us, define life, knowing what to say taking care of my hopes and dreams

Nurturing my every thought, eliminating the word "can't"
Wrapping me in a blanket of can, putting me down nestled in safety.
Letting me know they love me, wherever they are, I'll cherish them forever.
Cancer, diabetes, and old age can break a spirit, kill a dream, lose a life.
To those who know this pain, this road, this path know never to forget the fallen
Who cross the bridge, of life to be above us and below.

Bang! A gunshot to the other world. BEEP, BEEP the sound to the light
Vroom, crash! The fall of a lost life, all fall to whoever they love.
But none can escape their fate, to rise into blankness
The tears that are shed, for those who died, who walk among us as ghosts, but are still people.
The red blood shed, the cold hands, gray, pulse less, lifeless, nothing, but everything.
The coffin going down, down, down into the ground, the people we love.
The people who still wander in my head, the people who are gone but still in my heart.
My grandparents.

Austin Dalli, Grade 6
Nesaquake Middle School, NY

Where I'm From

I'm from Snowball from Jake to Sandy to Zorro to Leo
From Garfield to Batman
From PS1 to PS2 to PS3 to PSP

From football to basketball to baseball to track to dirt bikes to racing cars
From tree house to garage
From playing with my dog

From my great-great grandpa's wallet to my grandma's quilt
to my great-great-great cousins trophies to my great-great grandpa's hat to my grandma's best cup.

From my cousin Shelby to cousin Mackenzie to Aunt Stacy to great grandpa to grandma to pawpaw to nana

From "it is a hard life" to "life is not fair life stinks" to I killed my first deer
to I saw my first tiger to I went to my first zoo

From I went to Holiday World my first time to Virginia Beach to Ohio zoo with my pets to Six Flags

Mickey Heaton, Grade 6
Meredith-Dunn School, KY

My Dove

We both, staring, watching, waiting under the ancient peach tree.
I sat below, stopping my quiet reading to peer up at it.
While the dove, perched on the branch, knowingly looked at me.
I sat, amazed as the bird knocked down a peach, for anyone, for me.
As I began to bite in, the dove took off and a pure white feather floated gently to the ground.

Anna Talley, Grade 6
Chickahominy Middle School, VA

Space Dreams

We're going into space, we're gonna see the stars,
Once we are up, we're gonna go to Mars.

Then we'll fly to the sun,
It will be a lot of fun.
This ship we're on is kinda cool,
It even has a swimming pool.

What is that weird beeping sound,
Inside the pool?
Wake Up! Wake Up!
It is time for school.

Joshua Shealy, Grade 5
Fleming Island Elementary School, FL

Super Dreams for Super People!

I wish I had super powers
To fly high like a bird in the sky,
And saying, "Hi," to airplane passengers that pass by.
I wish!

I wish I had super powers
Lifting buildings as I please,
But watch out when I sneeze!
I wish!

I wish I had super powers
Reading minds when I want to have fun,
And deciding when to say, "I'm done."
I wish!

David Saran, Grade 6
Wyman Elementary School, RI

The Soccer Shot

When you walk on the field
you smell the freshly cut grass.
You're in starting position like a
rocket ready to lift off.
Then you hear the whistle blow.

Your opponents as fierce as tigers
running towards you.
You move left and right.
Suddenly you crave the cold,
refreshing taste of water.
Finally you push the ball forward,
and kick it hard.

The ball screams from the power
of your foot. SWOOSH!
Feel the excitement of the crowd
and realize you had shot the goal.

Danielle Akinyemi, Grade 5
Foxborough Regional Charter School, MA

Sticky Buns

Sticky buns I get at Christmas.
Yummy, yummy sticky ovals
Swirly, cinnamon brown and white
I hear it crackling in the oven all the time.
Sweet! Sweet!
Sticky bun! Sticky bun! Sticky buns!
Delicious, gooey sticky buns.
Hot, mushy, very sugary, too!
Sticky buns I get at Christmas.
Yummy! Yummy! Yum!

Abbie Reed, Grade 4
Watsontown Elementary School, PA

If I Could Fly

If I could fly
I would soar
above the clouds
and
above the heavens.
I would meet the rainbow bird
I would fly down through
the sky's cotton with him.
We'd sail in outer space,
then we'd shoot back down
with the north wind in our hair.
We'd touch the moon
then touch the sun.
We'd bounce off the stars
having so much fun.
If I could fly.

Aaron Butler, Grade 4
South Area Solomon Schechter Day School, MA

Green

Green is watermelon being eaten
Green is a shoe torn in the dirt
Green is a happy color
Green is a bug being squished
Green smells like fresh air
Green tastes like apples
Green sounds like grass swaying in the breeze
Green looks like dirty water
Green feels like your hand in goo
Green makes me feel like I'm sick
Green is a tree falling down

Joshua Trecannelli, Grade 4
Lincoln Elementary School, PA

Summer

The pitter patter of the rain taps on the ground
Sunlight pours through the clouds
Buds spring from underground
Bees buzz birds chirp
Chipmunks scurry

Kailey Casassa, Grade 6
Kelly Lane Intermediate School, CT

Erutan

Green trees blowing in the wind
Bluebirds sweetly chirping
To their babies, rabbits tend
Sound of brown worms slurping.

Bugs flying all around
Yellow flowers blooming
More bugs crawling on the ground
Bees buzzing and zooming.

Grasshoppers jumping into the air
A beautiful clear sky
Squirrels storing their nuts with care
Black falcons soaring high

Fish splashing in crystal blue water
Locusts making sweet noise
Climate slowly becoming hotter
Red birds with perfect poise

Ashley Russell, Grade 6
Blue Ridge Middle School, VA

Lightning Striking

Fast as a wink
In a fiery pink
Shoots a thundering,
Blundering
Lightning striking

From the high
Of the sky
To the mirth
Of the earth
Jets a shackling,
Crackling
Lightning striking

Down to the ground
With a boom-booming sound
Ends the snap-snapping,
Clap-clapping
Lightning striking

I wave farewell

Megan Schaller, Grade 6
The Bryn Mawr School, MD

Tomato

The tomato
Popped out of the ground
Then plopped down
Onto my burger.

Ben Lynch, Grade 6
Holmes Middle School, NC

Tornadoes

Tornadoes spin round and round
Destroying everything on the ground.
Destroying everything you love
Starting from the clouds above.
Once it's gone with only a little gust
Leaving nothing but a lot of dust.

Cole Trout, Grade 4
Bethesda Christian Academy, NC

Now Is Spring

This is time for beautiful weather
Spring is finally here
Time to go outside together
Time to have fun, play, and cheer

Brennan O'Brien, Grade 4
Ridgeway Elementary School, MD

Red

Red is the color of Mars
And fire engine red cars

A ripe cherry
And a strawberry

A tomato
And the reddish skin of a potato

A grape on a vine
And a hexagon shaped sign

A new red dress at the mall
And leaves in the fall

When you see red you feel excited
Red is the color of a fire just lighted

When you see red it may give you a fright
Like firelight in the dead of night

Red is all sorts of wonderful things
And what explosive joy it brings.

Jordyn Arakelian, Grade 4
Annie L Sargent School, MA

Baseball/Football

Baseball
Round, bumpy
Batting, pitching, catching
Spring, feet, yards, autumn
Tackling, sacking, sprinting
Rectangle, rough
Football

Kyle Scanlan, Grade 6
Juliet W Long School, CT

Fish and Chips

Fish and chips.
I'll wrap my lips around
Fish and chips.
Add a little lemon,
And some salt and pepper.
A little bit of ketchup,
And some tartar sauce.
Put the chips on the side.
Put it in the basket.
Hand it to me.
Squirt a little lemon on top,
And it is ready to eat.

Blake Bomboy, Grade 4
Watsontown Elementary School, PA

Snow!

Barefoot feet run across the cold floor
to the window near the door.
Small snowflakes that are
sure to stick, fall all over the yard.
Snowshoes, long pants, and
coats are thrown on in
the rush to get outside.
Little hands and noses
complain that it is too cold.
Mom makes hot chocolate
that fills me up with warmth.

Julia Graham, Grade 6
E T Richardson Middle School, PA

A Falcon

A falcon, a falcon
But on whom shall I snack on.
Maybe two mice
Or something nice.

A falcon, a falcon
With wings like horizon.
Flies through the air
Spotting children that are scared.

Matthew Sanders, Grade 4
Pike Creek Christian School, DE

Softball

S lamming softballs all day long
O utrageously nerve-racking
F earless of anything that is in your way
T houghtless of anyone else
B elieving that you can make it home
A lways aware of where the ball might be
L ittle time to go before you are safe
L ittle time for you to pace

Rosie Cochran, Grade 5
Princeton Elementary School, ME

Singing Is My Life!

I have an instrument with me,
no matter where I go,
whether it's my voice, or I have band that day,
I won't give up singing, no matter what you say.
You will always hear my singing,
it's my instrument of choice,
if you ask me, I will always choose my voice.
I will always use it,
I will never abuse,
because singing is my life!

Maiya Swan, Grade 6
Discovery School @ Reeves Rogers, TN

The Beautiful Garden

A wooden path leads to a garden of green.
Trees, ponds, and swamps created this scene.
I opened my eyes amazed by what I saw.
I looked around and stood there in awe.
A tree caught my eye as soon as we arrived.
It was struck by lightning and survived.
I tried to look up but could not see the sky.
The trees were like rooftops way up high.
There was a ray of sun peeking through the trees.
This shining light put my mind at ease.
No matter where I turned all I saw was green.
The arms of the tree were long and lean.
The cinnamon smell of spice bush filled the air.
I noticed it right when we got there.
The sudden smell of skunk cabbage filled my head.
This leaf smelled like fresh baked garlic bread.
A pond was covered in a blanket of moss.
There was a bridge that we walked across.
Nature is something that can brighten your day,
So don't ever let it slip away.

Alessandra Phelan, Grade 6
East Shore Middle School, CT

My Sister

My sister,
is my guardian angel.
She has a special way of making me feel like a star.
She knows my deepest secrets.
Clarissa lifts me up into the clouds,
until I am soaring on my own.
She is my guardian angel.

How can she be so kind
when I blow her out of her mind?
She almost never speaks with harsh words,
although she can be quite stern.
She has a special light that shines with all its might and glory.
It glows above the crowd.
It soars in all the clouds.
She is my guardian angel.

Hannah Capers, Grade 6
Gulfview Middle School, FL

Dancing in the Rain

Dancing in the rain
Prancing in the moonlight
In the dark night
Every dew drop splashes on the grass
Hoping the sun won't flash
You can hear the thunder clap
While the water taps
With every step you take you feel like your walking on water
As if it feels like the rain drops are talking to you
A great light gives me a clue that the sun will be up soon
I can see the sight of the sun
The rain has stopped pouring
And the rainbow is soaring across the sky
My, how I wish I could dance in the rain again

Celina Viravouth, Grade 6
Discovery School @ Reeves Rogers, TN

Fight of the Nightmares

O'er your house and into your head,
March the monsters from under your the bed.
Once again they come to your room
To show you all the fates of doom.
"Cease" you say, "you're scaring me!"
"Then we'll keep on scaring thee!"
You glance around as fast as can be,
Searching for the point or key.
But never ever look under your bed.
For what you will see you will dread.
To fight these monsters you need a foe.
Good things, good things let it be great.
Let these bad ones have their fate.
Then you hear a moan and spin around to see
That all your monsters have paid a large fee.
They were disappearing in the mist of day
And you hollered: "Yes! Hooray!"
Your mom wakes up and says, "Go to sleep."
And so you oblige without a peep…

Schuyler Firestone, Grade 5
Home School, NY

The Beach

The warm baked sand beneath my feet,
the sparkling glare from the ocean.
Children splashing in the water,
and the chirping from the birds above.
Sandcastles along the shore,
and the crunching shells when I walk.

Tiny bait fish nibbling at my toes,
and baby crabs scampering across the sand.
The ocean mist in my face,
there's no place better than the beach.

Ryan Walz, Grade 6
Gulfview Middle School, FL

Scooby-Doo

Scooby-Doo
Shaggy always finds you
eating a Scooby snack
and devouring the whole pack.

Bryan Hanks, Grade 6
Bedford Middle School, PA

Champ

Hyper, cute
Playing, running, cuddling
Loves to see me!
Boston Terrier

Alexandra Culberson, Grade 4
Glenwood Elementary School, MA

Imagination

The sun slips
Through the clouds
The wind gets slow,
And warm
The grass shimmers
And tumbles
In a sun awning
And then
I step, and...
Splash!
The sun and wind
Flow away
I shiver as a wind
Tickles my arm
My clothes dampen
And I hurry
Through the rain.

Anna Moore, Grade 5
Hamagrael Elementary School, NY

I Wish You Were Here

I wish you were here
With me now
To see what has changed
And to see what hasn't
I know you can't
But I wish you could
Because I miss you so dearly

I know that you are in a better place
But I wish you were here
To yell at me
When I do something wrong
I wish you were here to cheer me on
When I'm scared and have no one there
I wish you were here so I could say
That I love you
And I wish I never lost you

Akhila Kurian, Grade 6
E T Richardson Middle School, PA

Dreams

Sometimes it seems we'll touch that dream but things come slow, or not at all.
The ones on top may not come true, but don't give up.
Tomorrow your seeds will grow.

Sayvon Harris, Grade 5
Southern Pines Elementary School, NC

Red

Red reminds me of school.
It is warm not cool.

The color red tastes like church wine.
Red doesn't make me feel fine.

The red on our country's flag stands for our soldiers' lost blood.
A tale of truth is Red Riding Hood.

Red, juicy strawberries in summertime.
A sunburn that doesn't feel so divine.

When I see Cardinals I think of red.
It's a color I do not dread.

I see red five times a week.
Red is not the color for a sneak.

I love the feel of red Chinese silk.
You can find red on a carton of milk.

Freedom's colors are white and red.
Look at all the red I've said.

Kelley Pfeiffer, Grade 6
Freedom Area Middle School, PA

Saluting America

Dear Soldiers,
It was twilight in spring and you could hear the guns firing.
You could smell the blue ocean.
You could see the stars you got on your hat.
Even though it was hot and dry, that did not stop him from saluting the general
With green pants, blue eyes, brown hat, and red badges.
I am extremely happy that we are winning the war!
Thank you for defending our country!

Craig Krebbeks, Grade 4
Honeoye Falls-Lima Manor School, NY

Blue

Blue is the sky, friends of the clouds
Blue is the sea in the evening
Blue is the wind, people just don't know it
Blue is jazz a feeling of rhythm
Blue is a gloomy feeling that overcomes most poets, most people
Blue is a favorite color liked by many people
Blue is a crystal or a diamond ready bought

Devonté Francis, Grade 5
Speas Elementary School, NC

Our Young World

Every day is a good day
On our planet Earth
We see through our day and are happy
Because of our Earth

We all smile and say hello
To everyone we see
We talk and chat
From you to me

We all also let
The animals lead their life
We all will watch as birds will sing
Their songs about life

The Earth will soon start to turn
From day to night
We all will go straight back home
And enjoy our light

The time will come
When all of us say good night
And tomorrow we will wake up again
To a young world fresh and bright

Shivani Ramesh, Grade 5
Countryside Montessori Elementary School, FL

The Race of Owl, Gecko, and Snake

Owl, Gecko, and Snake look for a mouse.
Owl flies above the morass.
Gecko crawls on the smooth grass, towards the house;
he moves as fast as a young lass.

Moving along without any legs,
Snake makes his way across the ground.
Seeing a bird laying her eggs,
Owl suddenly swoops and wakes a hound.

Something's following Gecko, into the hay;
turns out it's a cat that sounds like hail.
Snake sees some corn, but veered away,
remembering the encounter in the dale.

Farmer thinks Owl is a dummy with a small head.
Owl decided to go it alone;
he spotted a barn and headed for it instead,
hoping to find a mouse on his own.

Snake hears some snickering from a grouse,
forgetting the race, he turns to eat that.
Reaching the house, Gecko finds the mouse,
he has a feast 'til he heard the cat.

Adam Antonini, Grade 6
East Shore Middle School, CT

Green

I taste crisp lettuce for a healthy body
I smell freshly cut grass in the air
I hear the sound of leaves holding on so tight to their trees,
Trying so hard not to be blown away by the wind in the storm
I feel all the clovers at my feet, tickling my toes
I see people recycling to keep the Earth clean
Now, that's green

Kassie Rimel, Grade 4
Spartanburg Jr Writing Project, SC

War

Walking down the street,
It's like a big war.
I stare at people, they look bizarre.
Wear your armor.
Grab your sword.
Because we have something big in store.
By the end of the street you'll be dead,
With lots of blood that was shed.
I can admit I am weak,
And you laugh at everything I have to speak.
But I won't go down without a fight,
I'll keep going till nothing's in sight.

Alyah Scott, Grade 6
Gulfview Middle School, FL

Dreaming

Soaring higher and higher
Flying with the birds, flying through the clouds
The feeling of being weightless rushes through my body
Wait, we're somewhere new now
Bright lights and loud people
I feel overpowered and I want to go somewhere new
Too much bustling around
I'm in the countryside with mooing cows and open fields.
I like this feeling but, it's too boring for me
I prefer flying seeing the world from afar.
The possibilities are endless, when you're dreaming.
I like dreaming the best in the night.

Kiersten Guy, Grade 6
Avon Grove Intermediate School, PA

Blue

Blue is the bright sky
Blue is the splashing sea
Blue is a light T-shirt
Blue is dark jeans
Blue smells like fresh picked blueberries
Blue tastes like cold refreshing water
Blue sounds like crashing waves
Blue looks like the top of a beautiful whale
Blue feels like a rough spinning globe
Blue makes me feel cooled down
Blue is my favorite color

Janet Rodriguez, Grade 4
Lincoln Elementary School, PA

Books

Take a good look,
inside a book.

The book might make you feel sad,
or it might make you feel glad.

The story might be really good,
like the book of "Red Riding Hood."

You might want a book of mystery,
or a good old book of history.

You can read the book of poems,
you can read the book at home.

Maybe you'll want a book that's funny,
maybe even on a day that is sunny.

A book is a great thing,
as good as a diamond ring.

Now, sit down and read a good book,
maybe a book about how to cook!
Sandra Zhao, Grade 4
Nelson Place Elementary School, MA

Seasons

Autumn
Chilly, colorful
Drifting, changing, hiding
Leaves, winds, warmth, creatures
Awakening, blossoming, venturing
Radiant, flawless
Spring
Faith Farina, Grade 5
Tucker School, AR

Soldier

Soldier
resolute, gung-ho
serving, fighting, saluting
in a foreign land
survivor!
Jerred Oney, Grade 4
Waynesburg Elementary School, KY

Lions

Lions
Very dangerous
Killing their prey
Furry, scary, giant, vicious
Majestic
Salvatore Rainone, Grade 4
Public School 207 Rockwood Park, NY

Paul the Ball

There once was a ball named Paul
He loved to roll down the hall
He was black and white
He could not fight
He was a soccer ball
Riley Schmitt, Grade 5
Tucker School, AR

The Bird Hound

My dog is a bird hound,
We got him at the pound,
How many birds he had killed,
Had me quite thrilled.

He likes to play,
And run all day,
He plays with peoples laces,
Which puts smiles on their faces.

He eats a lot,
From a pot,
When I give him a bath,
He always makes me laugh.

He went on the boat,
And got on the float,
He chased a cat up a tree,
Which made me hurt my knee.
Branden Ranoull, Grade 4
Harmony Community School, FL

Black and White

Black
Dark, dull
Scaring, creeping, trapping
Scary, dreary, shiny, blank
Comforting, gleaming, shining
Light, bright
White
Sean Nemes, Grade 4
Pike Creek Christian School, DE

I Will Always Care

Nature, I will always care.
The flowers, the trees
I will always care.
The animals, the birds,
I will always care.
The waters, the land
I will always care.
The green grass
I will always care…
Lindsay Brodeur, Grade 6
Kelly Lane Intermediate School, CT

Summer

S un beaming on your skin
U nder the water we swim
M ust try to not get burned
M issing friends from school
E very morning sleeping late
R eally enjoying vacation
Ally O'Brien, Grade 6
Kelly Lane Intermediate School, CT

I Am

I am bright and nice
I wonder why the sky is blue
I hear dinosaurs roar
I see a UFO
I want a little brother or sister
I am bright and nice

I pretend to be a queen
I feel weird about aliens
I touch a long snake
I worry about the day I will die
I am bright and nice

I understand math
I say I can be a lawyer
I dream about being a private eye
I try to get A's
I hope to grow up and be somebody
I am bright and nice
D'yanna Wallace, Grade 6
Kelly Lane Intermediate School, CT

I Am an Oceanographer

I am an oceanographer.
I wonder if I will be famous,
I hear the fish splashing,
I see stingrays,
I want to swim with the dolphins,
I pretend I touch creatures of the deep,
I am an oceanographer.

I touch sharks,
I worry that I will get hurt,
I cry when fish are harmed,
I am an oceanographer.

I understand not to throw trash in water,
I say I am an oceanographer,
I dream to swim with sharks,
I try to be safe,
I hope I keep fish safe,
I am an oceanographer.
Courtney Moran, Grade 4
Meadow Park Elementary School, FL

The Lonely Puppy

I see a puppy that is hungry
He is dirty and alone

I hear him cry for food
I hear him cry for a chance to have a family

I touch the soft golden fur of the puppy's back
I touch the dirt on his head that has stained the sunny glow

I smell a horrible wet dog smell
That won't go away

He tastes the dog food in my hand
He eats 'til I have no more food

Kerry Burstein, Grade 6
Suffern Middle School, NY

Blue Bird

The snow sleeps
Piled gently on the ground
A snowflake makes its way to where it shall be bound

Through the frozen sky
A sight that caught your eye
The blue bird perched on a tree
Where it wasn't supposed to be.

But with more to come, an eyesore yes to some
The sky now flooding happiness
You fly out like you've become
The blue bird perched.

Brendan Hyatt, Grade 4
Weston Intermediate School, CT

Dream Follower

Every day there's a new sensation,
Every second there's a new creation.
Good things come and go.
You have to reach for the stars when it's tough,
Soar for the clouds when it's rough.
New inventions never to fail,
Though life is no fairy tale.
You have to live it to the fullest.
Even when you're down,
Try to smile and never frown.
When opportunities knock at the door,
Open it or your life may fall to the floor.
With life there's love and with love there's life.
Some people follow their dreams,
Some people make up schemes.
I'm a dream follower and proud to be one,
Doing that can be lots of fun.
Do what you can to make your dreams come true,
Then life will be a pleasure for me and you.

Ella Denney, Grade 6
Discovery School @ Reeves Rogers, TN

I Don't Understand

I don't understand…
    Why the grass is so green,
The sun is so hot,
    The sky is so blue,
The snow is so cold,
    The dinosaurs are extinct,
Or why flamingos are pink.

But most of all…
    I don't understand why people are so different,
Or why the Earth is round,
    Or why we walk on the ground,
Or why the birds chirp,
    Or why we drive on the parkway,
And park in the driveway.

What I understand most…
    Is why 2 and 2 equal 4,
And why we wear clothes,
    And why we need a nose,
And why blue and red make purple,
    And why I love the color green,
And why I am who I am.

Raylen Shannon, Grade 6
Freedom Area Middle School, PA

Are You There

Are you there when I'm sad?
When I'm happy, or when I'm mad?
Do you see every tear drop I cry?
Or every scream I yell to the sky?
Are you there when I want to cheer?
Or when the sorrowful times are near?
Are you there when I fall and I need help?
Or should I yell for someone else?
I guess the question I want to ask is,
Are you there when I'm sad?

Alexis Wright-Hicks, Grade 5
Southwood Elementary School, FL

What I Am

I am…
A purple flower that is different from the bunch
A piece of chocolate that is sweeter than the rest
A rushing waterfall that is a mix of emotions
A scared hero that must be brave to face the consequences
An eagle that flies higher than others
Wings of a plane that guide people through storms
A green rubber band that holds things together
As fierce as a tiger, but as fast as a cheetah
A silver moon that comes out only at night
These are the things that make me…me!

Meagan Crumley, Grade 6
Lakeside Middle School, GA

Elly Has an Empty Belly

There was an elephant named Elly
Who liked to fill her belly
She ate two trees
And got stung by bees
Elly will never again fill her belly

Hunter Holden, Grade 6
Linkhorne Middle School, VA

Alaska

A white world all around,
Birds making all the sound,
Polar bears walking on ice,
Little foxes run like mice,
Seals go up for air,
Baby cubs leave their lair,
Acting like they're at a fun fair.

Evan Haines, Grade 4
Naquag Elementary School, MA

Kentucky Slideshow

Kentucky is,
lightning fast Thoroughbreds
galloping around the clay track
speeding toward the finish line,
Clip-clop, clip-clop, clip-clop

Kentucky is,
hard working farmers
rising early before dawn
to get their chores finished,
moo, moo, moo.

Kentucky is,
banjos, fiddles, guitars, and mandolins
playing a high lonesome sound
echoing through the mountains,
G, C, D.

Kentucky is,
salty country ham
creamy chocolate gravy and biscuits
a glass of ice cold milk,
um, um, um.

There's no place like Kentucky!

Blake Eldridge, Grade 4
Waynesburg Elementary School, KY

Hamsters

Hamsters
Puffy, cute
Hiding, climbing, walking
I love cute hamsters
Rodents.

Jody Shuey, Grade 4
Lincoln Elementary School, PA

Ode to Tacos

Tacos, I need you
Without you I would not know the taste of goodness.
Without you my taste buds would have no flavor for anything.
Without you I would not know what I would do.
It would take forever to describe your delicious taste.
When I take a bite out of you, of that juicy meat with the combination
of the lettuce and cheese it makes me want to eat more.
When I take a bite out of you it seems like there is a fiesta in my mouth.
Tacos, you give me the reason to live.
Tacos, I need you.

Yamian Rivera Moro, Grade 5
Melville School, RI

Cereal

O *Cereal*, I need you
O *Cereal*, if I didn't have you I do not know how I would survive
O *Cereal*, you give my life meaning
O *Cereal*, every morning you make my stomach go crazy from all your tasty flavors.
O *Cereal*, you make a frown turn upside down,
You make me happy when I am sad,
You make me feel relaxed when I am stressed.

O *Cereal*, I love you

Anthony G. Mele, Grade 5
Melville School, RI

The Magic Box

I will put into the box
The bright sunrise declaring the New Year,
An abandoned spider web, dripping with raindrop dew,
And waves, splashing the shore.

I will put into the box
The texture of wet rocks in a river,
The smell of flowers in a meadow,
The song of a robin in the morning,
And the mysterious hoot of a great snowy mountain owl.

I will put into the box
The light of a fairy,
An ant colony between tree roots,
A twisted branch for me to climb on,
A bright light deep in the forest.

I will put into the box
An angel so beautiful she makes the stars look like black dirt.

My box lid is fashioned from ice, lava, and gold.
The lid is the color of shimmering water with coral hinges and wishes on the edges,
Seasons and animals on the bow and rushing water down the front.
I shall make peace in my box
And then live in a peaceful home.

Brenna Jenkins, Grade 4
Ridgecrest Elementary School, FL

Play Every Day

Siss, Boom, Bah,
the karate kids, "Hiyah!",
hear the soccer players kick,
and the baseball players hit,
as they play, every day, outside,
Some kids are playing tag,
and slipping down the slide.

They don't have any worry,
while the happiness is churning,
until somebody gets hurt and then they cry.

Zavior Phillips, Grade 6
Discovery School @ Reeves Rogers, TN

The Color of Orange in Autumn

Orange is the big, booming, blazing color
    of falling leaves

Orange is the sound
    of whistling winds

Orange is the sweet taste
    of pumpkin pie

Orange is the bright, shocking color
    of the chrysanthemum

Orange is the happy smile
    of a disguised kid — Halloween!

Alex Cvecich, Grade 6
Hackley School, NY

Change of World

Now I can clap,
Now I can sing,
This change of world,
Does more than ONE thing!

It helps me smile,
And now I can breathe,
This change of world,
I bet you can't believe!

The better sights,
And a better smell,
This change of world,
I'm thinking it's very swell...

Now, you must know my story,
I've fallen, you see,
And this change of world,
Is for you, not me!

Anisa Anuar, Grade 6
Science & Engineering Magnet School, CT

Monsters Galore!

Ghosts and ghouls and monsters galore.
They climb up right out of the floor.
Giving little kiddies a fright
when they try to get to sleep at night.

Haunted houses and witches scare
the little children that would not dare
to go into the haunted house,
for there might be a giant, hungry mouse.

Each zombie comes up from its grave
because they crave and crave
the brains of little children.

The witches make poison mildred
and dew that people would like to drink or eat.
But when they eat it, they reach their feat.

Ghosts and ghouls and monsters galore.
They climb up right out of the floor.
Giving little kiddies a fright.
So be careful when you go to sleep TONIGHT!

Jakob Surber, Grade 6
South Woods Middle School, NY

Nature

The dripping water
Falling off the gutter
Feeding the seeds drip by drip
Growing to get ready to sprout
Before you know it boom there's a flower.

Kaileigh Tinnin, Grade 5
Avon Grove Intermediate School, PA

I Am a Poet

I am a poet.
I wonder how animals see the world,
I hear the sounds of rivers flowing,
I see nature as a playground,
I want to swim with dolphins in blue water,
I pretend I can fly and see the earth below,
I am a poet.

I touch the lives of many people,
I worry about animal extinction,
I cry when I see suffering,
I am a poet.

I understand the language of nature,
I say, "Take care of the injured,"
I dream about blooming flowers,
I try to inspire others,
I hope I show I care,
I am a poet.

Daniel Otero, Grade 4
Meadow Park Elementary School, FL

Summer Time Love

I love the skies that are so blue
especially in a summer new
in the summer it's nice and warm
so fill out that swim team form
it gives me time to spend with you
and makes me say I'm not sick of you
which just might mean, I love you!

Catherine Gaught, Grade 6
Amanda Gist Elementary School, AR

Land and Water

Land
Solid, dry
Comforting, thrilling, amazing
Large, crowded, open, lonely
Whisping, swimming, moving
Blue, hollow
Water

Brandon Holly, Grade 4
Pike Creek Christian School, DE

I Remember the Day…

I remember the day we got her
I was so excited
I thought she was so cute
I wouldn't let anyone play with her
I loved her

I remember the day she died
She was six
I was eleven
She had cancer

She had lived a good life
We loved her
We still love her

Sydney Wharton, Grade 6
E T Richardson Middle School, PA

Death Is Coming

The cloud cover is sodden black,
The rain about to fall.
The wind is roaring storming past,
He's coming for us all.
He who rides in his black coach,
Coming, he is death.
Here to take us all away,
On our very last breath.
The ravens shriek outside the house,
They hear him riding by.
My heart is pounding with the rain,
I am about to die.

Julia Beasley, Grade 6
Discovery School @ Reeves Rogers, TN

I Am Mad and Glad

When I am mad
I feel like a bear whose food got stolen
but when I am glad
I feel like a dog with a huge bone
when I am both mad and glad
I feel like I destroyed
the whole world.

Jabrea Holmes, Grade 5
Southern Pines Elementary School, NC

Love

What is love?
Well, I don't really know.
But I do know that,
Love is special.
Love is trust.
Love is an indescribable emotion.
Love is like a roller coaster.
You're up one day
And down the next.
The butterflies in your stomach.
A love filled hug
Love isn't only the boy-girl love
It's also the family love.
Love isn't mandatory.
It's optional.
It's okay if you'd rather live without love.
But it is nice to live with love.
Love is three words.
I LOVE YOU!

Anny Trejo, Grade 6
Gulfview Middle School, FL

Christmas

Christmas
Christmas trees,
Caroling people,
Gingerbread houses,
Scent of ham and cake,
Shredded wrapping paper,
Christmas

Ethan Wooding, Grade 4
Sacred Heart School, PA

The Watch

I'm sitting on a night stand
Waiting to be picked up
I'm feeling lonely tick-tick-tock
Hurray! I've been picked up!
I go to work with my fellow
He knows what time it is
Then back on the night stand I go

Christina Venator, Grade 4
West Frankfort Elementary School, NY

Angel

Angel
Fast, strong
Running, panting, jumping
Awesomeness, healing, crazy, catcher
Ball

Ben Mann, Grade 5
Avon Grove Intermediate School, PA

Easter

Easter is a happy time
People have fun and joke and rhyme
We'll have lots of fun this year
When Easter comes near
I know we'll make the sun shine.

Jennifer Carter, Grade 5
Coral Park Elementary School, FL

Wendy

W ake me up an you will see
E arly morning's not for me
N ever can go back to sleep
D ay is cranky and a creep
Y awn sleepily yes indeed,
Wake me up and you will see

Wendy Novoa, Grade 6
Normandin Middle School, MA

Books

Stories come to life
Take you any place you want
The best adventures

Anjna Nair, Grade 6
Fairfax Collegiate School, VA

Trees

Trees blossoming now.
Leaves falling in the autumn.
Trees bare in the cold.

Dana Stopinski, Grade 6
Discovery School @ Reeves Rogers, TN

A Question

You may question me.
Whether or not you like me,
doesn't bother me.
You can take pictures
and call me,
but not after nine.
When I die,
you can't question me.
But you can question
what I leave behind.

Dominick Anthony Biagetti, Grade 6
Gulfview Middle School, FL

Friends or Foes?

A friend is someone who is very sweet
They are the kind of people you want to meet.
They pick you up when you're feeling down,
And their words you hear are a happy sound.
A foe is someone who doesn't care.
Every day they are never fair.
They're mean, and nasty, and mad, and rude.
In this case they are never nice to you.
The time has come for me to say,
To never be a foe that way.
Be nice and kind from head to toe.
To be a friend and not a foe.

Rylie Barnes, Grade 6
Freedom Area Middle School, PA

Anger

The trees are rumbling with a type of fury
the trees are trying to stand through the madness.
All animals are silent,
as if,
they're mad.
Anger is rising.

No one is outside,
no one is playing.
Someone's angry.

Fires are smoking up from the chimney,
all houses are dark.
Something is angry.

Rain is coming down,
hard as rocks.
The Heavens are angry.

Anger is rising.
Anger is all around.
Anger is powerful.

Brittney Evans, Grade 6
Haynes Academy for Advanced Studies, LA

The X

"X marks the spot"
Yelled the pirate lot,
They knew just what to do,
They grabbed their shovels all 22,
They dug and dug and found their treasure,
To them it was a mighty pleasure,
They got back on the ship,
Up the anchor went "sip,"
They all went home
And they all got something made of chrome,
The sad part was that it was Firebeard's treasure,
And his ghost haunted them forever.

Maria Clark, Grade 4
Crestwood Elementary School, KY

Lost

My souls were buried in the deep, dark ground
No matter how I try they won't ever be found

They are lonely, ill, lost, and cold, too
Fighting for a house inside of my shoe

I will never find them ever again
Though there are way too many of ten

I can't find them with my right eye
So then some of them started to die

But I had forgotten I was dead
I then discovered my souls had fled

Brooke Davis, Grade 5
Avon Grove Intermediate School, PA

Jewels

Sparkling Shimmering Shining
In the late afternoon sun
Sitting there embedded in gold

Shining many different colors
Red, Blue, Yellow and Green
Throwing multicolored light upon the ground

Shining in the sun
They are flowers
In a Caribbean Paradise

Atticus Ignelzi, Grade 5
New Garden Friends School, NC

The Performance

I sat backstage, dreaming,
Of what was yet to come.
Then my predecessor exited the stage.

I stood up, prepared myself,
And walked onto the stage.
There it stood, gleaming, black, and glossy.

I sat down on the bench,
And placed my music on the stand.
Then I began, opening the piece slowly.

Fingers flying, crawling, creeping,
Across the keys of the piano.
Then, I was done, and I rose from the bench.

From the audience came thunderous applause,
Clapping, whistling, screaming, and yelling.
And then, I left, and disappeared backstage.

Raleigh Browne, Grade 6
Chickahominy Middle School, VA

Snow and Sand

Snow is fluffy and white,
As it takes flight,
Like a kite,
Soaring through the trees,
In the soft, quick breeze,
It is snow I like,
You don't have to be psyche,
To tell the light, fluffy snow,
From the hard, crunchy sand,
Especially on land,
It's easy to tell snow from sand.

Kaytlynn Nixon, Grade 5
Calvary Chapel Christian School, PA

The Squirrel

Leaping from tree to tree,
A squirrel seeks its meal to-be.
High up in the treetops
The squirrel hops,
As he sees
Acorns.

Spring!
The squirrel leaps to grab his find.
Leaving only the shell behind,
The squirrel enjoys his food.
He spots another acorn,
And runs across a field,
Where he renews
His favorite
Meal.

Raymond He, Grade 6
Allen-Stevenson School, NY

Vampires

Vampire
Cold, sparkly
Chasing, following, hunting
Blood, stillness, stone, fangs
Pouncing, drinking, running
Parasite

Tara Gardner, Grade 6
Freedom Area Middle School, PA

War

Gory fights
days and night
as the war never stops.
Men and women die
and dead bodies lie
on the battle grounds.
The brave step up to fight
with all their might,
in the fierce battle of war.

Spencer Dehnz, Grade 6
Gulfview Middle School, FL

The Deadly War

The Nazis came along and ruined it all —
The Danish peoples' happiness that they thought would never fall.
The Nazis from Germany came and invaded the places —
Their main goal was to create sad faces.
To the Jewish people they did horrible things,
They occupied Denmark after overpowering the king.
The Danish wanted to help their friends;
The Jewish who were in trouble.
They started smuggling them onto their boats to Sweden
To freedom on the double!

The Jews kept their heads held high:
They didn't give up their pride.
Nobody could take it away; it was on the inside.

The Danish people risked their lives;
To save their friends they would strive.
Then finally one day there was freedom at last,
And the deadly war had finally passed.

Sumedha Sahay, Grade 5
Foxborough Regional Charter School, MA

Katie Shannon

Katie
Friendly, intelligent, talented, shy
Sister of Annie Shannon
Lover of my Boston Terrier, Thor, God, the ocean, and performing
Who feels stressed when busy, happy when with family, and
relaxed when watching a movie
Who fears death, getting in trouble, and forgetting my line, dance,
or the words to a song
Who would like to become a star, travel the world, and go to SCAPA
Resident of Lexington
Shannon

Katie Shannon, Grade 6
Morton Middle School, KY

Just Because

Just because I'm short
Don't think I can't make big accomplishments
Don't make fun of me if I can't reach something you can
You can still ask me to play basketball

Just because I'm short
It doesn't mean I'm a freak
It doesn't give you the right to push me down
It doesn't stop me from reaching my goals in life

Just because I'm short
Remember big things come in small packages
Can't wait till I grow a few inches
Just because I'm short, remember my heart is the same size as yours

Kristian Cunningham, Grade 5
Hamilton Avenue School, CT

Dawn of the Sun or Dusk of the Dark

Always there is playful Light
and dull, dejected Darkness.
Light looks with a blissful view,
and Dark looks with distress.

Every day, Light reaches up at dawn,
driving Dark away bitterly.
During the day Light watches life keep going.
As he tires he falls away proudly.

Darkness shows up cold as always.
He curses Light for his good fortune.
"Light enjoys a ton of fun"
Darkness longs for the shouts and yells that make a tune.

Gleeful Light smirks at Dark
as they pass at dawn.
Dark resents Light's freedom.
Light gives him a sardonic yawn.

Light fights for "his right."
Dark will try and come down on him.
This never ending contest we call day
where neither Light nor Dark can win.

Simon Nickerson, Grade 6
Trickum Middle School, GA

If I Were in Charge of the World

If I were in charge of the world
There would be no more broccoli,
Spinach and green beans, or being grounded.
And also no more homework.

If I were in charge of the world
There'd be more ice-cream,
Healthier dogs, and back handsprings easier to do.

If I were in charge of the world,
You wouldn't have bedtimes.
You wouldn't have school.
You wouldn't have death,
Or "You better eat your vegetables."
You wouldn't even have vegetables.

If I were in charge of the world
Shoving everything on the floor under your bed
Would be cleaning.
All places would be for kids.
And a person who sometimes forgot to clean,
And sometimes forgot to turn off the water,
Would be the only person allowed to be
In charge of the world.

Kimberly Powell, Grade 6
Morton Middle School, KY

The Chase

I scamper and scurry,
Just like a bunny in such a hurry.
I must run from this scene,
There is an animals, soft and so mean.
To him I'm a nice treat.
I stop and stand still. My heart skips a beat,
Like a puma, he leaps.
I get scared because he gives me the creeps.
He runs really fast toward me.
Like a hawk, the predator can see me.
My tail smacks off a tree.
Whoopee! Now I will finally be free,
As he cannot eat me.
I sit and rest, up in that snakelike tree.
He then whimpers and cries.
I can see disappointment in his eyes.
He then says to his meal,
He will not eat me as long as I feel,
That he is a cutie.
Oh, what a creature! Oh, such a sweetie!

Jacqueline Fernous, Grade 6
East Shore Middle School, CT

My Walk

I went for my walk in the meadow,
Under the deep blue sky,
And out in the meadow,
I saw a blue jay flying by.

As I went for my walk in the meadow,
Out among the tall green grass,
I passed by a clear blue lake,
That looked like sparkling glass.

As I continued my walk in the meadow,
Under the shady trees,
Under a certain oak tree,
I saw a hive of bumble bees.

And as I climbed my walk in the meadow,
At the end of a tall steep hill,
I looked up into the deep blue sky,
And saw a tiny little butterfly.

Felicity Van der Putten, Grade 5
The Holy Name of Jesus Academy, NY

NL East Rivals

Phillies
Champions, MVP
Scoring, hitting, stealing
Home run, phanatic, disgrace, disappointment
Losing, building, striking
Choke, Citi
Mets

Brett Hardy, Grade 4
Pleasant Valley Elementary School, PA

Fear

Fear is like being seconds from death, trying to hold onto life when life is letting go.

Fear is losing a loved one after complicated times, even if they were strangers, or knew each other for years.

Fear is responsibility, taking care of another when they can't fill the needs of themselves.

Fear is self-consciousness, not knowing what they can push them self to do, being afraid that if they do harsh ridicule and whispers will come their way.

Fear is love, pouring their heart and soul to another isn't as easy the second time, when the first was when they had their heart broken.

Fear is knowledge, fearing that it can lead to tragedy, and everything they love and hold dear will collapse around them.

Lastly, fear is an illusion; fear is not self-consciousness, love, or even knowledge. It is just preventing from doing our best in life and fulfilling our dreams.

Michael Greene, Grade 6
St Augustine School, RI

The Trees

"Swish…Swish…" went the tall vertical logs with their green feathers swaying while birds sit upon the branches and sing the last tune. Soon, lightning strikes and a branch falls, although the trees' power is strong enough to stay in place, but that's too bad for the leaves. They are falling off, blowing from left to right, until the storm starts to slow down. The leaves start to cry because they want to go back home to their warm branches. They start to blow away into the dark, wet woods. It starts to get a light breeze while the trees start their cycle all over again.

JJ Polityka, Grade 4
Litchfield Intermediate School, CT

A Day by the Waterfall

In the woods a small waterfall approaches.
Its waters run long, slim and fast down large rocks,
over branches and twigs until it reaches its end.
Trees of all colored leaves rest by the young waterfall.
As the wind blows and the leaves fly away, they dance in the air
and make a rainbow in the sky with colors of amber, sunset, maize, emerald and copper.
You can hear the rustling waters as it falls down the long rocky slide.
You hear the crunching leaves as you walk more and more down the waterfall.
The wind blows and the trees shiver as their leaves fly away
and they once again hear the rustling of the waterfall.
You feel the cold, wet rock against the waterfall,
as the fast flowing water hits your finger like a sharp dagger.
You touch the hard, warm bark of the narrow trees lying side by side across the waterfall.
You inhale the freshest air and the sweet scents of the flowers against the bend of the waterfall.
You taste the sunsweet berries on the bushes on the edge of the waterfall.
They taste sweet and tangy as they slide down your throat.
This is all that happens as you go, walk side by side down the waterfall.

Claudia Cherrington, Grade 6
Suffern Middle School, NY

I Have a Dream

I have a dream that someday this world will be decorated with happiness.
I have a dream that someday wars will end and that peace comes.
I have a dream that violence will stop.
I have a dream that people will be worshiped for the good deeds they do and not the bad deeds.
I have a dream that rainforests will be built and not burned.
I have a dream that the homeless will find super homes.
I have a dream that the hungry will get as great of food as I do.
I have a dream that one day a woman will run for president and succeed.
My final dream is that everyone will and always be happy and peaceful.

Meg Whelan, Grade 4
St Joseph School, KY

Moon

The orbit of the moon is slow
So you might see the magnificent glow
The moon is a beautiful, bright white
It has a sparkling light
But, it only peaks out in the dead of night.

Alison Schultz, Grade 5
Avon Grove Intermediate School, PA

Soccer

Game begins
Ball flies to corner
We get the ball
I fly towards the middle
I attempt a header…
Hits the post!
Other team gains possession
Dribble, dribble, dribble
The intensity is picking up
They pass it perfectly…and score!
They have the 1-0 lead at the half
But we are determined, we don't quit,
We get the ball and pass it to the man at the 18 yard line
He heads it…GOAL!
The other team gets the ball and shoots…SAVE!
I get the ball with 10 seconds left
I dribble up the field
I get a clear look and shoot…
GOAL! The game is over!
I win!

Griffin Stone, Grade 6
St Stephen's School, NY

Wind, Water, Fire, Earth

W ild and
I ndefinite
N ot controlled by man, it can
D estroy

W ill not stop
A nd will always move
T oward the beaches toward
E veryone looking
R ight at them

F un at first but when
I gnited it cannot be stopped, everyone
R unning away
E veryone scarred that they will get burned

E verything that makes our world
A ll around us
R ight below us and sometime right on
T op of us
H iding us but still making its way around

Allen Kujrakovic, Grade 6
Canterbury School, FL

America

I wish for world peace
I am brave and strong
I feel proud and daring
I am safe and secure
I have rights for my religion
I am valiant and helping
I feel joyful and honored to be an American

Ramishah Maruf, Grade 4
Coral Park Elementary School, FL

Sunset

Colors mix as the sun hides beyond the horizon
Calmness fills your peaceful body
Light reflects on the motionless water

Cold sand wiggles under your toes
The sliver of a dull moon
Takes the place of the warming sun

Since the star called the sun has disappeared
Coldness replaces the peacefulness

You run inside a small hut to your awaiting mother
With hot soup and a hug.

Samantha Houle, Grade 4
John Lyman School, CT

Baseball

I put on my catcher's helmet
I grab my catcher's mitt
My knee and leg pads are on now
I am nervous a bit.

My team of twelve depends on me
To not let a ball pass
The wild pitches must be stopped
No balls let in the grass.

The first pitch was fast and too high
I leapt up to catch it
The next pitch was over the plate
The batter got a hit.

The next pitch was wild in the dirt
I dove to block the ball
A catcher with fast reflexes
Sometimes needs to crawl.

Being catcher is a big job
I've earned the position
After years of playing baseball
My dreams and ambition.

Eric Merten, Grade 5
Hunters Woods Elementary School for the Arts & Sciences, VA

A Ride at the Fair

The ride at the fair
That gave me a scare.
I think my heart stopped.
Especially when we dropped
And when we got off I could barely walk.
I could not talk
The ride at the fair
Was very rare.

Savannah Allen, Grade 5
Southern Pines Elementary School, NC

Life on the Farm

Life on the farm is,
the big red international tractor
pulling a large load of hay
up the long wide path,
Clink, clank, clunk.

Life on the farm is,
grandpa sitting in his old wooden rocker
drinking a steaming cup of coffee
by the warm fire,
Ummm, ummm, ummm.

Life on the farm is,
black and white Holsteins
grazing in the wide open field
waiting to be milked,
Moo, moo, moo.

Life on the farm is,
the gigantic red barn
filled with clover and fescue
to bed and feed the hungry cattle,
Munch, munch, munch.

Life on the farm is fantastic!

David Williams, Grade 4
Waynesburg Elementary School, KY

Friendship

If I want *more* friends,
I will NOT be annoying.
I will be nicer.
Being kind is really important
Loving is also important and kind.
Be kind to people
That's all I'm saying!

My lesson of the poem is,
If you want more friends
You have to be a friend!

Isabella Mariacher, Grade 5
Jamestown Elementary School, PA

What's in the Ocean?

What's in the ocean?
a leaping dolphin
a feeding shark
a squishy squid
a curious school of fish
a group of salty sardines
a very grumpy grouper
a creepy angler fish
a tiny, little shrimp so very
small

Derek Zepeda, Grade 5
Parkside Elementary School, FL

Salmon

The hopeful salmon jump and leap
As they travel up the stream
The waters here are quite deep
But they make it as a team.

Jennifer Coppa, Grade 6
Kelly Lane Intermediate School, CT

My Dog, Trevor

My dog's name is Trevor,
I won't forget that day.
When I was at my dad's,
When Trevor went away.

Even though he was the best,
I still can't complain.
All I want to know,
What was Trevor's pain?

When someone was at the door,
All he'd do was bark.
Does he have a history,
Black, deep, inside his heart?

I guess I'll never know.
My new pet, hermit crab,
Is not close as fun
As Trevor, the black Lab.

Hunter Burgess, Grade 6
Chickahominy Middle School, VA

Bob and Fluffy

Bob
Small, fish
Tricks, swim, jump
Scaly, scale, hair, fluffy
Leap, catch, love
Big, cat
Fluffy

Gladys Huichapa, Grade 5
Avon Grove Intermediate School, PA

Clouds

They float through the air,
drifting in the summer wind.
Snow falls down,
raindrops on the ground,
thunder they make.
One answer,
clouds.

Madison Garbinski, Grade 4
Abraham Pierson School, CT

Scott

I have a dad named Scott,
He works in the army a lot,
He is a very great guy,
Who loves us a lot,
That's why I love my dad
Named Scott.

Alexis Yeager, Grade 5
L Ray Appleman Elementary School, PA

Fire and Water

Fire
Hot, warm
Spreading, burning, damaging
Orange flame, volcano, ocean, lake
Sliding, hosing, flowing
Wet, cold
Water

Kyle Gomez, Grade 6
St Agatha School, NY

The Jungle

Apes swinging in jungle trees
Buzzing angry bumblebees
Caterpillars making cocoons
Donkeys playing with baboons
Elephants playing games; such fun
Fox's time is almost done
Giant monkeys eating bananas
Hyenas name Joannas
In the jungle, things go on
Just lying around is a very small fawn
Kangaroos are excitedly jumping
Lion hearts are thump, thump, thumping
Monkeys hanging from the trees
Now getting stung by bumblebees
Octopuses are not here
Putting ink in water clear
Quacking ducks in the water
Running with the kangaroos daughter
Seeing sites in the jungle
That's worth quite a bundle

Lindsey Fried, Grade 5
J F Kennedy Middle School, MA

What's the Meaning of Cleaning Your Room

What's the meaning of cleaning your room?
Clothes to the heavens
Including my leggings
Pants to the sky
And shirts so high
Shoes all over the world in different places
Everything is tangled up with the laces
What's the meaning of cleaning your room
When it looks like it exploded with a huge KABOOM!!!
Rotten food is all over the floor
Sometimes it looks like it's punching the door
It seems like everything comes alive
And it looks like it's even dancing the jive
Uh! Oh! I think it'll explode
You better take cover before it erodes
So…
What's the meaning of cleaning your room?
When everything will be gone when it goes KABOOM!!!
Meghanne Potter, Grade 5
Jamestown Elementary School, PA

Summer Beach

Kids splashing in the water
Parents are resting under colorful umbrellas.

The sand tickles my feet as I walk into the water
I feel a sudden shock from the cool water
As I swim up to my waist I feel the hard shells on my feet.

I can't stand the water anymore
And get out and see that the waves crashed my sand castle.

I don't rebuild it but…
Decide to look for sea glass and shells,
I find so many big and colorful ones I cannot take anymore.

The warm sun has faded my sunscreen away,
As the seagulls take my jelly sandwich.

Finally the sun has now set.
Kimberly Ripa, Grade 5
Melville School, RI

Waves

The waves are wild and free
Some people ask how could they be
But certain people will always know
Because they sit under the moonlit willow
Some people think that waves are just waves
But some people will be brave
That is just like me
I believe that the waves are wild and free
Jennifer Healy, Grade 6
Kelly Lane Intermediate School, CT

How Not to Have People Reading Your Diary*

If you don't want people
to read your diary,
don't lock it up,
you'll lose the key.
Don't carry it around
'cause people can see.
If you don't want people
to read your diary,
don't write in it!
That's as plain as can be!
Efrayim Sperber, Grade 4
South Area Solomon Schechter Day School, MA
*Inspired by "How Not to Have to Dry the Dishes"
by Shel Silverstein

Basketball

Time for the tip-off
Your nerves are going crazy
The ball is tossed
You win the tip
Pass, dribble, shoot, and score
Opponent gets the ball
Fans cheering
Blow horns are blowing
But your mind is in the game
The score is 32-14 in favor of you
The other team makes a comeback
The score is tied at 45
10 seconds left in the championship game
You get the ball, and shoot the three at the buzzer
Swoosh!
You win the championship
You become a legend.
Justin Figler, Grade 6
St Stephen's School, NY

The Gems of the Winter Sky

We weigh the clouds in the cold, humid air,
Only dancing there on chilly days.
Cheerful or gloomy, we don't really care,
Fall we do, each blowing different ways.

Wintertime is chilly, frigid, and cold.
Each snowflake holds a different shape.
Snow's a delight, oh, that's what I'm told,
We look like we're covered with glossy tape!

Children catch us on their tongues all the time,
Some kids mold us into many fine things.
People think we're so pretty and sublime!
I fly as if I have two graceful wings.

Snowflakes glisten in the sun's yellow light,
And look out for us on cold winter nights!
Faazilah Mohamed, Grade 6
Al-Hamra Academy, MA

Eagle Nest

Big nest
above the road
high in the sky
swaying
swaying
swaying
clear sky,
bright sun,
and perfect temperature
lots of cars driving
but peaceful
I felt amazed,
excited,
happy,
and tired
how big is the nest
and how many babies
did the mother eagle have?

Terric Fobbs, Grade 4
Grace Lutheran School, FL

Baylee

There once was a girl named Baylee,
Whose friend's last name was Haley.
She had a friend named Michelle,
She sang like a bell,
If only her name was Kaley.

Ranette Toothman, Grade 5
Tucker School, AR

Freedom

Freedom is like the birds flying
In an open, free sky
Soaring freely
Nowhere to go
Nowhere to fly.

Freedom is like having
No worries of fears.
No problems.

It cannot be owned,
But it can be found!

Natasha Crepeau, Grade 4
PS 10, NY

World War II

World War II
Dangerous, treacherous
Fighting, bombing, hurting
Bombs, weapons, people, life
Living, freeing, choosing
Liberty, independence
Freedom

Angela Huston, Grade 4
St Joseph School, KY

Ice Cream

Ice cream, ice cream
We all scream for ice cream.
Vanilla is a flavor and so is chocolate.
But it is better with marshmallows on top of it.
You can add colorful sprinkles or a piece of chocolate or two.
Anything on ice cream will always do!

Meghan Whiting, Grade 6
Gulfview Middle School, FL

The Outdoors

The first thing we did was see three turtles: wood, spotted, and box.
The cute spotted turtle looked like it had the red chicken pox.
Wow, did you know that all turtles' spines are part of their back shells.
But surely almost all turtles don't live in those scary wells.
When turtles get really scared, they bring in their heads, arms, and legs.
When turtles bring them in, their toenails look like sharp little pegs.
We came upon a white pine tree with five needles in each bunch.
A cute, little brown chipmunk can have the pine cone seeds for lunch.
There was a pond covered in disgusting algae and duckweed.
If someone cleaned the pond out, they would be doing a good deed.
There was lots of skunk cabbage that smelled bad, like dirty diapers.
This is surely not a habitat for birds, sandpipers.
African millipedes have 275 feet.
His skin felt like plastic; when you touched it, it felt super neat.
We saw a gray tree frog that lives high in canopies of trees.
Sometimes to others he is just a leaf, not a pod of peas.
Desert leopard geckos eat insects and sometimes baby mice.
Farmers thought corn snakes ate their corn, so they would kill them…not nice.
Barn owls are endangered because the loss of their habitat.
If any more are killed, their species could be gone, just like that.

Emily Sabo, Grade 6
East Shore Middle School, CT

Turtles Everywhere

I'm very excited to see the turtles coming out of their crates.
They are all different shapes and sizes how many are there, maybe eight?
Oh, but I was wrong; there really were only three.
A wood turtle, a box turtle, and a spotted turtle, I see.
A wood turtle looks like a piece of driftwood.
If he wanted to hide in wood, that would be good.
The wood turtle smells of water, and he lives in rivers and streams.
The wood turtle won't live in any saltwater; do you know what I mean?
The box turtle, shaped like a box, has a square shell.
Not a circle, or triangle, or hexagon, it's easy to tell.
When he goes in the water he makes a loud splash and does not shiver.
Living on land, he's not a very good swimmer.
The spotted turtle lives in the water and is a good swimmer.
He has very sharp claws, like a knife, he uses to cut his dinner.
His shell is a piece of glass; it feels flat but tough.
The spotted turtle can flip itself over if things get too rough.
So you can see the wood, box and spotted turtles are really cool.
I wish I could have them all in my swimming pool.
I know I cannot do this, but it is OK to have a dream.
Wood, box, and spotted turtles are very interesting, so it seems!

Jake Kasuba, Grade 6
East Shore Middle School, CT

The Big Blue Monster

I walked outside as the sun beat down on me.
The sticky sand rubbed against my feet.
As I walked towards the big blue monster,
a tiny red creature scrambled by me pinching its tiny claws.
The blue monster reached for me but grabbed the red creature instead
I was too far away. I moved closer the monster reached again.
It left tiny pebbles behind
I reached for one just as the monster came back for me
This time I let it carry me away
I could feel its other prisoners swimming at my feet.
It slowly swallowed me but I didn't care. I felt as if I had all the time in the world.
Then one of the prisoners crawled out. It made him angry
His waves of anger thrashed at my side. I dove in his mouth
Hoping not to make him even angrier for my slowness.
His prisoners seemed to greet me.
Where has this place been all my life I wondered.
A beautiful prisoner swam by. I saw more tiny pebbles
I felt as if I could live there in the big blue monster's mouth for the rest of my life.
A hand reached in for me. I knew my amazing experience was over…
For now, as I left, I promised my new friend the big blue monster
I would come back and visit him and his prisoners very soon!

Bailey Gagel, Grade 4
Crestwood Elementary School, KY

Leopard in a Tree

On one lazy afternoon Lizzie the leopard was just laying there in her tree. Lizzie was very hot because it was spring. And her fur coat wasn't helping. Birds were chirping happily and the wind was whistling beautifully. But Lizzie was just being lazy. The air was filled with pleasant and unpleasant scents. The weather was very warm out. Lizzie's fur was white and a beautiful mustard yellow. Her tree was the tallest tree of all so Lizzie is all you could see. Lizzie was very content and comfortable. She was kind of lonely and tired. At 9:00 pm before she went to bed she said, "This was the best day ever!"

Amanda Pazyck, Grade 4
Honeoye Falls-Lima Manor School, NY

One Last Look

As I sit in the empty classroom, I look out the window for reassurance.
I look at the clock and it ticks slowly, but I know in my heart that time has stopped.

As I stand in the empty hallway, I stare down the corridor for lingering hope.
I remember the once-crowded halls of traffic, and wait for them, but know they are not coming.

As I wander in the abandoned parking lot, I glance around for perhaps a little while too long.
I seem to see the busy area flowing to life but know it is just a look into the past.

As I stride through the old dead field of grass, I close my eyes and watch a game.
Running and yelling and panting for breath, I see the players, but know they are there no more.

As I walk through the old cafeteria, footsteps now echoing, the roaring of the whole scene fills my ears.
I remember the once-long line for lunch, but when I look up, it is no longer there.

As I find the musty old storage closet, I look back on seeing it have no importance.
But now as I stand in the doorway, it holds the utmost importance as I take one last look.

Nicole (Niki) Crawford, Grade 6
Joseph L Carwise Middle School, FL

Just Because I Have a Sister

I'm not her twin
I'm not exactly like her
I'm not able to always be responsible

Jut because I have a sister
I'm not always going to act my age
I'm not always the center of attention
I'm not sometimes able to handle the pressure

Just because I have a sister
I know that I look like her
I can't be perfect
I'm not my sister
Just because I have a sister — don't treat me like my sister.

Katie Shvach, Grade 6
Freedom Area Middle School, PA

Life's Candle

Life's beginning flame is growing,
A bud begins to form,

Wax is bubbling, flame is heating,
Petals begin to explore,

Smoke is meandering, flame is dancing,
A fiery flower in full bloom,

Fire is waning, wax is running, pouring down like rain,
Petals begin to fall,

Smoke receding, wax is bleeding,
The end is drawing near,

Light is flickering,
Flower is wilting, life is almost gone,

Light was once a gift,
Flower is decaying, life is gone,

Poof!
All this comes too soon.

Christian Frost, Grade 6
Haynes Academy for Advanced Studies, LA

My Model

Non-perfect size.
Never tries to hide from others.
Never teases, or tarries in work.
Criticizes carefully while judging.
Tries to be immaculate while modeling.
Makes great decisions.
Helps others head for better, not the worse.

Crystal Hawkins, Grade 6
Berry Middle School, AL

Happy Birthday

Happy birthday to the one and only
I wrote this poem for you, so you won't be lonely
People can see your smile from half a mile
And you absolutely have great style
Your brown eyes make you look shy
And when I look up I see you in the sky
You're huggable
And lovable
You're so very sweet
And you can dance to a good beat
I hope that you run and have some fun
On this day, you're loved a ton.
Happy birthday!

Kaliyah Poe, Grade 6
Linkhorne Middle School, VA

Home

I come home from school
    all sweaty and wet.
I take a shower, do my work,
    and go to bed.
I wake up to smell a delicious scent.
I wonder what it could have meant.
A special dinner or a family night,
    simply so we can reunite.
It's midnight and dark.
I'm sleepy and tired.
It's time to go to bed.
We give kisses and hugs
    and say, "Good night."
And then we all turn off the lights.

Alexandra Lubin, Grade 6
Gulfview Middle School, FL

Index

Author Autograph Page

Author Autograph Page

Author Autograph Page

Author Autograph Page